Law and Gospel

SELECTED WRITINGS OF C.F.W. WALTHER

Law and Gospel

Herbert J.A. Bouman, Translator

Aug. R. Suelflow, Series Editor

Publishing House
St. Louis

Quotations from *The Book of Concord* translated and edited by Theodore G. Tappert, copyright 1959, Fortress Press, used by permission.

Copyright © 1981
Concordia Publishing House
3558 South Jefferson
Saint Louis, Missouri 63118

Manufactured in the United States of America

1   2   3   4   5   6   7   8   9   10   90   89   88   87   86   85   84   83   82   81

Library of Congress Cataloging in Publication Data

Walther, C. F. W. (Carl Ferdinand Wilhelm), 1811-1887.
    Law and gospel.

    (Selected writings of C. F. W. Walther)
    Translation of: Die rechte Unterscheidung von Gesetz und Evangelium.
    "A considerable abridgment and condensation of the original."—Pref.
    1. Law and gospel—Addresses, essays, lectures.
I. Bouman, Herbert J. A. II. Title. III. Series: Walther, C. F. W. (Carl Ferdinand Wilhelm), 1811-1887.
Selections. English. 1981.
BT79.W3413 1981   230'.41322   81-3079
                                             AACR2

ISBN: 978-0-7586-1824-5

Contents

Introduction

It is an ambitious project to permit C. F. W. Walther (1811—87) to address English readers. Efforts to do so have occurred in the past from time to time. But this English edition constitutes one of the most significant contributions made to the study of the theology of Lutheranism in America within past years. The stereotype of Walther heretofore imposed upon him by those who were unable to read his German writings will now be significantly altered! It is to be regretted that a rich treasury of many other works from Walther's pen still await a future project.

Dr. Henry E. Jacobs (1844—1932), late president of Lutheran Theological Seminary in Philadelphia, Pa., said of Walther:

> He is as orthodox as John Gerhard, but as fervent as a pietist, as correct in form as a university or court preacher, and yet as popular as Luther himself. If the Lutheran Church will bring its doctrines again to the people, it must be as faithful and as definite in its doctrine and as interesting and thoroughly adapted to the times in form, as is the case in Walther. He is a model preacher in the Lutheran Church ("Dr. Walther as a Preacher, *Lutheran Church Review,* III [October 1889], 319).

In each of the volumes a special effort was made to select the most significant and relevant materials and to have Walther speak contemporary English. We have further endeavored, wherever possible, to quote from the American Edition of *Luther's Works* and to utilize the Revised Standard Version of the Bible for Scriptural references. Quotations from the Lutheran Confessions were keyed to the Tappert edition of the *Book of Concord.* It was helpful to be able to consult some resources which Walther had in his own library.

Walther was an exceedingly involved church leader. A founding father of The Lutheran Church—Missouri Synod, he served as its first president 1847—50 and 1864—78. He was Concordia Seminary's (St. Louis) foremost instructor from 1849 until his death in 1887, and served as its president 1850—87.

His concern for Lutheran unity is demonstrative. He conceived the "Free Conferences" in the aftermath of the confessional crisis in 1855. Later, in 1872, he was elected the first president of a new pan-Lutheran federation, the Evangelical Lutheran Synodical Conference.

The project to translate Walther into English received support from The Lutheran Church—Missouri Synod in 1962, when a special committee was formed. When funds were not available, the project was transferred to Concordia Publishing House. It has now become a pioneer in publishing both Luther's and Walther's select works in English.

Walther's classic *Law and Gospel,* generally considered one of the most important books produced within American Lutheranism, deserves a volume of its own. In it we see him as theological professor, with his students gathered around him.

Another volume acquaints us with Walther the preacher. He made a great impact on his hearers, and much of his sermonic and homiletical material was published in German during his lifetime and in the years following his death. In spite of this, several thousand sermon manuscripts still remain untouched.

In a further volume we see Walther the convention essayist. None of these essays, presented to Western District conventions between 1873 and 1886, with their ever-recurring theme "To God All Glory!" have seen the English light of day until now.

Of particular importance were Walther's writings on the church, and one of our volumes brings a condensation of these. *Church and Ministry* (1852), *The Proper Form* (1863), and *The True Visible Church* (1866) give the theological foundation for the Missouri Synod's strong emphasis on the congregation and on lay involvement.

We include a volume of Walther's correspondence. It lets us see him in his intense and complex relationships with many different people. Concordia Historical Institute, with funds provided by the Aid Association for Lutherans, has in recent years transcribed several hundred original *Fraktur* letters. Only a few have been published in English heretofore, and we too can bring only a selection.

Finally we take a look at Walther the editor—one of his most important functions. Through *Lehre und Wehre* (from which we bring articles never before presented in English) and *Der Lutheraner* Walther exerted a strong influence toward orthodox Lutheranism.

The translators of this edition hope that readers and users will develop a new appreciation for this 19th-century hero of faith, but above all, that Walther, as the preceptor of Luther in America, will direct the readers to the very cross of our Lord Jesus Christ, his and our only hope.

Aug. R. Suelflow, *Series Editor*

Translator's Preface

In 1577 the Formula of Concord, last of the 16th-century Lutheran Confessions, declared: "The distinction between Law and Gospel is an especially brilliant light which serves the purpose that the Word of God may be rightly divided and the writings of the holy prophets and apostles may be explained and understood correctly" (Solid Declaration, Art. V, par. 1; Tappert, p. 558). Ever since then Lutheran theology has given much space to this approach to Scripture.

Dr. C. F. W. Walther was a Lutheran theologian in the classic mold. By his writings and lectures he did much to introduce Lutheran theological classics to the Lutheran Church in the new world. This is evident also in this book, particularly in his extensive quotations from Luther.

In addition to his regular schedule of classroom lectures to the students at Concordia Seminary, St. Louis, Walther set aside Friday evenings of the school year for series of informal lectures on a variety of theological topics. The longest, most detailed, most noteworthy, and also the last was the series on the proper distinction between Law and Gospel, in 39 lectures, from Sept. 12, 1884, to Nov. 6, 1885, thus spanning all of one school year and part of a second. A student, Th. Claus, made a stenographic record of the entire series. Another student, L. Fuerbringer, edited the material for its initial publication in German, 1897. A third student of Walther's, W. H. T. Dau, offered the lectures in English translation, 1928.

The present translation was prepared on the basis of the German original, occasionally borrowing a felicitous phrase from Dau. The current work represents a considerable abridgment and condensation of the original. Many of Walther's extensive citations from Luther and other authors were either reduced to their essential point or deleted entirely. As a rule, the Bible passages were retained, or at least the references were given, while much of Walther's running comment was condensed. These cuts in the material were dictated by the publisher's space limitations.

It is, nevertheless, this writer's belief that nothing essential has been omitted. Walther's lectures were delivered freely from extensive notes and are often quite rambling and diffuse, even repetitious. It was possible, therefore, to reduce the volume very extensively without sacrificing any of

Walther's lines of thought. In many cases where Walther quotes from Scripture we added the reference, putting it into brackets.

As Luther spoke relevantly and incisively to issues, problems, and heresies of his day, so Walther dealt vigorously and uncompromisingly with the ills of church and theology as he saw them in his time. If we would be true to our heritage, we must deal with contemporary issues responsibly by translating the great Biblical and theological insights of our fathers in Christ into relevant application today. Then we shall let the "brilliant light" of the distinction between Law and Gospel illuminate the darkness of this age.

Herbert J. A. Bouman

First Evening Lecture

(Sept. 12, 1884)

My dear friends: If you want to become able teachers in church and school, you must necessarily become thoroughly acquainted with all teachings of the Christian revelation. But that is not all that is necessary. You must also know how to *apply* these teachings correctly. Not only must you clearly grasp them with your mind, but they must also have penetrated deeply into your hearts and exerted their divine, heavenly power. They must all have become so precious, so valuable, so dear to you that you cannot help affirming them with glowing hearts and saying with Paul, "We believe, and so we speak," and with all the apostles, "We cannot but speak of what we have seen and heard." To be sure, you have not, like the apostles, seen it with physical eyes and heard it with physical ears, but you must come to experience it with spiritual eyes and ears.

Since it is the objective of my courses in dogmatics to ground you and give you certainty in every doctrine, these Friday evening hours are designed to make you thoroughly practical theologians and speak Christian doctrine into your hearts in such a way that you will one day take your place as living witnesses "in demonstration of the Spirit and of power"; not stand in your pulpits like lifeless statues, but confidently and cheerfully dispense your help wherever possible.

The first and foremost teaching is the doctrine of justification. A close second is the right way to distinguish Law and Gospel. Let us give this matter our serious attention at this time.

Luther says that one who has mastered the art of distinguishing the Law from the Gospel should be given the top place and be called a doctor of Holy Scripture [St. Louis Edition, IX, 802; cf. *Luther's Works,* American Edition, Vol. 26, p. 342]. But, please, do not think that I want to assume that position. That would be a big mistake, even though people at times accuse me of this. But I, too, want to remain a humble pupil of Luther and sit at his feet, just as he learned this doctrine from the apostles and prophets. Whenever you come to these lectures, do so with the silent prayer that God would richly grant us His Holy Spirit to aid you in hearing and me in effective teaching. Let us, then, go to work in full confidence that God will bless us in our own souls and the souls of those whom we are to save.

As we compare Holy Scripture with other writings we note that no book appears to be so full of contradictions as the Bible, and not only in peripheral matters but in the central issue, in the doctrine of how we may come to God and be saved. In one place forgiveness of sins is offered to all sinners, in another, the sins are retained for all sinners. In one place eternal life is offered to all gratis, in another, man is ordered to do something himself. This riddle is solved when we bear in mind that Scripture contains two completely different teachings, the doctrine of the Law and the doctrine of the Gospel.

Thesis I

The doctrinal content of all of Holy Scripture, both Old and New Testaments, consists of two diametrically opposite teachings, namely the Law and the Gospel.

My aim during these hours is not to treat the doctrine of Law and Gospel systematically but rather to show you how easily they can be mingled in spite of their great difference, to the detriment of your hearers, thus frustrating the purpose of both. However, you will be interested in this point only after you see clearly just what the difference between Law and Gospel is.

Law and Gospel must not be differentiated as if the Gospel were a divine teaching but the Law of human origin, the product of human reason. No, what Scripture has to say about both of them is all the Word of the living God Himself. Again, the difference is not that only the Gospel is necessary but not the Law, as if it were merely an addition we could do without. No, both are equally necessary. Apart from the Law we do not understand the Gospel, and apart from the Gospel the Law is of no use to us. Nor is this the difference, as is often naively supposed, that the Law is the teaching of the Old Testament and the Gospel that of the New. No, the Gospel is in the Old Testament and the Law in the New. In the latter the Lord opened for us the seal of the Law by purging it of Jewish ordinances. Again, the difference is not that each has its own final goal, as if the Gospel were given for salvation and the Law for damnation. No, the ultimate goal of both is man's salvation, except that since the fall the Law cannot bring us to salvation; it only prepares us for the Gospel. And subsequently the Gospel gives us the power to keep the Law to some extent. Nor is this the difference, that these doctrines contradict each other. There are no contradictions in Scripture. These doctrines are merely different and yet in complete harmony. Again, it is not that only one of these two is intended for Christians. The Law continues to apply also to the Christians. In fact, whoever no longer makes use of the one or the other is no longer a true Christian.

14

The difference between Law and Gospel consists of the following: They are distinguished: 1. In the manner of their revelation to mankind; 2. in their content; 3. in the promises offered by both; 4. in their threats; 5. in the function and effects of both; 6. in respect to the persons to whom the one or the other is to be proclaimed.

All other differences can be subsumed under these six points. Now we shall offer proof from the Word of God.

First of all, then, Law and Gospel are different in the way they were revealed to mankind. The Law was written in man's heart at his creation. To be sure, because of the Fall this writing in the heart has become greatly blurred, yet not entirely erased. Therefore when the Law is proclaimed to even the most ungodly person, his conscience tells him, "This is true." But his conscience will not tell him this when he hears the Gospel; he may even become incensed. The most depraved person understands that he ought to do what the Law demands. Why is this? Because the Law is written in his heart. It is different with the Gospel. It contains the proclamation and revelation of nothing but free acts of God's grace, and these are by no means self-evident. What God has done according to the Gospel He was not forced to do, as if He could not do otherwise if He wanted to remain just and loving. No, God would have remained eternal Love even if he had let all people go to the devil.

The apostle testifies that also the blind heathen have the Moral Law in their hearts and consciences, even without a supernatural revelation (Romans 2:14-15). The Ten Commandments were given to restore the faded writing in the heart. In Romans 16:25-26 it is clearly stated that since the beginning of the world the Gospel could not be discovered. It has become known only because the Holy Spirit gave it by inspiration to holy men of God.

But how important is this difference! All religions know something of the Law. Some heathen even recognized that also an inner cleansing of the soul, of thoughts and desires, was required. But nowhere is there anything about the Gospel except in the Christian religion. If the Law had not been written in men's hearts, no one would listen to the preaching of the Law, but everyone would turn away and exclaim, "That is cruel! Nobody can live up to it!" But go right ahead and preach the Law! Even if the people blaspheme, they do it only with their mouth; for what you preach is what their conscience tells them every day. And we would not convert anybody with our Gospel if the Law had not first done its work, if the Law had not been written in the heart. . . .

Secondly, Law and Gospel differ in their content. The Law tells us what we must do, while the Gospel speaks only of what God does. The Law talks of our works, while the Gospel proclaims the great works of God. The Ten Commandments tell us ten times: "You shall!" The Law has nothing more to say to us. The Gospel, on the other hand, demands nothing at all. Don't think, "But the Gospel does demand faith." Imagine you are inviting a hungry person to come to the table and eat. He surely will not say, "I don't have to take orders from you!" He will accept your "command" as a kind invitation. So it is with the Gospel. It is a kind invitation to partake of heavenly blessings.

A very important passage is Gal. 3:12: "The Law does not rest on faith, for 'He who does them shall live by them.' " The Law knows nothing of forgiveness or of grace. The Law does not say, "If you are sorry, if you amend your life, the rest will be forgiven you." Not a word of it. The Law only orders and demands. The Gospel only offers; it wants to take nothing, it wants only to give. Accordingly, the apostle says: "The Law was given through Moses; grace and truth came through Jesus Christ" (John 1:17). The Gospel contains nothing but grace and truth. How important that is! As we read and study the Law and measure ourselves by it, we are appalled by the many demands made upon us and we would despair and be lost if we had nothing more. But, God be praised! we have another teaching, the Gospel, and we cling to that.

Thirdly, Law and Gospel differ in their promises. The Law promises something just as great as what the Gospel promises—eternal life and salvation. But there the great difference becomes manifest: The Law promises everything under certain conditions, on condition that we keep it perfectly. Therefore, the greater the promise, the more tragic it is. The Law offers us food but keeps it out of our reach. It offers salvation to us as to Tantalus (always just beyond reach). To be sure, it says to us, "I will quench the thirst of your soul and satisfy your hunger," but it is unable to do so, for it always says, "If you do what I tell you, you will have it." How different it is with the lovely, sweet, consoling Gospel! It promises us God's grace and salvation without any condition at all. It is a promise of free grace. It makes no demands; it just says, "Take it, and it is yours." However, that is not a condition but purely a kind invitation.

God says: "You shall therefore keep My statutes and My ordinances, by *doing which* a man shall live" (Leviticus 18:5). Hence none can be saved by the Law except he who keeps it. In telling the self-righteous Pharisee: "Do this, and you will live" (Luke 10:28), the Lord is saying that only one who keeps the Law can obtain salvation. Even so, there would be no merit in the fact that those who do God's will would be saved; it would be God's goodness. As for us, this condition attached to the Law plunges us into despair.

16

"Go into all the world," Jesus instructs His disciples, "and preach the Gospel to the whole creation. He who believes and is baptized will be saved" (Mark 16:15-16). No condition is attached to the Gospel; it is a promise of grace. (See also Romans 3:22-24; Ephesians 2:8-9). What a precious difference! When the Law has struck us down, we may again cheerfully lift up our heads; for alongside the Law we have a teaching that makes no demands whatever. If we were to ask the Lord Christ, "What must I do to be saved?" He would answer, "No works! I have done everything. You need not drink one drop of My cup." My friends, if you truly grasp that, you will leap and jump for joy that this glad message has come also to you. One who nevertheless remains downcast and thinks, "I am a disgraceful person; there can be no forgiveness for me," well, he rejects the Gospel, he rejects Christ. And even if I had committed the most heinous sins and would have to say with Paul, "I am the foremost of sinners," and had committed the sins of Judas or of Cain, I should still accept the Gospel, for it demands nothing of me.

Fourthly, Law and Gospel differ in their threats. The Gospel has no threats at all, only words of consolation. Wherever you find a threat in Scripture, you can be sure that it is Law. How blessed that person who properly consoles himself with this fact! However, the Holy Spirit must effect this in each person; otherwise a human being remains unbelieving. But we must not think that the Gospel lulls into security because it has no threats. By no means. The Gospel removes from the believer the desire to sin. The Law knows nothing but threats. As Abraham gave Hagar a piece of bread and some water and sent her into the desert, so the Law hands us a piece of bread and drives us into the desert.

The Law lays a curse on all who do not keep it perfectly (Deuteronomy 27:26). In fact, man is ordered by the Law to curse himself. Only one surrounded by the darkness of hell believes that he can cope with the Law. The Gospel acts quite differently. Paul shows that even the foremost sinner receives no threat but only the sweetest promise (1 Timothy 1:15). In His address to the assembly in the Nazareth synagogue (Luke 4:16-21) the Lord defines the content of His teaching, that is, the Gospel, as if to say, "I did not come to impose a new Law, but to proclaim the Gospel." His preaching is pure consolation and salvation for sinners. How blessed is the person who knows that! May God grant us all this knowledge!

Second Evening Lecture

(Sept. 19, 1884)

My friends, as long as a person still wants to be a Christian but actually is not yet one, he will be quite content with knowing Christian doctrine in a superficial way. All else, in his opinion, is for pastors and theologians. A non-Christian is not interested in gaining a clear understanding of all that God has revealed. But as soon as one becomes a Christian he has a lively longing for the teaching of Christ. Even the most uncultured peasant is suddenly aroused when he is converted. He begins to reflect on God and heaven, on salvation and damnation, etc., and occupies himself with the greatest problems of human life.

Think, for example, of the many Jews, as well as the apostles, who came to Jesus. The crowd heard Christ with great pleasure and were astonished that He spoke with authority and not as the scribes. Yet most of them did not go beyond this benevolent attitude and admiration. How different it was with the apostles, who were also unlettered men! They did not rest but came to Christ with various questions and requests for an interpretation of His parables. Similarly, the Beroeans examined the Scriptures daily [Acts 17:12]. What the Apology says is, therefore, quite true: "Good consciences cry out for the truth and proper instruction from the Word of God. For them even death is not as bitter as being in doubt about one point. For that reason they must seek where they may find instruction" (Apology, Art. XII, par. 129, German text; *Concordia Triglotta*, p. 290; our translation).

If it is a necessary mark of any Christian that he strive for the truth and divine certainty, it is even more necessary for a theologian. A theologian who is not keenly interested in Christian doctrine is unthinkable. Anyone who has made only a beginning of faith in his heart will consider no point unimportant, and every doctrine will be gold, silver, and precious jewels to him. God grant that this may be so with you also! Then you will not come to these lectures with a blasé attitude but will ask again and again, "What is truth?"—not like Pilate but like Mary, who sat at Jesus' feet and listened to every word. Then this hour will bring great blessing also to you, no matter how lowly the instrument through which the truth is being brought to you.

We come now to the fifth difference between Law and Gospel. It deals with their function and effect. What is the effect of the Law? It is threefold.

First, the Law tells us what we must do but gives us no power to do it. On the contrary, it has the effect of increasing our aversion. To be sure, many handle the Law as if it were a mathematical rule. But once the Law penetrates the heart, the heart rebels against God and rages against Him who demands the impossible. Indeed, in his heart he curses God and would murder Him if he could, cast Him down from His throne if that were possible. Hence the effect of the Law is to increase the desire to sin.

Secondly, the Law uncovers a person's sins but offers him no way out and thus plunges him into despair.

Thirdly, the Law indeed produces contrition, fear of hell, of death, and of God's wrath, but it has not one drop of comfort for the sinner. If nothing else is added to the Law, man must despair and die and perish in his sins. Since the Fall the Law can have no other effect in man, as Romans 7:7-9 shows.

No heathen knows that already the evil desires of the heart are sin. The greatest moralists among them have said, "That is not my fault; I can do nothing about it, I can't help it." But the divine Law says: "You shall not covet!" We are to be free even of inbred lust. Apart from the Law sin goes in and out and the person is not even conscious of sinning. Ask a child of the world, and he will be surprised and answer, "I have done no wrong. I have killed nobody, I have not committed adultery, I have not stolen, etc." He is quite unaware of the sin that dwells within him.

But when the Law strikes him like lightning, he discovers what a great sinner he is, what dreadful, godless thoughts he harbors. Therefore the apostle says that "sin revived" when the Law came. It uncovers sin but gives us no comfort. If we had nothing else and nothing more, we would have to perish eternally in hell. The penalties and curse of the divine Law will be felt only in hell; for the Law must be fulfilled, and it must keep its divine authority.

"The written code kills" (2 Corinthians 3:6). The apostle calls it the written code, or the letter, because God wrote it on tablets of stone. Even heathens have observed that the Law effects the opposite of what it commands. You may be familiar with what the immoral poet Ovid said: "We are always after what is forbidden and crave what is denied." Ovid was himself a swine, and he puts his attitude bluntly: "See, this is the way I act; I always do what others consider forbidden."

When the Israelites received the Ten Commandments at Mt. Sinai, the whole mountain quaked. As nature trembled, so their hearts trembled within. God wanted to show at the outset that this is the effect of the Law. We also recall the rich young man who came to Christ and asked how he might obtain eternal life. He was so thoroughly blinded that he did not recognize his sinful corruption at all; "he went away sorrowful" (Matthew 19:16-22). Christ could not yet offer this young man the Gospel, for He first had to convince him of his inability to keep the Law. When Paul preached to Felix the governor, about justice and self-control and future judgment,

Felix was alarmed and said: "Go away for the present; when I have an opportunity, I will summon you" (Acts 24:24-27). But he never did summon Paul again, because he wanted to be rid of the thunder and lightning of the Law. When Peter preached the Law at the first Pentecost the hearers "were cut to the heart." But then they asked, "Brethren, what shall we do"—that is, to be saved? Peter answered, "Repent, and be baptized every one of you in the name of Jesus Christ for the forgiveness of your sins; and you shall receive the gift of the Holy Spirit" (Acts 2:37-38).

The effects of the Gospel are totally different. First of all, the Gospel calls for faith but grants and bestows faith in the demand. When we preach: "Believe in the Lord Jesus Christ!" God gives people faith through our preaching. We preach faith, and whoever does not willfully resist receives faith. It is, of course, not the mere sound of the words but the content that achieves this result.

A second effect of the Gospel is that it does not punish the sinner at all, but removes all terror, all fears, all anxiety and fills the sinner with peace and joy in the Holy Spirit. When the prodigal son returns home, the father does not in a single word refer to the son's dreadful and disgraceful conduct; he says nothing, nothing about that, but simply embraces and kisses the prodigal and prepares a splendid banquet for him. That is a glorious parable, showing us what the Gospel accomplishes. It removes all alarm and fills us with a blessed, heavenly peace.

Thirdly, the Gospel demands nothing good of man whatever, no good heart, no good will, no improvement, no piety, no love, either to God or to man. It issues no commands, but it transforms man, implants love in his heart, and equips him for all good works. It demands nothing but gives everything. Doesn't that make us want to leap and jump for joy? (These effects of the Gospel are clearly set forth, for example, in Acts 16:30-34; Romans 1:16; Ephesians 2:8-10; Galatians 3:2).

Finally, in the sixth place, Law and Gospel differ in respect to the persons to whom the one or the other must be addressed. Both the persons and the purposes are entirely different. The Law must be preached to secure sinners and the Gospel to terrified sinners. Certainly both must be proclaimed, but we must ask about the persons to whom the Law, not the Gospel, must be preached, and vice versa.

In 1 Timothy 1:8-10 the apostle describes those to whom only the Law is to be proclaimed without one drop of Gospel. As long as a person is comfortable with his sins and is unwilling to give them up, only the Law that curses and condemns him must be preached to him. But as soon as he is terrified, the Gospel must come at once, for then he is no longer a secure sinner. Hence, as long as the devil still holds you captive in *one* sin, you are still a person to whom not the Gospel but the Law applies.

Isaiah 61:1-6 speaks of the afflicted and brokenhearted to whom the good news of the Gospel is to be proclaimed. Not one word of Law must be preached to them. Woe to the preacher who still applies the Law to such a famished sinner! To him the preacher must say: "Just come! There still is room! Oh, come to Jesus!" Such people are the proper addressees for the Gospel.

[*Editorial note:* Here Walther cites passages from Luther's *Sermon on the Distinction Between Law and Gospel.* St. Louis Edition, IX, 802 f.; see also the extended discussion in Luther's *Lectures on Galatians,* 1535, ch. 3, *Luther's Works,* American Edition, Vol. 26, pp. 186 ff.]

We see that Luther does not develop this teaching scientifically but bears witness to it like a prophet. For that reason he made so deep an impression. If he had written a scholarly Latin book on this subject and had systematically divided and subdivided the material according to a strict outline, the people would have said, "What a learned scholar that man is!" But it would not have made the same impression. In the writings of the church fathers we find hardly anything on this distinction between Law and Gospel.

Third Evening Lecture
(Sept. 26, 1884)

The way of pure doctrine is as narrow as the way to heaven of which Christ speaks, for pure doctrine is nothing else than the teaching concerning the way to heaven. But as easy as it is for a person to stray off a narrow, little-traveled path through a dense forest, either to the right or to the left, without wanting to stray or even being aware of it, so easy is it to stray off the narrow path of pure doctrine that is also little-traveled and leads through a dense forest of false teachings. The person who strays will plunge either into the swamp of fanaticism or the abyss of rationalism. This is no joking matter. False doctrine is a poison dangerous to the soul. Just as a large company of people at a table may drink physical and temporal death if the common cup contains arsenic, so a large number of hearers can incur spiritual and eternal death if false teaching is mixed in with the sermon. Even only one false comfort, even only one false reproof may deprive a person of his soul's salvation. This can happen even more easily because all of us are by nature much more accessible to the blinking and blinding light of reason than to the truth. "The unspiritual (natural) man does not receive the gifts of the Spirit of God, for they are folly to him, and he is not able to understand them" (1 Corinthians 2:14).

From this you may see how foolish, indeed what a dreadful delusion, it is when so many people nowadays ridicule pure doctrine and say to us, "Will you finally quit with your clamor for pure doctrine! Pure doctrine! That can only lead to dead orthodoxy. Be more concerned about a pure life, and then you will establish a proper Christianity!" That is just as if I would say to a farmer, "Quit being concerned all the time about good seed and be more concerned about good fruits." The concern for good seed is precisely the concern for good fruits. Just so, concern for pure doctrine is the proper concern for a genuine Christianity and for a decent Christian life. False doctrine is the weed seed, sown by the enemy, from which the children of wickedness will sprout. The wheat seed is the pure doctrine; that is the seed of the children of the kingdom, who belong into Christ's realm already in this life and will one day be received into the kingdom of glory. Oh, that God would even now implant in your heart a profound fear, yes, a true loathing of false doctrine, and by grace grant you a holy yearning for the pure truth, revealed by God Himself and leading to salvation! That's primarily what these evening hours are for.

We must say a few more things about our first thesis. We have already seen how Law and Gospel differ from each other. Now we must also offer an example of how both teachings are to be presented without mingling them. Let us hear a passage from Luther's *Sermon on the Gospel of St. John,* chs. 6—8, from the years 1530—32. (Young people as a rule are more interested in beauty of language and style than in content. But that is very dangerous. You must always ask more about the What rather than the How.) The Law must indeed be preached in all its severity, but the hearer must be able to note, "That is for the good of the person who is still secure in his sins." And the Gospel must be preached in such a way that the people can notice, "That applies only to those who have been struck by the Law and need comfort." This is the most important thing to consider in a sermon.

Now, Luther says about the words of Christ in John 7:37: "These two points must be made: The Law creates a thirst and leads us to hell; the Gospel, however, satisfies the thirst and leads to heaven. The Law states what we must do, but that we have fallen short of doing it, no matter how holy we may be. Thus it produces uncertainty in me and arouses this thrist" *(Luther's Works,* American Edition, Vol. 23, p. 270 ff.).

Such a thirsty person must do only one thing: Drink, receive the comfort of the Gospel. How a truly thirsty person is refreshed by even one small glass of water! But if he is not thirsty, you may pour glass after glass down his throat, and it won't do him any good; it won't refresh him. [The quotation from Luther about spiritual thirst continues at length. Walther comments:] One who has not experienced being refreshed by the Gospel after the Law has driven him to thirst is a sound without meaning, "a noisy gong or a clanging cymbal" (1 Corinthians 13:1). But when a preacher has himself gone through this experience and his message now comes *from* the heart, it will also find its way *to* the heart. It is purely by accident if someone is awakened and converted by an unconverted preacher. The preacher must prepare a battle plan in order to gain his hearers for the kingdom of God. Otherwise, the hearers might well say, "That was a lovely sermon," but that is all. They will leave the church with an empty heart. [The long quotation from Luther about the difference between Law and Gospel continues. Walther concludes:] Thus Law and Gospel must be presented without any mingling.

One who does not preach in simple words preaches himself, and he who preaches himself preaches the people into hell, even if they say, "That was beautiful! He is quite an orator!" Even a true and honorable preacher will have such proud thoughts suggested to him by his sinful flesh. But as soon as he becomes aware of it, he casts the suggestion from him and asks God to rid him of such accursed thoughts of pride. He will then enter the pulpit a humble man, and the people will be able to notice whether his preaching comes from the heart or not. You will, of course, not have the ability of a Luther, yet you must give heed to the question, "How can I preach the Law to secure sinners and the Gospel to stricken sinners?" Both teachings must have a place in every sermon. If either one is missing, the other is false, for a sermon that does not offer all that belongs to salvation is a false sermon.

You must not think, however, that all is well when one part of the sermon preaches the Law an the second part the Gospel. Such a topographical division is meaningless. Both may be contained in the same sentence, but every hearer must be able to say, "That is meant for me!" Every sermon, no matter how comforting and winsome, must also contain the Law.

In his commentary on Psalm 23:3, "He restores my soul," Luther says: "But because our Lord has a twofold Word, the Law and the Gospel, the prophet makes it sufficiently clear that he is speaking here not of the Law but of the Gospel when he says, 'He restores my soul.' " When you come across words that contain threats and penalties you know they belong to the Law. If they are words that console, give, bestow, offer, they are Gospel. You will not find any Gospel lesson on the basis of which you could not preach both Law and Gospel.

Luther continues: "The Law cannot restore the soul, for it is a Word that makes demands on us and commands us that we shall love God with all our hearts, etc., and our neighbors as ourselves (Matt. 22:37, 39). It damns him that does otherwise. . . . The Gospel, however, is a blessed Word. It demands nothing of us, but announces everything that is good" . . . *(Luther's Works,* American Edition, Vol. 12, pp. 164 f.).

One might ask why it is that the Law produces the horrible sin of despair. That is a purely accidental feature of its function. In and of itself also the Law is good.

[*Editorial note:* Here Walther offers further support for his thesis from Luther's comments on Galatians 2:13-14 *(Luther's Works,* American Edition, Vol. 26, pp. 113—17).] Our own righteousness is for this life, but that bestowed by the Gospel is a heavenly righteousness.—As we will hear later, one must rightly divide Law and Gospel not only in the sermon but above all in one's own heart.

Fourth Evening Lecture
(Oct. 3, 1884)

If a theologian refuses to yield or make concessions in a single point of Christian doctrine for the sake of finally bringing peace to the church, his behavior looks to reason like intolerable stubbornness and even open malice. As long as they live such theologians will, therefore, be loved and lauded by very few. In fact, they will be denounced by most people as disturbers of the peace, yes, destroyers of the kingdom of God. They are regarded as utterly detestable. In the end, however, it becomes manifest that a decided, inexorable insistence on the pure doctrine of the Word of God by no means wrecks the church. In the midst of the greatest strife this is what builds the church and ultimately brings true peace. Therefore woe to a church that does not have such men who will stand as watchmen on the walls of Zion, announce the charge of every enemy trying to gain entrance, and enlist under the banner of Jesus Christ for the holy war!

Try to picture this to yourselves: Suppose Athanasius had yielded just a little in the doctrine of Christ's deity, made a compromise with the Arians, and quieted his conscience with the thought that, after all, the Arians said they, too, believed Christ to be God, except that He had a beginning ("there was a time when He was not") and then became God; but they added, "Nevertheless He is to be worshiped because He is God." What do you think would have happened? Already then the church would have fallen from the Rock on which it is founded, and that Rock is none other than Jesus Christ.

Again, picture this: Suppose Augustine had yielded just a little in the matter of free will, or rather of man's total impotence in spiritual things, had made a compromise with the Pelagians, and quieted his conscience with the Pelagians' statement that, of course, no one can be saved without the help of God's grace—if God's grace is understood as a divine endowment given to everyone. What would have happened if Augustine had given in? Already then the church would have lost the heart of the Gospel, and nothing but the empty, hollow shell would have been preserved; yes, the church would have kept nothing of the Gospel but the name. For the teaching of the Gospel that man is righteous before God and will be saved by the pure, unadulterated grace of God through the merits of Jesus Christ is the most important teaching of all, the heart and kernel of Christian doctrine. Where this teaching is not proclaimed there is no Christ, no Gospel, no salvation. There people are lost; there the Son of God has come into this world in vain.

Finally, picture this: Suppose Luther backed down just a little in the doctrine of the Lord's Supper, made a compromise with Zwingli at Marburg, and quieted his conscience with the word of the Zwinglians, "We, too, believe a kind of presence of Christ's body and blood in the Lord's Supper, but not a physical presence, for God does not expect us to believe what is beyond comprehension." By this declaration Zwingli called all of Christianity into question, so that even Melanchthon, who was usually inclined to make concessions, said that Zwingli had relapsed into paganism. What do you think would have happened? Already at that time the church would have succumbed to rationalism, which places reason above the clear Word of God.

Therefore blessed be all the faithful warriors who fought for every point of Christian doctrine without concern for men's favor or fear of their displeasure! Although the disgrace they suffered was great, it was not in vain. They went their way until death as accursed, but now they wear the crown of glory and enjoy the most blessed fellowship of Christ and of all the angels and elect. Also their labor and their fierce battles were not in vain, for after more than 1,500 years, or several centuries, as the case may be, the church is still reaping what they sowed.

My friends, we too must cling to this treasure of pure doctrine! Do not be surprised if we must then also bear the disgrace those men bore. Bear in mind that we too will then experience the truth of the statement: "Strive even to death for the truth, and the Lord God will fight for you" (Ecclesiastes 4:28). Let that be your motto! "Strive even to death for the truth, and the Lord God will fight for you."

We now come to a thesis that tells us: Since both doctrines, Law and

Gospel, are so different from one another, we must distinguish between these doctrines also in our sermons.

Thesis II

Only he is a pure teacher who not only presents all articles of faith in accordance with Scripture but also correctly distinguishes between Law and Gospel.

This thesis has two parts: The one asks that a pure teacher present all articles of faith in accordance with Scripture. In our day such a demand is unheard-of. People, even among the so-called believers, are shocked when someone says, "I have found the truth and have come to certainty in every teaching of revelation." Such a claim is regarded as arrogance. Certainly, people say, a young student should not talk that way. "Just don't close your mind," they cry in Germany; "don't you believe that you have already discovered the truth! Keep on studying until you have reached the goal!" But the goal is never reached, for if anyone would say, "I have reached it!" he would be highly suspect.

There are people who do not seek gratification in eating and drinking or in riches and pleasant days, but in appeasing their quest for knowledge. To be sure, this attitude is not exactly approved, and yet this is basically what professors do when they warn their own students, "Don't come to final conclusions about Christian doctrine!" They are afraid that theologians will be finished with some article, instead of trying eternally to roll the stone uphill (like Sisyphus). For that reason Kahnis, once a faithful Lutheran, tried to justify himself in the preface to his wretched *Dogmatics* with the words, "One day teaches the next" *(Dies diem docet).* That is to say, "A year ago I believed so and so, but since then other ideas have come to me and I have discovered other teachings." What a wretched and horrible attitude! No, God's Word demands that we preserve it altogether clean and pure, so that when we leave the pulpit we can say, "I can swear that I have preached God's Word correctly; yes, even if an angel came from heaven, I could still say, I have preached correctly!" This is why Luther made the paradoxical statement that when a preacher descends from the pulpit he should not pray the Lord's Prayer. He should do that before the sermon. But after the sermon an orthodox preacher need not pray, "Forgive me my trespasses." Rather he should say, "I have proclaimed the pure truth." Anyone saying that nowadays would be taken for a half lunatic. To such a degree people have become immersed in skepticism.

The Lord says through the prophet Jeremiah: "Let him who has My Word speak My Word faithfully. What has straw in common with wheat?" (Jeremiah 23:28). Hence our sermons should contain only wheat and no straw. Paul warns the Galatians: "A little leaven leavens the whole lump" (Galatians 5:9). He means to say that a single false doctrine destroys all doctrine. Moses warns: "You shall not add to the word which I command you, nor take from it" (Deuteronomy 4:2), and John closes the whole Bible with the same words [Revelation 22:18-19]. Now, if anyone says, "It is impossible to reach the point where articles of faith can be presented in accordance with Scripture," he is teaching a devilish doctrine. Especially when students hear it, a truly infernal poison is injected into their hearts; for then they will not be diligent to get to the bottom of the truth and to gain clarity in it.

However, even if one could say, "There was no false doctrine in my sermon," all of it can be wrong. Can you believe that? The second part of our thesis says just that. "Only he is a pure teacher who . . . also correctly distinguishes between Law and Gospel." This is the ultimate test of a proper sermon. It is not only a matter of having drawn all statements in the sermon from the Word of God and conforming them to it, but also of properly distinguishing between Law and Gospel.

Two builders can be given exactly the same building material, yet the one erects a beautiful structure while the other botches the whole job with the same material. If he is out of his mind he might begin with the roof, put all the windows in one room, or take the building stones and pile them on top of one another in such a way that everything is crooked. The one house is thoroughly botched and it collapses, while the other stands firm and is comfortable and beautiful. Thus in two sermons all doctrines may be stated, but the one is lovely and precious, while the other is wrong from beginning to end. Be sure to bear that in mind!

When you hear the sermons of Enthusiasts you may say, "He preached the truth," and yet feel unsatisfied. The key to this mystery is that the preacher failed to distinguish Law and Gospel, and that makes everything wrong. He preached Law truth when he should have preached Gospel truth, and vice versa. Whoever follows this preacher will go astray; he will not reach the sure ground of divine truth and will not come to certainty with regard to grace and salvation. This often happens also with the sermons of students. There are comforting statements to the effect that "it is all by grace," and then we are told, "You must do good works," and then again, "We can do nothing by our own efforts." Everything is mixed up and no one understands it, least of all the one who needs the one more than the other. Law and Gospel must be properly distinguished. Take care that you work out your sermons according to this rule! Perhaps, for once, the words flowed smoothly; but now reread the sermon and check whether Law and Gospel are properly distinguished. Often you will find that you have failed at this point. Then the sermon is wrong even though there is no false doctrine in it.

For Bible passages in support of this teaching I refer you to 2 Timothy 2:15; Luke 12:42; Ezekiel 13:18-22; Zechariah 11:7.

Also nature teaches that certain things simply cannot be mixed if they are to retain their salutary power. Certain substances are in themselves beneficial but turn into poison when mixed with each other. So it is with Law and Gospel. Or look at the colors. Mix yellow and blue together, and you get neither blue nor yellow but green. And if in a sermon Law and Gospel are mingled, you get a third something that does not belong there. In fact, it causes both Law and Gospel to lose their effectiveness.

You may formulate quite correctly what Law and Gospel say, but if you say it in such a way that they are mixed together, you produce poison for souls. Law and Gospel are indeed God's Word, but they are two kinds of teaching. Whoever does not know the real difference has nothing. Of course, merely knowing and learning this difference does no good either—for such knowledge can be acquired in a few hours, well enough to pass an examination—but experience must be added. Only then will the discovery be made that the difference between these two doctrines is a glorious one! (See Luther's *Sermon on the Distinction Between Law and Gospel,* St. Louis Edition, IX, 799 f.)

Fifth Evening Lecture
(Oct. 17, 1884)

It is marvelous and beyond comprehension that God does not govern the kingdoms of this world directly but through human beings, even though, aside from all else, they are far too shortsighted and far too weak. Yet is is incomparably more marvelous that God does not plant, manage, enlarge, and preserve even His kingdom of grace directly, but does it through human beings who are totally unfit for the task. This is a testimonial to God's loving-kindness and condescension, but also to His wisdom which no human mind can grasp or fathom. Who can measure the greatness of God's love which is revealed in the fact that God not only wants to save the world that has fallen away from Him but also that He determines to use human beings themselves, hence fellow sinners with others, for this purpose? Who can estimate the riches of God's wisdom, that He knows how to accomplish His work of salvation through people who are totally unfit and unqualified, and that He has hitherto accomplished this work so gloriously and continues to do so?

O my friends, you have every reason not only to be humbly astonished but also to be heartily joyful and enraptured that God desires to make such instruments of His grace also of you! Just think: If you could learn here how to prolong by 50 years the life of those entrusted to you, or even to restore the dead to a new earthly life, how exalted and glorious your calling would appear not only to you but to all people! How they would mob you! What extraordinary men they would consider you to be! What a treasure they would think they have if they could get you!

And yet all of this would be as nothing compared with the grandeur and glory of the calling for which you are being prepared here. You are not to prolong the poor earthly life of those entrusted to you, but to give them the life that includes all blessedness, the life that is eternal and therefore without end. You are not to resurrect your people to this earthly existence, from physical death to this poor life, but to snatch them out of their spiritual and eternal death for entrance into heaven.

Oh, if you would properly reflect on the high honor God has thereby bestowed on you, you would daily, yes hourly, fall on your knees; yes, you would throw yourself face down into the dust of the earth and say with the psalmist: "O Lord, what is man that Thou dost regard him, or the son of man that Thou dost think of him?" (Psalm 144:3). At the same time this would spur you on to offer yourself daily and hourly to the merciful God and say: "Here, Lord, I am Thine with body and soul and all my powers! I want to be consumed in Thy service." How eager you would be to sacrifice all on behalf of your calling and let yourself be formed into an instrument of God!

Yet the most important thing for you is that you first come to a thorough and living knowledge of what God has revealed through His prophets and apostles for man's salvation before you impart it to others. Therefore let us joyfully continue in the consideration of our highly important subject.

John Gerhard, though without the divine rhetoric to speak of matters of experience as only Luther could, had studied Luther carefully and presented his teaching in a systematic way. He wrote: "Although the Law and the Gospel must be distinguished everywhere"—mark well, everywhere! There is no doctrine in which their proper distinction is not called for at once—"yet the distinction must be observed above all in two points. First, in the doctrine of justification, since our justification does not come from the Law. Because of the corruption and weakness of our flesh a certain although accidental impotence is ascribed to the Law in this matter, Romans 8:3."—The Law has no place in the doctrine of justification. How important that is! We cannot be saved through the Law, and so God provides us with another means through which we may be saved. It only depends on whether we accept it, namely the Gospel, this joyful message. If you remove the doctrine of justification from the Bible, it becomes merely another ethical book.—Gerhard: "Justification comes from the Gospel, in which the righteousness which counts before God is revealed apart from the Law, Rom. 3:21, because the Gospel is 'the power of God for salvation to everyone who has faith,' Rom. 1:16. Therefore the people must be exhorted, indeed urged, to do good works in accordance with the Law, but these must not be brought into the arena of justification before God, for there is here a constant antithesis between doing and believing, between faith and works, between Law and Gospel."

Woe to us if we set out to offer the Gospel and then mix in the Law! But that is what we do if we say anything more than "Accept it!" Then it would be Law. The Gospel demands nothing of us at all but only says, "Come, eat and drink!" The Gospel brings us the great supper. Here is where most preachers go astray. They are afraid that, if they preach the Gospel too clearly, the people will fall into sin and the preachers will be to blame. That will only feed the flesh, in their opinion. It is indeed true that the Gospel becomes "a fragrance of death to death" [2 Corinthians 2:16] for many, but that is not the fault of the Gospel. On the contrary, it happens only because such people do not accept the Gospel in faith. The idea, "I believe," is not yet faith. My whole heart must be captured and must rest in the Gospel. Then I will be transformed, then I cannot do otherwise than love God and serve Him. Even after people have come to faith they must continue to be most earnestly admonished, but these admonitions must not be brought into the arena of justification. First the Law must perform its office so that the hearers, starving and parched, will receive and drink the Gospel in big gulps. As soon as a person has become a poor sinner, as soon as he understands that he cannot save himself, and even when there is not yet any love in him, Christ says, "There is My man! Come to Me just as you are. I will help you, I will remove the burden that oppresses you, and the burden I place upon you is light and My yoke is easy." This is the chief thing when I tell a person how he can become righteous, that I proclaim God's free grace, hold back nothing, say nothing but what God says in the Gospel. A hedge must be built around Mt. Sinai, but none should be put around Mt. Calvary. There God's wrath has been appeased for all.

Now, the Lord has given the church two keys, and through the church to all preachers: the binding key and the loosing key. The binding key locks the door to heaven, while the loosing key unlocks it. The preacher holds these two remarkable keys in his hand, for when the church gave him the office of preaching, it equipped him with these keys.

[*Editorial note:* Here Walther cites Gerhard on the necessity of distinguishing Law and Gospel in the use of the keys, the second point where this is most necessary. See Gerhard, *Loci theologici, De Evangelio* (On the Gospel), par. 55. Walther comments:]

It would be a disgraceful mingling of Law and Gospel if the latter were preached to the impenitent, just as if I wanted to keep on stuffing food into the mouth of a person who already had too much.—If I know that a person is in no condition for the Gospel to help him, I must not proclaim it to him. However, it is different in public, where I must give chief consideration to God's elect children. Yet I must preach the Law even there. In fact, a sermon without Law is worthless. In every assembly there are some who are still impenitent, and these must be shaken out of their sleep of sin.— One who says, "Don't bother me with that stuff," proves that his heart has not yet been broken.

[*Editorial note:* Here follows another section from Gerhard's chapter on the Gospel, par. 52. Gerhard lists three reasons why the distinction between Law and Gospel must be rigidly obseved: "1. The article of justification will not and cannot keep its integrity if the distinction of these doctrines is neglected, as the history of the early church amply demonstrates; 2. The blessings of Christ are greatly obscured if the doctrine of the Gospel is not strictly delimited against the doctrine of the Law; 3. The confusion of Law and Gospel necessarily entails the disturbance of consciences, since no true and firm consolation remains for great and serious terrors of conscience if the gracious promises of the Gospel are adulterated." Walther concludes:]

The mingling of Law and Gospel leads to disturbed consciences. No matter how consoling the message, it will do the people no good if a sting is added. The honey of the Gospel will at first taste sweet, but if a sting of the Law is mixed in, everything is spoiled. The conscience can have no peace unless I say, "God accepts you by grace." If the preacher says, " 'Come, for all is now ready,' but—you must first do so and do," I will be lost, for then I must always wonder, "Have I really done what God wants?" Then nothing will do me any good.

Sixth Evening Lecture
(Oct. 24, 1884)

A pious old Lutheran theologian said of students of theology, "When they come to the university, they know everything. In the second year they discover that there are, after all, some things they do not know. At the end of their last year they are convinced that they don't know anything." It is easy to see what that old theologian wanted to impress on his students, namely that no delusion is worse than the idea that one has come a long way in his knowledge, and that being conceited about one's knowledge is a sure indication that it must be very superficial. No doubt the old theologian was entirely right. His judgment agrees fully with what the apostle Paul says: "If anyone imagines that he knows something, he does not yet know as he ought to know" (1 Cor. 8:2).

For that reason all the great pedagogs and teachers have told their students, *"Non multa, sed multum"* ("Not many different things, but much of one thing"). It is not so much a matter of what and how much a person knows, but of *how* he knows it. The more he gets into his field of study, the more quickly he will come to the conviction that he still has much to learn. He does not parrot the watchword of our time, "Look how much we know!" but, on the contrary, he echoes the word of a great philosopher, "How much there is that we do not know!" The more learned a man is in truth, the more modest he is, because he knows how much he still lacks, and how narrow are the boundaries in which his knowledge is contained, and how much more there is that has never been explored.

If this is true of all knowledge, of every area of learning, it is true to a far greater degree in the field of theology. Here the cited statement of the apostle Paul applies, which refers not to genuine knowledge but to the knowledge a conceited person claims to have. For that reason Luther exhorts every lazy student: "Study and keep on reading! You cannot read Scripture too much; and what you read you cannot understand too well; and what you understand you cannot teach too well; and what you teach well, you cannot live too well. Believe one who has had experience!"

True understanding, true knowledge in theology is connected with great difficulty, great labor. But this is especially true of the doctrine with which we are dealing in these evening hours. To become clear on this, the third thesis now gives us an excellent opportunity.

Thesis III

To distinguish properly between Law and Gospel is the most difficult and exalted skill of Christians and theologians, a skill that only the Holy Spirit teaches in the school of experience.

Some of you may perhaps think, "What? Is that really true? I have already heard five lectures on the subject and am perfectly clear on it. Can this be the most difficult skill? I have mastered it." But, my dear friend, you are badly mistaken! Bear in mind, the thesis does not mean that the doctrine of Law and Gospel is so difficult that it could not be learned without the assistance of the Holy Spirit. It is easy, even for children. Every child can grasp this teaching; it is stated in every catechism; it is not strong meat but milk; it belongs to the ABCs, the first principles of Christianity, for without this teaching no person can be a Christian. Even a little child soon observes: "The first chief part treats of the Ten Commandments and the second of the Creed. First we are told what we must do, and then, that we must only believe in order to be saved, for nothing is demanded here." The circumstances of this doctrine are entirely different from those of the doctrine concerning the properties by which the Persons of the Trinity are distinguished. This teaching differs altogether from the doctrine of predestination with its many impenetrable mysteries; it is totally different from the doctrine concerning the communication of the properties of Christ's deity to His humanity. Those are teachings that children cannot grasp, for they are beyond their understanding. It is a different matter when we come to Law and Gsopel. You, too, now know this doctrine.

But here we are speaking about its application and function. It is the practical application which is so difficult that no human being can achieve it on the basis of his own reflection. The Holy Spirit must teach it to us in the school of experience. First of all, it is so difficult and such a high art for the preacher as a Christian, and secondly, it is so difficult and such a high art for him as a preacher.

First, then, properly to distinguish Law and Gospel is so difficult and such a high art for the preacher as a Christian. In fact, this is the greatest skill a human being can acquire.

In Psalm 51:10-11 David prays for a "right [or steadfast] spirit." He lacked certainty since his dreadful fall into the sins of murder and adultery. When he acknowledged his sin, he received absolution, and yet we do not read that David cheered up immediately, but we gather from many psalms that he experienced great misery and trials. When God's messenger told him, "Your sins have been taken away," he said within himself, "No, that is impossible; my sin is too great." He soaked his bed with tears, walked around bowed and stooped, his body wasted away, and his strength was dried up as by the heat of summer (Psalm 32:3-4). This exalted and royal prophet knew the doctrine of Law and Gospel very well. His psalms are full of the difference between the two. But when he himself fell into sin, he was unable to put his knowledge into practice. He cried, "Put a new and right spirit within me."

That is characteristic of Christians. They accept Scripture as true, as God's infallible Word. But when they need comfort they cannot find it and they cry for mercy and get down on their knees before God. And God let David taste the bitterness of sin. We observe, in general, that after his fall

David experienced more grief than joy and that one calamity upon the other struck him. God did not do this as though He had not forgiven him his sin, but in order to preserve him from a new lapse. God acted out of pure love and mercy. Naturally, one who is still dead in sins will think: "How stupid of David to keep on tormenting himself, even though God had forgiven him his sins!" Such a person turns the Gospel into a soft pillow; he continues to live in sin, and he thinks he will get to heaven anyway. But that is a carnal Gospel.

Luke 5:1-11: The Lord came to His disciple whom He called *Petros,* the "Rockman," and told him and his companions to let down their nets, even though they had caught nothing all night. Peter obeyed, although he perhaps thought he would not catch anything anyway. But behold, they caught so many fish that the nets began to break. Then Peter was afraid and thought, "That must be the almighty God Himself! That must be my Creator! That must also be the One who will one day be my Judge!" He fell down at Jesus' feet, saying, "Depart from me, for I am a sinful man, O Lord." Is this not remarkable? Peter thinks the Lord will say to him, "Look, you have committed so many sins and are therefore a man worthy of condemnation."

Whence this fear? Why did he not fall down at Jesus' feet and thank Him? Because his sins were vividly before him, he could not be joyful and grateful, but was driven in fear and trembling to his knees, where he uttered those dreadful words to his Lord and Savior: "Depart from me!" It was the devil who had robbed him of all comfort and induced him to speak thus to Christ. He thought nothing else than that the Lord would annihilate him. He was unable to distinguish Law and Gospel. If he could have done so, he could have confidently approached Jesus, knowing that He had forgiven him all his sins. How often he must have thought later on, "What a big fool I was then! I should have said, 'Abide with me, O Lord, for I am a sinful man.' " Indeed, that is what he did later on when he had fallen once again. Then he was filled with inexpressible joy when Jesus looked upon him full of grace.

1 John 3:19-20: "By this we shall know that we are of the truth, and reassure our hearts before Him whenever our hearts condemn us; for God is greater than our hearts, and He knows everything." When our heart does not condemn us, it is easy to distinguish Law and Gospel. And that is the state of a Christian. Yet he, too, will get into situations where his heart condemns him. Do what he will, he cannot silence this voice. It constantly calls to him and reminds him all at once of former sins. He suddenly remembers a sin he had long forgotten, and a terrible fear assails him. If a person is then able to distinguish Law and Gospel, he will fall down at

Jesus' feet and be consoled by His merit. But this is difficult. It seems foolish to one who is spiritually dead to be tormented about past sins. He becomes ever more indifferent to all sin. A Christian, however, is conscious of his sins and also feels the witness of his conscience against them.

Finally, however, when Christians correctly practice the distinction between Law and Gospel, they will say with St. John: "God is greater than my heart; He has rendered a different verdict, and that applies to me too." But that is so difficult! Blessed are you if you have learned this skill! And once you have learned it, do not think you have mastered it; you will always remain a pupil. There will be hours when you will be unable to distinguish Law and Gospel. But when the Law condemns you, you must reach for the Gospel at once.

Luther treats this subject more gloriously than anyone since the days of the apostles, and yet he confesses that in practice he often succumbed. The devil often tormented him, even though he had committed no gross sins and had led a virtuous life. The devil often assailed him about spiritual sins so that he did not know where to turn. Frequently he then went to his father confessor, Bugenhagen, made his confession, knelt and received absolution. Then he departed in good cheer.

[*Editorial note:* Here follow quotations from Luther's *Sermon on the Distinction Between Law and Gospel*, St. Louis Edition, IX, 806 f.; 808 f.; 802.]

In his *Table Talk*, Luther says: "There's no man living on earth who knows how to distinguish between the Law and the Gospel. We may think we understand it when we are listening to a sermon, but we're far from it. Only the Holy Spirit knows this. . . . Because I've been writing so much and so long about it, you'd think I'd know the distinction, but when a crisis comes I recognize very well that I am far, far from understanding. So God alone should and must be our holy master" *(Luther's Works,* American Edition, Vol. 54, p. 127). Note that this confession comes from Luther, who had for so many years written large volumes on this subject! We are always more inclined to listen to the Law rather than to the Gospel.

[*Editorial note:* Walther quotes from Luther's commentary on Psalm 131—St. Louis Edition, IV, 2077 f.—to the effect that dying persons are often frightened by the Law. Walther continues:] In the agony of death the devil comes and seeks to snatch the poor Christian away from the Gospel in his last hour. When Christians are about to enter eternity, they wonder, "Am I really fit for it?" They recall many Bible passages, among them, "If you would enter life, keep the commandments," and they forget that that is Law. Then their hearts will say, "You are not fit, you cannot be saved." In that moment they simply cannot distinguish between Law and Gospel.

Therefore it is good for you to learn it already in your youth. Don't think: "We have been thoroughly instructed on this doctrine. Hence, in case I experience the agony of death, I will resort to it." Yes, if that were within our power! The devil will throw you into such confusion that you won't know where to turn. Nor must you think, "I'm still young!" How often God snatches away a person in the full bloom of his youth in order to remind others of the necessity of giving thought to their death!

We are still talking about how a preacher as a Christian should distinguish between Law and Gospel. For he should be a Christian; otherwise he should not be a preacher. Whoever has not arrived at knowing and practicing this distinction is still a heathen or a Jew. It is of the very essence of being a Christian that he knows how to seek his salvation in Christ and thus to escape from the Law.

Let me cite Luther again: "But when it comes to experience, you will find the Gospel a rare guest but the Law a constant guest in your conscience, which is habituated to the Law and the sense of sin; reason, too, supports this sense" *(Lectures on Galatians,* 1535, *Luther's Works,* American Edition, Vol. 26, p. 117). Unless we learn it by experience, we will not learn it at all. . . . When the comfort of the Gospel is in your heart, those are glimpses of light on a certain day; sometimes there are none at all for several days. But one should always keep in mind: "For poor sinners like me, the Gospel, the sweet Gospel, is available. I have forgiveness of sins through Christ."

[*Editorial note:* Walther again quotes Luther, to the effect that there is a proper time for everything—a time to hear the Gospel, and also, when public duties are to be performed, a time to hear the Law and perform the duties according to it. Walther continues:]

So, when one is to do in public what is right, then is not the time to hear the Gospel but the Law, when one is thinking of his calling. When it is not a matter of your relationship to God, then you must act according to the Law—however, not like a slave but like a child.

Seventh Evening Lecture

(Nov. 7, 1884)

When I told you 14 days ago that Luther says no one is able to distinguish Law and Gospel without illumination by the Holy Spirit, and that even Luther was himself only a humble beginner in this high and glorious art, it was by no means my intention to depress and discourage you. On the contrary, I wanted those who had thought it a skill very easily acquired to be cured of this great self-delusion and, on the other hand, I wished to hearten and encourage the faint-hearted among you who think, "Well, if even Luther had such a hard time acquiring this skill, my chances are very much smaller."

Remember: If a person can learn how properly to distinguish Law and Gospel only in the school of the Holy Spirit and genuine Christian experience, he may have studied in all kinds of other schools and still not have acquired this skill. He dare not think that the remarks about the difficulty of this matter apply only to weak people, but not to gifted and knowledgeable young men. On the contrary, the more gifted and knowledgeable a person is, the more easily he flatters his own ego and trusts in himself; he does not take the matter seriously and will probably never learn to know how these teachings must be related to one another and distinguished from one another.

Just think of Chrysostom, a great scholar and so outstanding an orator that he was called John Goldenmouth. He appeared to have the ability to move his hearers any way he wanted. He could make them happy, if he wanted; he could make them sad, if that is what he wanted; he could make them shout for joy, or mourn, weep, or sigh. Yet this good man accomplished very little, on the whole, because he was so poor at distinguishing Law and Gospel and constantly and dangerously mingled them.

Another example is Andrew Osiander, a learned and astute man, an orator without an equal. At first he distinguished Law and Gospel very well, as may be seen from his preliminary draft of the Augsburg Confession. However, this situation continued only as long as he was willing to be Luther's pupil. He became proud of his fine gifts and splendid learning and was finally entirely blinded in his judgment. As a result he became guilty of the most horrendous mingling of Law and Gospel. He taught that man is justified before God not because of the righteousness won for him by Christ through His bitter suffering and death, but because Christ dwells in man with His essential, divine righteousness. Therefore be on your guard!

Now, once a person has learned in the school of the Holy Spirit how to distinguish Law and Gospel correctly, the weakest people—if only they are true Christians, if only they themselves have felt the force of the Law and the comfort of the Gospel, the power of faith—will be the best equipped to apply to others what they themselves have experienced. For that reason the least gifted among preachers are often the best ones. Without a doubt, at the time of Chrysostom many a simple, poor, unheralded presbyter in the hinterland distinguished Law and Gospel better than the great orator in the world metropolis Constantinople, better than the philosophically trained Clement of Alexandria, better than the many-sided scholar Origen.

The same holds true at the time of the Reformation. A simple pastor named Cordatus, a close friend of Luther, undoubtedly distinguished Law and Gospel a thousand times better than Melanchthon, the "teacher of all Germany," even though the latter derisively called Cordatus *Quadratus,* a clumsy "square," because he had unmasked Melanchthon when he went astray in the doctrine of free will. Therefore one who has come to the love of his Lord Jesus and has experienced the power of the Law and of the Gospel will become the most proficient in the art of distinguishing them, no matter how difficult it is.

We are now ready to consider that the correct distinction of Law and Gospel is also the highest and most difficult skill for the *theologian,* and that all else he must know is inferior to this skill.

2 Timothy 2:15: "Do your best to present yourself to God as one approved . . . rightly handling the Word of truth." "Do your best" suggests that it is a high and difficult art to distinguish Law and Gospel properly.

In Luke 12:42 the Lord calls that steward faithful and wise who gives the members of the household "their portion of food at the proper time"— not when he speaks the Word of God in general, or, to stay with the picture, when he gives everyone a little of the food he was authorized to distribute. No, the steward is commended when at the proper time he gives each person his proper portion, precisely what he must give to correspond to each one's spiritual condition. And this must be done at the proper time, for he is a poor steward who gives the members of the household some morsel and after a lengthy interval repeats the process without asking how much he should give them and how often. Thus a preacher must know the art of giving each person at the proper time what he needs, be it Law or Gospel.

This skill is acquired only through the Holy Spirit, as 2 Corinthians 2:16 and 3:4-6 show. The apostle says that "our competence is from God" alone for this high and difficult art. The "written code" is the Law, while the "Spirit" denotes the Gospel. We are clearly told that both must be proclaimed side by side. And by nature no one has the ability to do this; God Himself must supply it. Therefore a pastor must no longer have the spirit of this world. One who still has this spirit within him can never learn how to make this distinction properly. For the Spirit of God cannot dwell in a heart where the spirit of the world is still in control. Hence the world cannot receive the Spirit. Anyone, therefore, who desires to be a servant approved by the Lord must first become a Christian. He may be able to present all the dogmas correctly, but that is not enough. He must also know how to give each soul in his audience what it needs. This is possible when the preacher can investigate the condition of each soul. Of course, that is extremely difficult, just as the diagnosis is the most difficult task for the physician.

It is not enough for you to use the living and sharp Word of God. With this sharp sword you could easily kill the souls if you did not give them what they need. For that reason a preacher must be able to perceive whether he is dealing with a hypocrite or an honest Christian; whether it is one still spiritually dead or one aroused from the sleep of sin; whether it is one assailed by the devil and the flesh, or one who because of his willful malice has been consigned to the devil. One who has no experience may easily mistake a hypocrite for a genuine Christian, etc. You must preach in such a way that every hearer thinks, "That applies to me! He has pictured the hypocrite exactly the way I am." Or the pastor has described the person suffering from trials in a way so true to life that he cannot but think, "That's how it is with me." Also the penitent person must quickly become aware, "that word of comfort is for me, and I must make it my own." The terrified one must think, "Oh, that is a sweet word! That's for me." Even the impenitent must be able to say to himself, "Yes, that is exactly a picture of me."

Hence the preacher must know how to present an accurate portrait of each hearer. If he merely sets forth the various doctrines in an objective way, that will not be enough. One who is indeed orthodox and has comprehended the pure teaching but is not himself in communication with God, has not yet come to terms with God, has not yet become sure as to whether his sins are forgiven or not—how can he produce a Christian sermon? Here too the pagan proverb applies, "It is the heart that makes one eloquent." Indeed, only in the school of the Holy Spirit and through trial can we learn how to distinguish Law and Gospel correctly.

For that reason people love to read Luther's sermons. To be sure, at first his sermons have little appeal. But once people overcome their dislike (perhaps bringing themselves to overcome it because the preacher recommended the collection as "the most precious sermon book"), they like these sermons so much that they want nothing else. And it is indeed a joy to read Luther's sermons. You find yourself on every page. First he scares the living daylights out of you and hurls you down into the depths. But he has hardly done that when he says, "Do you believe that?" "Yes." "Good, come back up!" There is thunder and lightning, but then immediately the gentle breath of the Holy Spirit in the Gospel. It is impossible to resist. We are compelled to say, "This is good, invigorating daily bread, the proper food for my soul." Luther does not prescribe a long journey, nor does he offer detailed instructions on how to get out, but once he has led a person to acknowledge himself a poor sinner, he says, "Stop; Christ's grace is greater than all the world's sin." He constantly preaches Law and Gospel side by side, so that the Law is illustrated in a far more terrifying way by the Gospel, and the Gospel is made far sweeter and more consoling through the Law. You must learn this from dear father Luther. Then the people will listen to you. This will interest them. It will make them feel that in this hour the preacher wants to bring them up from destruction, so that they must leave the church rejoicing.

But how careful the preacher must be not to say something wrong! Therefore you must always go over your sermon once more and ask, "Is all this entirely correct? Is it neither against the Law nor against the Gospel?" So, for example, it would be wrong to say, "Whoever is still afraid of death is not a Christian; for a Christian is not afraid of death." That is a great lie. It may well be true that Christians are not afraid to come before God, but they are still afraid of decaying and moldering in the grave, etc. A preacher must delete such a sentence at once. Furthermore, young preachers who like to be active and accomplish something (a very fine ambition!) enjoy speaking about a Christian's salvation to children of the world. But often they go too far and say, "Those poor people, those children of the world, have no pleasure, no peace, no rest at all." That is not true. When children of the world hear this, they will think, "That simple-minded preacher! What does he know? We have lots of pleasure and peace." The preacher must express it differently. He must say that the children of the world indeed have joys and pleasures, but then all at once thoughts such as these will come to them: "What if the Christians' words are true? What if they are right? What will happen to me then?" In the midst of high living the thought of death intrudes like a ghost and turns joy into bitterness. Then such people must admit: "Yes, the preacher really knows how to draw a true picture of us!"

Or, if you picture Christians as people who are always happy and never have any trouble, that too is false. Christians have more anguish and trouble and tribulation than the world. And yet the Christian is far more blessed. If God should come during this night to take his soul, he will think: "Praise God, it is finished! I will soon be with my Savior." In tribulation he will think: "It won't last very long; then I will reach home, and all the misery and grief of this earth will vanish and be forgotten." Christians weep, and the angels rejoice over them. Christians experience anguish and terror, and God has their best interests at heart and says to them, "You are My dear children." These are just a few examples to show that you dare not go too far, even with the best intention.

Your second concern in preparing your sermons must be not to say anything that can be misunderstood. For example, "One who sins deliberately and knowingly falls from grace." That is subject to misunderstanding, for at times even true Christians sin knowingly and willingly, but in a state in which they are, so to say, *overcome* by sin inwardly or also outwardly. These are called rash sins. Someone has a hot temper but is otherwise amiable. Suddenly something crosses his path, and he gives vent to his temper. Then the Spirit of God reproves him, "Look what kind of person you are!" and he begs God for forgiveness. It is true, when a Christian sins knowingly, he grieves the Holy Spirit, and the Holy Spirit wants no part of it. Therefore you must tell the people: "That is a dangerous path! The Holy Spirit will draw back, and you will suffer a relapse instead of going forward. And unless you proceed in true repentance, this sin can lead you to destruction."

It would be just as misleading to say, "Good works are not necessary, but faith alone." If I say, "They are not necessary for salvation," it is correct. But if I do not do good works I cannot stay on the right path. After all, God has commanded them. It is His will that we do good works.

Again, it is misleading to say, "Sin will not hurt a Christian." To be sure, a sin of weakness will not at once subject the person to God's disfavor, but it still does damage. "There is ... no condemnation for those who are in Christ Jesus," says Paul [Romans 8:1]. He does not say, "there is nothing sinful." In short, we can't be too careful in our preaching.

However, it is also wrong if at times a subject is not sufficiently explained. When Aegidius Hunnius was still at school, he once heard these words in church: "There is, however, one sin that cannot be forgiven. It is the sin against the Holy Spirit." These words pierced his heart like a dagger. He thought at once that he had committed this sin. In fact, he thought of taking his own life. He recalled that the Holy Spirit had repeatedly knocked at the door of his heart during the sermon but that in youthful frivolity he had put it out of his mind. But God in a wonderful way delivered him from the agony of conscience. One day, taking his seat, he found a page torn out of a fine book of devotions by Spangenberg. On this page there was a discussion of the sin against the Holy Spirit, stating that a person guilty of that sin *refused to his dying day to repent.* So Hunnius was rescued. Because of that he became a great theologian, since he had to experience such great trials already in his youth.

It is even more difficult to distinguish Law and Gospel in the pastoral care of the individual. In the pulpit the preacher may say various things and think, "That will surely knock on the door of their hearts." But when people come to him as their pastor, it is much more difficult. He will soon realize, "That one is a Christian and that one is not." This is not to say that he could not be mistaken in the case of someone who puts on a very pious mien and yet is a hypocrite. But if the pastor can properly distinguish Law and Gospel, some people may still deceive him, but it will not be his fault. He will assume a dreadful burden of responsibility only if he himself is to blame when people misunderstand him. If, however, people act like Christians in order to deceive me, it is not I who am deceived, but those people themselves. There the preacher must treat a person as a Christian if he appears so to him, and vice versa.

But non-Christians are not all alike. One is a coarse scoffer and a despiser of the Bible, another is orthodox with the dead faith of the intellect, but the preacher notices that he is still blind and in a state of spiritual death. One who is still caught up in sin will naturally not know how to judge such a person. Now, when an unchristian man is thoroughly alarmed and full of unconscious dread because of his many sins, yet still unbroken, the pastor must note that he must still be crushed. One person is a slave of vice, another is self-righteous. And this is the great difficulty, namely to discover these different classes of the unconverted and to apply the proper treatment to each. My purpose is to convince you that only the Holy Spirit can properly prepare a preacher.

Finally, it is still more difficult to treat genuine Christians in accordance with their specific spiritual condition. One is a weak Christian, another is strong; one is cheerful, another is dejected; one is lukewarm, another is aglow with zeal; one has scant spiritual knowledge, another is deeply grounded in the truth.

One more thing: It is extremely important for a preacher to recognize different temperaments if he wants to judge people fairly and deal with them accordingly. My spiritual eye must not be allowed to be blind to good traits because of faults of temperament. For example, a person of sanguine temperament may always be cheerful and not trouble himself with sad thoughts, and yet not be a Christian; it is simply his nature. If, then, you discover that he is a sanguine character, and he becomes sad when you preach the Law to him, you will know that the Word has been effective. And if you then preach the Gospel to him, you must discern whether his becoming cheerful again is merely due to his nature or not. Or you may run into a melancholy person and note that he is very sad and downcast. Then you must not immediately conclude that he is sad because of his sins. But if the Gospel suddenly animates him and you see him act contrary to his temperament, you may be sure that the Gospel has reached him effectively. Or you may be dealing with a phlegmatic person who always loves to take it easy and hates to be disturbed in his thoughts. If you have calmed him, you must not think at once that you have done so through the Gospel. Or you have before you a choleric individual. If he becomes despondent, you may be sure that the Word of God is responsible.

Eighth Evening Lecture

(Nov. 14, 1884)

If Scripture were really so obscure that no certainty could be obtained as to the meaning of those pasages on which the articles of the Christian faith are based, and that without some other authority it would be impossible to determine which of several possibilities is the only correct interpretation—then Scripture could not be the Word of God. What kind of revelation would that be that leaves us in the dark particularly as to its essential content? In the Middle Ages Jewish Biblical scholars said the literal sense was obvious, but there was a hidden meaning of prime importance which could be discerned only by means of the Cabala. They stated that the Hebrew letter Aleph occurred six times in both the first and last verse of the Hebrew Scriptures. An ordinary person could not know what that signified, but the Cabala provided the answer. It meant that the world would remain for 6,000 years.

This is, of course, ridiculous, yet even within Christendom, in the papacy, it is taught that Scripture is so obscure that it is largely unintelligible, or at least that many important teachings of the Christian religion cannot be demonstrated from Scripture. Therefore tradition is indispensable. But that is blindness! To them applies the word of Paul that "the Gospel is veiled only to those who are perishing" (2 Corinthians 4:3). Luther is right in saying: "No book on earth is as plain as Holy Scripture; compared to all other books, it is like the sun compared to all other lights" *(Interpretation of Psalm 37;* St. Louis Edition, V, 334; see also Luther's *Address to the Councilmen of All Cities in Germany That They Establish and Maintain Christian Schools, Luther's Works,* American Edition, Vol. 45, pp. 363f.; for similar statements see *Luther's Works,* American Edition, Vol. 39, pp. 164 f.).

Luther is entirely correct. Holy Scripture is far clearer than the most lucid human writing, for it is given by the Holy Spirit, the Creator of languages. Therefore, as long as we remain with the words of Scripture, we cannot possible cite an error or a contradiction in Scripture. Therefore that precious Communion hymn states: "Firm as a rock this truth shall stand, unmoved by any daring hand or subtle craft and cunning" *(The Lutheran Hymnal,* 306:3).

Yet although anyone who knows the language can grasp the historical-grammatical sense of Scripture, no one—be he ever so great a linguist, ever so famous a philologist, ever so logical a thinker—can understand Scripture for his salvation without the Holy Spirit. The apostle Paul says, "The unspiritual man does not receive the gifts of the Spirit of God, for they are folly to him, and he is not able to understand them because they are spiritually discerned" (1 Corinthians 2:14). "We preach Christ crucified, a stumbling block to Jews and folly to Gentiles" (1 Corinthians 1:23). But to gain a saving knowledge of Scripture one must, above all, understand the distinction between Law and Gospel. With this understanding all Scripture becomes clear; without it, the whole Bible remains a book sealed with seven seals.

Now before we go on to our fourth thesis, listen to a few quotations from Luther. When we hear the sermons of inexperienced preachers, we perhaps cannot say that they misstated the Law or the Gospel, and yet we must often observe that Law and Gospel have been intermingled. In his *Sermon on the Distinction Between Law and Gospel* Luther states: "It is quite easy to show that the Law is a word and teaching different from the Gospel. But to distinguish them in practice is difficult and arduous. St. Jerome wrote much on the subject, but the way a blind man speaks of color" (St. Louis Edition, IX, 806 f.). Luther had great respect for the learned. He cherished Erasmus for reviving the languages. But Luther never called him a doctor of theology. Why not? Because he did not have *this* skill. And even though a most talented person were to spend 50 years in preparation for the holy ministry—but had not received the Holy Spirit— he would not rightly distinguish Law and Gospel. This is indeed the Scylla and Charybdis. On both sides one can lead souls to destruction and grievously sin against poor Christians.

Commenting on Galatians 2:14, Luther says: "Whoever knows well how to distinguish the Gospel from the Law should give thanks to God and know that he is a real theologian. I admit that in the time of temptation I myself do not know how to do this as I should" *(Lectures on Galatians, 1535, Luther's Works,* American Edition, Vol. 26, p. 115). A simple preacher can be an excellent theologian, while another, who has mastered all Oriental languages and has studied who knows what else, perhaps does not yet deserve that title. It all depends on whether God has made him a theologian or not.

As for you who object that this is really going too far, you are still blind! If you had experienced it, you would admit that this art is exceedingly difficult.

Thesis IV

The true knowledge of the difference between Law and Gospel is not only a glorious light for the correct understanding of all of Holy Scripture, but without such knowledge Scripture is and remains a closed book.

Paging through Scripture before we know the difference between Law and Gospel makes us think it contains nothing but contradictions, even more than the Koran. At one place the Bible pronounces a person blessed, at another place it condemns him. When a rich young man asked Jesus: "Teacher, what good deed must I do to have eternal life?" he was told: "If you would enter life, keep the commandments" [Matthew 19:16 f.]. When the jailer at Philippi put the same question to Paul and Silas, he was told: "Believe in the Lord Jesus, and you will be saved, you and your household" [Acts 16:31]. In Habakkuk 2:4 we read: "The righteous shall live by his faith"; John says: "He who does right is righteous" (1 John 3:7); and the apostle Paul replies: "Since all have sinned and fall short of the glory of God, they are justified by His grace as a gift, through the redemption which is in Christ Jesus" [Romans 3:23-24]. In one place Scripture says that God does not want sinners; in another place: "Everyone who calls upon the name of the Lord will be saved" [Romans 10:13]. In one place Paul exclaims: "The wrath of God is revealed from heaven against all ungodliness and wickedness of men" [Romans 1:18], and Psalm 5:4 says: "Thou art not a God who delights in wickedness; evil may not sojourn with Thee." Yet Peter tells us to "set your hope fully upon the grace that is coming to you" [1 Peter 1:13]. In one place we are told that the whole world is under God's judgment (see Romans 3:19), while at another place the message is, "God so loved the world that He gave His only Son, that whoever believes in Him should not perish but have eternal life" [John 3:16]. Also noteworthy is 1 Corinthians 6:9-11. . . .

On reading all this, one who has no idea of the difference between Law and Gospel can only be thoroughly confused and ask, "What? This is supposed to be God's Word? A book full of such contradictions?"

Nor is it true that the Old Testament reveals a wrathful God, while the New shows us a gracious God; or that in the Old Testament salvation is by works, while in the New it is by faith. We find statements of both kinds in both testaments. But as soon as we know the difference between Law and Gospel, the sun rises over Scripture. Then we discover the most beautiful harmony. We learn that the Law was not given that we might be righteous through it, but that we might see our impotence, that we might see what weak people we are. Then we will note what a sweet message the Gospel is, what a glorious teaching it is; then we will accept the Gospel with thousandfold joy.

Church history also demonstrates the importance of this knowledge. The church's downfall set in when Law and Gospel were mingled, as the writings of the church fathers show. To be sure, up to the sixth century we still run across beautiful statements, but then we also note that this light is going out and this distinction is being forgotten more and more. This is evident also in the monastic life, which became more and more prominent. The monastics even regarded as necessary for salvation what the Lord had told that rich young man. They proclaimed the Law when they should have proclaimed the Gospel.

At the height of papal rule the knowledge of this distinction was completely snuffed out; a truly infernal darkness descended, so that bald paganism and idolatry came into the church. Think of our dear Luther! Compared with the prevailing darkness, he was quite enlightened, even at the beginning, but he did not yet know how to distinguish between Law and Gospel. How he tortured himself! He scourged himself, he fasted, almost to the point of death. What he found most difficult and terrifying was the statement that the righteousness of God is revealed in the Gospel [Romans 1:17]. "How dreadful!" he thought. "The Law demands fulfillment, and now the Gospel also orders us to become righteous!" He even entertained blasphemous thoughts. But then he was suddenly enlightened as to what kind of righteousness is revealed in the Gospel. Henceforth he became aware of the distinction between Law and Gospel throughout Scripture. [*Editorial note:* See Luther's own account of his experience, in his *Preface to the Complete Edition of Luther's Latin Writings, Luther's Works,* American Edition, Vol. 34, pp. 327 ff., esp. pp. 336 f.]

From the moment Luther understood this distinction he became the Reformer. That is why he was so remarkably successful. By this knowledge he delivered the poor people from the wretchedness to which they had been driven by the Law-preaching of their priests.

You, too, must know how important this is for you, especially when you must act as pastor. Whenever someone comes to you wretched and afraid, it is always because the Law has had its effect and he does not remember that he can be saved through the Gospel. All he can think of is, "I am a poor sinner who has deserved hell." Then you must say to him: "True, you are a lost and condemned sinner. But that is Law. However, there is another teaching in Scripture. The law has done its work in you to bring you to a knowledge of your sin. Now leave Sinai and come to Golgotha! Behold there your Savior bleeding and dying for you." Yes, when you assume the pastoral office you will learn for the first time how significant and important the distinction between Law and Gospel is, and how an understanding of this difference alone enables you to conduct the office that is to save the world. Naturally the most important thing is for you to have experienced this distinction in yourself. I am not thinking of those who have never been terrified by their sins, who imagine that because they have grown up in a Christian family they are orthodox, but I am thinking of those who are concerned about their salvation. At times you will feel you are God's children, and then again you will think your sins have not been forgiven. In that case you can have peace only by understanding the distinction between Law and Gospel.

The Apology tells us that "rightly to understand the benefit of Christ and the great treasure of the Gospel (which Paul extols so greatly), we must separate, on the one hand, the promise of God and the grace that is offered, and, on the other hand, the Law, as far as the heavens are from the earth" (Ar. IV [III], par. 185 [65], German text; *Concordia Triglotta,* p. 173; cf. Tappert, p. 132). Formula of Concord Art. V is devoted to the importance and nature of the distinction between Law and Gospel (Tappert, pp. 477 ff. and 558 ff.). If these two doctrines are not kept separate, the Gospel is darkened and the merit of Christ is obscured. If I fear the threats of the Law, I have forgotten Christ, for He says to me: "Though your sins are like scarlet, they shall be as white as snow. Come to Me, all who labor and are heavy laden, and I will give you rest." The preacher will proclaim this correctly only if he has received an indelible impression of the distinction between Law and Gospel. Only such a one can calmly take to his deathbed. In whatever way the devil assails him, he will say to the devil, "You are quite right, but I have another doctrine, which tells me something different. I am glad the Law dealt with me as it has, for now the Gospel tastes all the better."

[*Editorial note:* Walther cites Formula of Concord Art. V, par. 27 (Tappert, p. 563), which speaks of the danger in mingling Law and Gospel. He continues:] We are in the same danger. Read the writings of those who claim to be the best preachers! They are so harsh because they mingle Law and Gospel, so that the people are assailed by doubts on their deathbed. Many a one will think, "I wonder if God will accept me." But to die in such uncertainty is not to die a blessed death. And who is to blame in many cases? The preacher.

Nor may the preacher say that the Law has been repealed, for that is not true. The Law stands and is not repealed. But we have another message. God does not say: "Through the Law comes righteousness," but "through the Law comes knowledge of sin" [Romans 3:20]. Indeed, in the Letter to the Romans [4:5] it says: "To the one who . . . trusts Him who justifies the ungodly, his faith is reckoned as righteousness." Hence, just when I realize that I am ungodly, I am on the right road, the road to salvation.

Luther on Galatians 3:19: "Unless the Gospel is clearly distinguished from the Law, Christian doctrine cannot be kept sound. But when this distinction is recognized, the true meaning of justification is recognized. Then it is easy to distinguish faith from works, and Christ from Moses, as well as from the magistrate and all civil laws" *(Luther's Works,* American Edition, Vol. 26, p. 313).

As Chemnitz says *(Loci theologici,* "On Justification," 206), no other light has dispelled the darkness of the papacy but the fact that the distinction between Law and Gospel became prominent. Mighty emperors tried, great councils of the church attempted a reformation, but what did they accomplish? Nothing! In fact, matters became worse. How, then, could a lowly monk accomplish it? Without a doubt because he restored this candlestick to the sanctuary. Without that distinction he might have preached ever so evangelically, but the Christians would not have been comforted. For when they found the Law they would have thought: "I was mistaken after all! I must keep God's commandments if I want to enter life." Most preachers fall short here. Hus preached the Gospel very well, but he did not correctly show the difference between Law and Gospel, and so his work did not endure.

May God preserve to us this light which He has kindled for us! I am thinking especially of you. We older people will soon lie in our graves. In our time this light has begun to shine again. See to it that it is not extinguished! If you think you will have mastered it in a few hours, you are on the wrong track. If this light is not diligently guarded, it will soon be extinguished. Thus we find this light burning only in the writings of the earliest church fathers. They are followed by others who have nothing definite to say on the subject. For that reason the papacy invaded the church so rapidly. But the same danger threatens us too.

Our thesis rests principally on Romans 10:2-4. The Jews had an unenlightened zeal for the Law, because they were "ignorant of the righteousness that comes from God." they failed to understand that "Christ is the end of the Law"; otherwise they would not have become enemies of the Gospel, and the dreadful darkness surrounding them would have been dispelled.

Ninth Evening Lecture

(Nov. 21, 1884)

According to the latest statistics [1884], the present population of the world is about 1,400,000,000, of whom less than a third acknowledge Christ, in whom alone there is salvation. Equally lamentable is the fact that of the approximately 400 million nominal Christians, nearly half are still adherents of the pope, the Antichrist. This is so gruesome and tragic a mystery that true Christians are afraid to gaze into this abyss of indescribable misery and wretchedness.

To be sure, nowadays many, if not most, of those claiming to be Lutherans no longer regard the pope as the Antichrist and the papacy as the kingdom of Antichrist. If the orthodox Lutheran church in our country still seriously asserts this view together with the whole church of the Reformation and in agreement with the Confessions of this church, this is regarded, at best, as a queer notion of narrow-minded people who refuse to keep up with the times.

Why should this be? Primarily because people no longer realize what it is that makes Antichrist what he is. They say: "We concede that especially in the Middle Ages there were many popes who were veritable monsters and who, even in the opinion of papistic authors, were swallowed up by hell." People admit that also today there are still many evils there, and yet they say: "Show us a church where there are no errors and even Judases." It is granted further that many horrible heresies hold sway in the papacy, and yet it is pointed out that even there the three ecumenical creeds are firmly adhered to. When the Council of Trent opened in 1545 those creeds were recited. Furthermore: "Also the popes believe that the Bible in both testaments is God's revealed Word, that God is triune, that Christ is God and man in one Person and the Savior of the world. Like ourselves, they acknowledge a resurrection of the dead and a final judgment on all flesh; they also believe that there is a heaven and a hell. Therefore, far from being the realm of Antichrist, it is rather a strong dike against the dreadful deluge of unbelief threatening Christendom." Pantheism, materialism, atheism, socialism, nihilism, anarchism, and the like—these dreadful heritages of our age are regarded as the realm of Antichrist. But I ask again, why is it that people draw the conclusion that therefore the papacy is not the kingdom of Antichrist, and the pope is not the Antichrist?

People do not bear in mind that the pope wants to be the vicar of Christ on earth and the visible head of all Christendom. To achieve that he must confess many Christian doctrines, he must wear a mask, or else an Antichrist could not possibly exist within Christendom. Yes, he has to declare war on the enemies of all religions and the enemies of the Christian religion, for he knows that if Christ falls, Antichrist must also fall. For if He whose vicar he claims to be falls, then his own position is also finished. Thus, when the pope seemingly fights for Christ and Christianity, he is really fighting for himself and his kingdom. Most important of all, the pope is the only one in all of Christendom—I do not regard as Christians those groups that deny the triune God—who is a foe of God's free grace in Christ, an enemy of the Gospel under the guise of Christianity, while aping Christian institutions. To this we are led by our next thesis.

Thesis V

The first and most glaring way of mingling Law and Gospel is the teaching of the papists, Socinians, and rationalists that makes of Christ a new Moses or Lawgiver and turns the Gospel into a doctrine of works and, conversely, like the papists, condemns and anathematizes those who teach the Gospel as a message of God's free grace in Christ.

Two months before Luther's death the Council of Trent opened for the purpose of rebuilding the papacy that had been mortally wounded by Luther's Reformation. Session IV states that the council's purpose was "that the purity of the Gospel may be preserved in the Church after the errors have been removed. This [Gospel], of old promised through the Prophets in the Holy Scriptures, our Lord Jesus Christ, the Son of God, promulgated first with His own mouth, and then commanded it to be preached by His apostles to every creature as the source at once of all saving truth and *rules of conduct*" (H. J. Schroeder, ed. *Canons and Decrees of the Council of Trent*. St. Louis: B. Herder Book Co., 1941, p. 16).

This does not, at first, sound too bad. [They] speak of the Gospel as containing salutary teachings, but they immediately add that it also prescribes rules of conduct. That is what Christ is said to have had in mind when He commanded: "Go into all the world and preach the Gospel to the whole creation" (Mark 16:15), as if to say, "Tell them the Gospel, tell them what morals and what works are expected of them." Here we see that they do not want to accept the Gospel in the true sense of the word. In their view it is, at best, a law like that of Moses. Furthermore, they do not promote God's commandments so much as the commandments of the church. If someone transgresses God's commandments, he is left in peace; but let him transgress the commandments of the church, and he will be harassed until he confesses that he has committed a mortal sin in, for example, eating meat on Friday.

Session VI, Canon 21: "If anyone says that Christ Jesus was given by

50

God to men as a redeemer in whom to trust, and not also a *legislator* whom to obey, let him be anathema" (Schroeder, p. 44). That destroys the whole Christian faith. If Christ came into the world to bring us new laws, we might say He could just as well have stayed in heaven. Moses has already given us so perfect a Law that we cannot keep it. If Christ had brought us new laws in addition, we would have been driven to despair.

The very word "Gospel" contradicts such a view. From Mark 16:15 we know that Christ Himself called His Word Gospel, concretely, "he who believes and is baptized, etc." If Christ's teaching were Law, it would not be an evangel, a message of joy, but rather a message of gloom.

We see the same thing in the Old Testament, already in Genesis 3:15 ... which has been called the Protevangel, the first Gospel. It informed the Old Testament believers that Someone will come not only to tell us what we must do to get to heaven. On the contrary, the Messiah Himself will do everything. If, then, the devil's kingdom has been destroyed, there can be no question about what I must do. I have been set free, and there is nothing for me to do but accept that freedom. That is what the Biblical word "believe" means: "Make your own what Christ has won."

Many more prophecies could be cited to prove this. But I will remind you of only one, which shows us clearly what the doctrine of the Gospel really is.

Jeremiah 31:31-34 tells us that God will make a *new* covenant, not a Law covenant like the one at Sinai. On the contrary, "I will forgive their iniquity, and I will remember their sin no more." That is the sum and substance of Christ's Gospel, forgiveness of sins by free grace for Christ's sake. Anyone who thinks Christ is a new Lawgiver, bringing us new laws, crosses out the whole Christian religion. For that is what distinguishes Christianity from all other religions of the world. They all say, "This is how you must be and what you must do to get to heaven." But the Christian religion says, "You are indeed a lost and condemned sinner who cannot save himself. But do not despair. Someone has obtained salvation for you. Christ has opened the gates of heaven, and He invites you: 'Come, everything is ready. Come to the marriage feast!' "

For that reason Christ also says: "I am a physician for the sick and not for the healthy; I have come to seek and to save the lost; I have come not to call the righteous, but sinners to repentance." Wherever we see the Lord Jesus, He is surrounded by sinners, while the Pharisees lurk in the background. But the sinners crowd around Him, hungering and thirsting, for He has won their hearts. And even though the divine majesty shone forth from Him, they have the courage to approach Him and trust Him. The Pharisees complain bitterly: "This man receives sinners and eats with

51

them"[Luke 15:2]. The Lord heard what they said and would have known even if He had not heard. What does He do? He does not try to defend Himself and say, "I do not want sinners but righteous people," but He confirms their statement. "Yes indeed, I want sinners." He supports His attitude by means of the parables of the lost sheep, the lost coin, and the lost (or prodigal) son. "This is my teaching," says the Lord. "I came to seek and to save the lost" [Luke 19:10].

Examine the whole life of Jesus, and you will discover that He does not go around like a proud philosopher, a moralist surrounded by so-called "decent" people whom He teaches how to attain to the highest degree of philosophical perfection. On the contrary, He goes after the lost sinners and even says that harlots and tax collectors will get into the kingdom of heaven before the proud Pharisees. Here He shows clearly what His Gospel is, and all apostles say the same thing. (See John 1:17; John 3:17; Romans 1:16-17; 1 Timothy 1:15.)

How dreadful that in spite of these clear passages it is taught in the papal church that what Scripture calls the Gospel is nothing but a new law! Elsewhere they add that many laws came from the mouth of Jesus of which Moses knew nothing. They include loving one's enemy, not taking revenge, etc. Yet even Moses said, "You shall love the Lord your God with all your heart, and with all your soul, and with all your might"[Deut. 6:5] and "You shall love your neighbor as yourself"[Lev. 19:18]. Christ did not repeal this Law of Moses, but neither did He offer any new laws. Rather, He expounded the Law in its spiritual sense. He did not come to abolish but to fulfill (Matt. 5:17), so that we may have the benefit of His fulfillment.

[*Editorial note:* Walther offers additional citations from the Canons and Decrees of the Council of Trent to demonstrate the papal teaching of justification by works, thus manifesting its antichristian character. Walther thinks the papal church is worse than all the sects. His lecture continues:]

But Christ says: "Take My *yoke* upon you . . . for My yoke is easy, and My burden is light" (Matt. 11:29-30). Hence Christ does impose a yoke. And this yoke, say the Romanists, this self-denial and cross-bearing is far more burdensome than the Law of Moses. They say that Moses prohibited only gross outward deeds and therefore think that Christ had Moses in mind when He said: "You have heard that it was said to the men of old . . ." [Matthew 5]. However, Christ means to say, "The men of old taught you in their precepts that if you refrain from the outward deed you have kept the Law." Then He proceeded to explain the Law of Moses in its true sense.

[*Editorial note:* Walther cites Luther's *Glosses on the Gospel of Matthew*—St. Louis Edition, VII, 143. Here Luther identifies the "yoke of Christ" with the Christian's cross and repudiates every reference to an "evangelical law." Walther comments:]

As soon as someone has come to a living faith through true repentance, he is a blessed person, already standing at the gates of heaven; and at the moment of death the gates open and he enters. But since it is dangerous for a Christian to have only pleasant days in this world, the Savior has made provision to lay a cross upon him. As soon as a Christian confesses his faith in word and deed, he makes enemies. Although the hostility may not become overt, it is nevertheless noticeable and causes the Christian much distress. How many people have suffered martyrdom for Christ!

But how much easier is the yoke of Christ than the yoke of the Law! Under the burden of the Law a person exclaims, "I am the most wretched of creatures!"—in fact, he falls into despair. One who lives neither under the Law nor under the Gospel simply lives like an animal; but woe to him when his eyes are opened after death! A Christian, on the contrary, can rejoice that God will deliver him from the grief and misery of this life; then he can sing Hallelujah! Think of the martyrs. They did not go weeping and wailing to their martyrdom, but with joy and jubilation. There Christ's word: "My yoke is easy and My burden is light," had its fulfillment. Please don't just listen to this; apply it to yourselves. For the chief purpose of these lectures is to advance you in the Christian faith. God grant that it will not be in vain!

Tenth Evening Lecture

(Nov. 28, 1884)

A person's resolve to become a true Christian is certainly praiseworthy and important, but yet this resolve is not a blessed one if he is not really serious about it. Many thousands have resolved to forsake the world and choose the narrow path of the children of God after draining the cup of worldly pleasure to the dregs; many thousands have resolved to renounce their sins, even their pet vices, after experiencing the truth of the statement that "sin is a reproach to any people" (Proverbs 14:34); many thousands have resolved to seek God's grace and the forgiveness of their sins after being tormented day and night by uncertainty as to God's grace and the forgiveness of their sins. In terror they asked themselves: "If you should die today, will you have a blessed death?" And what happened? Most of those who formed this resolve did not live up to it, but rather kept postponing action for a day, a week, a month, year after year. Nothing came of their resolve, and finally death caught up with them and they were lost eternally.

Why? Because they did not take their resolution seriously. God is indeed so patient, so friendly, and so gracious that He daily and richly forgives His Christians their sins of weakness and frailty—but those are only the ones who are serious about their Christianity. Those with whom this is not the case are not genuine Christians.

Much the same applies to a person who resolves to become a servant of Christ, of His church and His Word. This important and praiseworthy resolve will not be a blessed one if it is not taken seriously. One who wants to become a preacher must have an attitude that moves him to say: "Dear Lord Jesus, You are mine and I want to be Yours. To You and You alone I want to dedicate all that I do and have, my body and soul, my powers and talents, my whole life. Impose on me what You will; I will gladly bear it. Lead me anywhere, through grief or joy, through good fortune or ill, through disgrace or honor, through popular favor or contempt, through a long life or an early death: I am content. Just lead the way, and I will follow!" So our dear Paul Gerhardt sings:

> Now I will cling forever to Christ, my Savior true;
> My Lord will leave me never, Whate'er He passes through.
> He rends Death's iron chain, He breaks through sin and pain,
> He shatters hell's dark thrall—I follow Him through all.
>
> *(The Lutheran Hymnal, 192:6)*

This was the attitude of the dear apostle Paul from the moment the Lord appeared to him and spoke to him. When he had received the command to go to the heathen and preach the Gospel of Christ, he did not, as he himself said, "confer with flesh and blood" (Galatians 1:16). How blessed he was! And how unspeakably blessed his ministry! Now he is with his God and Savior these 1,800 years to see Him face to face and praise Him eternally.

O my dear friends, you have all chosen to enter the service of Christ, His church and His Word. Be sure to be entirely serious about it, or else your resolve means nothing. In fact, if you fail to execute the decision to which God has led you, if you quickly stifle the voice of the Holy Spirit in your heart, all those blessed moments will appear as your accusers before the throne of God. But how blessed you are if you carry out this resolve! You will never complain about having experienced so much grief and fear and distress, but you will rejoice when the Lord will one day with His pierced hand place the crown of glory on your head.

But what is really your chief obligation if you want to assume this holy office? You must proclaim Law and Gospel to a sinful world, but do it clearly and completely and with an ardent spirit. This leads us to our next thesis.

54

Thesis VI

Secondly, God's Word is not properly divided when the Law is not preached in its full severity nor the Gospel in its full sweetness, but when Gospel elements are mingled with the Law and Law elements with the Gospel.

. . . Let us consult Scripture. What does it say, first, of the Law? How does it tell us to avoid mixing Gospel elements into the Law?

An important and precious passage is Galatians 3:11-12. We are told that a person is justified before God by faith alone. Consequently the Law cannot justify, for it knows nothing of justifying and saving faith. That is the exclusive message of the Gospel. In other words: "The Law knows nothing of grace."

Romans 4:16 shows us that faith is not demanded of us for the purpose of giving us at least something to do (lest there be no difference between those who go to hell and those who go to heaven); no, righteousness depends on faith in order that "the promise may rest on grace." It amounts to the same thing. When I say that a person is justified before God by faith I mean to say that he is justified gratis, by grace, as a gift. Here nothing is demanded of a person, but he is told: "Take it, and you have it." This act of taking is faith. One who hears the Gospel, rejoices over it and puts his trust in it, accepts it and consoles himself with it, such a one has true faith, even though he has never heard anything about faith. Hence no Gospel element may be mingled with the Law. Whoever expounds the Law and injects grace—the grace, friendliness, and patience of God, who forgives sins—has shamefully perverted the Law. He acts like the nurse who sugarcoats the bitter pill to make it palatable to the patient. The result is that the medicine is ineffective, and the patient remains ill. The medicine should not have been sweetened and diluted. So the preacher must speak the Law in such a way that nothing sweet remains in it for us lost and condemned sinners. Whatever sweetness is injected into it is poison that neutralizes this heavenly medicine and makes it ineffective.

On the basis of Matthew 5:17-19 you must know that the Law makes no concessions. It only makes demands. The Law says: "do this! If you don't, there is no patience, no kindness, no leniency; you must go to hell." To make this perfectly clear the Lord says, "Whoever relaxes one of the least of these commandments and teaches men so, shall be called least in the kingdom of heaven." This does not mean that they will have inferior positions in the kingdom, but that they will not enter it at all.

As Galatians 3:10 shows, it is an accursed teaching, a shameful perversion of the Law, to demand good works and add the comforting assurance: "You are indeed supposed to be perfect, but God does not demand the impossible. Just do the best you can in your weakness and be sincere about it." God did not say one word about this on Mt. Sinai.

Romans 7:14: "The Law is spiritual; but I am carnal, sold under sin." For God's sake, whenever a preacher proclaims the Law, he must bear in mind that it is spiritual and exerts its influence on the spirit, not on some member of the body, but on man's spirit, his will, his heart, his attitude. This is always the case. When the Law says, "You shall not kill," this seems to concern only the hand. But no, it concerns the heart, as we see from the Ninth and Tenth Commandments. This must also be included when the Law is preached from the pulpit. It is not only a scolding about the shameful vices that may prevail in the congregation. Constant scolding does not good. People may briefly refrain from what was condemned, but in two weeks they do it again. Of course, the preacher must with great earnestness oppose these sins, but he must also tell the people: "Even if you quit your cursing and swearing, etc., that does not yet make you Christians, and you can still go to hell. God looks at the state of your heart." This can be stated calmly and very clearly. "When God says, 'You shall not kill,' this does not mean that you are not guilty of murder as long as you don't kill someone, attack and rob him, and so endanger his life! Don't think you have then kept the Fifth Commandment. No, the Law applies to the heart and the spirit." If you mention only by the way that "the Law is spiritual," the people will not get the point. You must go into detail, as if you were using a sharp knife. It cuts into life, and the people will go home as if struck in the face. They will fall on their knees at home and exclaim, "I am not what God wants me to be. I must become a different person."

Romans 3:20: "Through the Law comes knowledge of sin." God did not put the Law into your hands in order to make the people good. When the Law really begins to work, it drives man to rage against God all the more. He hates the preacher who has preached the Law into his heart; he can't get rid of it. You will hear people say, "I won't ever go back to that church. It scares the daylights out of a person. I'd rather go to hear Rev. N. N. He makes me feel good because he shows me what a good person I really am." To be sure, when they are in hell, they would like to get even with this false prophet who plunged them into hell.

There was nothing kind or comforting on Mt. Sinai. Already on the previous day Moses told the people that God was coming. And God came amid thunders and lightnings. The whole mountain began to quake, and the Lord descended on it in fire. Then there was a loud, dreadful trumpet blast that could be heard far and wide. Most terrifying of all was the voice of Jehovah speaking the Ten Commandments: "You shall! You shall! You shall!" "I the Lord your God am a jealous God, visiting the iniquity of the fathers upon the children, etc." All Israel trembled with fear.

Surely all this was no accident. Already the day before, Moses had set bounds around the mountian and had told the people that anyone coming too close and touching the mountain would die. Only Moses, under God's protection, could approach.

There God indicated how we are to preach the Law. How beneficial is a sermon in which the preacher begins with the Law in all its severity and expounds it spiritually! Many people will think: "If what he says is true, I am lost!" To be sure, some will think: "That is no way for an evangelical preacher to act!" Yes indeed, he must act that way, or else he is no evangelical preacher. If the Law does not precede, the Gospel will not succeed. First Moses, then Christ; or, first John the Baptizer and then Christ. At first the people will think, "Oh, how terrible that is!" But then the preacher, with eyes aglow, comes to Gospel. Now the people are glad and they understand why the preacher first proclaimed the Law, namely so that they could see how polluted they are with sin.

So you must deal also in catechetical instruction. Children, too, must be made afraid. Failure in this repsect has led so many to think of themselves as quite good Christians, when in fact they are wretched Pharisees. That is the way their parents raised them; they did not make them aware that they are poor sinners. The vilest sinner feels struck when he hears the Law, but not the Pharisees, who are much more difficult to convert. That was the worst evil of papists to the present day. The Jews mixed Gospel elements into the Law when they said; "As long as you do not actually kill someone, you are no murderer; as long as you are not guilty of open fornication, you are no adulterer!" Even man's evil desires were regarded as something quite natural. The papists say the same thing. They must indeed admit that Christ's exposition of the Law contains many items that cannot be considered gross transgressions of the Law. However, they assert that such statements are merely good counsels which people might observe to obtain a high position in heaven. They are called works of supererogation.

[*Editorial note:* Walther quotes Luther's comments on Matthew 5:21 ff., *Luther's Works,* American Edition, Vol. 21, pp. 74 f. Walther continues:]

The Jews, who boasted of the Law, emptied it of its content and kept only the outer shell. That is what the rationalists of our time do also. They are concerned about honorable conduct and steering clear of the disgraceful vices of which every citizen must be ashamed. They are only concerned about preaching public decency. Even so-called Christian preachers do this. The papists, too, followed in the footsteps of the Pharisees and are just like them. As the Jews turned Christ over to the civil government, so the papists say, "the church does not thirst for blood. True, many people who were our enemies and heretics were put to death, but the responsibility is the government's, not ours." However, when the government refused to execute their verdict, it was excommunicated. They desire to wash their hands of the martyrs' blood, but in vain. This blood will one day testify against them before God. As for the Jews, if they had grasped the spiritual meaning of the Law, they would also have realized: "We killed Christ, for we cried, 'Crucify, crucify Him!' "

[*Editorial note:* Here Walther continues the quotation from Luther and then cites Chemnitz, *Loci theologici,* Part II, listing the 12 so-called "evangelical counsels," such as voluntary poverty, celibacy, obedience, etc. Walther continues:]

You can see how horribly the Law has been perverted and robbed of its true spirit.... When the Jesuits appeared on the scene, they said that the poor Christians had been overburdened with moral precepts. Therefore they, the Jesuits, had formed a society to relieve Christendom of this burden. They were so successful that even the worst scoundrel could be a good Christian according to their ethical standards. Their moral code is a Decalog in reverse, so that they can perpetrate the most heinous crimes, if only they have a good intention.... But when Christ says: "Whoever says, 'You fool!' shall be liable to the hell of fire" [Matthew 5:22], He shatters this entire papistic and Jesuit moral code.

Eleventh Evening Lecture
(Dec. 5, 1884)

The words of Jeremiah 23:22, "If they . . . would have proclaimed My words to My people . . . they would have turned them from their evil way," are perhaps the most devastating against false teachers. By false teaching a preacher can become responsible for the souls entrusted to his care not being converted, and thus—horrible to say!—being lost forever. To be sure, those led astray by false teaching are also guilty, for in countless places in His Word God has warned against false teachers and prophets and has identified them in detail. Therefore one who despises these divine warnings will have only himself to blame for being lost. Yet this does not excuse the false prophets and teachers. On the contrary, their guilt is all the greater because they not only went astray themselves but also misled the souls entrusted to them. God will hold them accountable (Hebrews 13:17).

... Then every false teacher will wish he had never been born and will curse the day of his ordination. Then it will be seen that false doctrine is not so insignificant and harmless as is supposed in our day.

My dear friends, heed what God tells us through His prophet Isaiah: "This is the man to whom I will look, he that is humble and contrite in spirit, and trembles at My Word" (Isaiah 66:2). Not only are we to love God's Word, but also to tremble at it, be afraid to depart from it in a single letter, or add or subtract anything. We must be prepared to shed our blood rather than yield in any letter of the Word of God. Take our dear Luther as your model. He said: "One Bible passage makes the world too small for me." That is: "If I discovered that a single passage contradicted my teaching, I would have no rest day or night; I would not know where to go; it would be too dreadful for me!" Therefore strive to have the attitude of the royal prophet David, who said: "My flesh trembles for fear of Thee, and I am afraid of Thy judgments" (Psalm 119:120).

But you certainly cannot have or follow such an attitude as long as you do not possess a clear and thorough knowledge of all teachings of Holy Scripture. How can you preserve what you do not have? That is the purpose of your studies here, to enable you to become acquainted with all of Scripture and learn to know each article for itself and in its connection and relationship to the other doctrines. This is also the purpose of these Friday evening hours, as we treat the distinction between Law and Gospel. For everything depends on rightly dividing Law and Gospel. Unless you become apostate, I am not afraid that you will set up new articles of faith; but I am afraid that you will not distinguish Law and Gospel correctly. Here it is essential that you deviate neither to the right nor to the left, neither to despair nor to laxity.

Thesis VII

God's Word is not rightly divided, in the third place, when the Gospel is preached first and then the Law, first sanctification and then justification, first faith and then contrition, first good works and then grace.

Here we are dealing with proper sequence. Failure to observe this order can do great damage in the hearts and understanding of the hearers. Four false approaches are possible.

First, when the Gospel is preached before the Law. Perhaps you may say, "Who would be so confused? Every pupil of the catechism knows very well that the Law comes first, and then the Gospel." However, it can happen all too easily, and we can point to entire church bodies that fell prey to this error. At Luther's time there were the Antinomians under the leadership of Agricola, and in the last century there were the Herrnhuters.

These would have liked having nothing to do with the Law at all. Their basic principle was: "First the Gospel must be proclaimed, first the suffering and bleeding of Christ must be presented." That was completley wrong. It may well be true that the Herrnhuters made a deep impression on many, but it was only superficial. Their hearers were never made to realize man's deep sinful corruption; they never understood that they were God's enemies worthy of being cast into hell.—In this context we, of course, speak of the Gospel in the narrower sense, in distinction from the Law. Mark 1:15, Acts 20:21, and Luke 24:47 all demonstrate that the Law must be preached first, and then the Gospel.

Second, the proper order is inverted when sanctification of life is preached before justification, which consists of the forgiveness of sins. When Christ's righteousness becomes my righteousness, then I am justified. Psalm 130:4, Psalm 119:32, 1 Corinthians 1:30, John 15:5, and Acts 15:9 are some passages which clearly show that the proper order is first justification and then sanctification. Mingling them is one of the worst errors. In that case the sermon is a complete failure, no matter how eloquently it is delivered. Only a strict distinction between justification and sanctification can make it clear to a poor sinner and give him certainty that God is gracious to him, and equip him with strength for a new life.

Third, the proper order is inverted when faith is preached first and then contrition, as the Antinomians did and as the Herrnhuters still do. They insist: "Faith must come first, and then you must repent of your sins." How foolish! How can faith come into a heart not yet crushed? How can one who loathes the food hunger and thirst? No, if you want to believe in Christ, you must first become sick; for Christ is a physician only for the sick. First you must become a poor, lost sinner; for He came to seek and to save the lost. First you must become a lost sheep; for He is the Good Shepherd who seeks the lost sheep. When the Jews asked Peter and the other apostles, "Brethren, what shall we do?" Peter answered, "Repent, and be baptized every one of you in the name of Jesus Christ for the forgiveness of your sins" (Acts 2:38). Consequently, repentance comes first, then faith. "Repentance to God and faith in our Lord Jesus Christ" (Acts 20:21) clearly establishes the proper order and refutes all who invert it.

Fourth, it is wrong to preach good works first and then grace. All these points are related; one is as false as the other. Note Ephesians 2:8-10. What a golden passage! The apostle does not say, "We must do good works, and then God will be gracious to us," but the very opposite: "By grace you have been saved! But by grace you have been created for good works." First you must receive grace, and then God has made you a new creature; then you must do good works and can no longer remain under the dominion of sin.

Titus 2:11-12 shows that grace must be preached first, and then it trains us. This is the divine pedagogy inherent in grace. As soon as a person accepts the grace which God has brought from heaven, it begins its training function, teaching people to do good works and lead honorable lives. As we know, the Old Testament is primarily legal, although it also contains the Gospel, while the New Testament is predominantly evangelical, although the Law certainly is not absent. The solemn revelation of the Law first took place in the Old Testament, while the solemn revelation of the Gospel was given in the New Testament. Although the Gospel was present already in the garden of Eden, its solemn revelation came later. At Sinai, amid thunder and lightning and earthquake, the Law was fully revealed; and it seemed as if the earth would be destroyed. In the New Testament, when the Holy Spirit was poured out at Pentecost, there was fire also, but it burned nothing. Tongues of fire appeared above the heads of the apostles but did not singe their hair. A mighty wind rushed from heaven, but nothing was destroyed or blown over. This was to indicate that a completely different revelation was about to take place, one of comfort.

Now look at the epistles, especially Romans, which contains the whole of Christian doctrine. Chapters 1—3, an incisive proclamation of the Law; chapters 4 and 5, the doctrine of justification; and from chapter 6 on, sanctification. There you have a good model of the correct sequence: First, Law, God's wrath and threats; then the Gospel, God's promises and consolations; and then instructions on what we are to do, now that we have become new people. As often as the prophets preached for the purpose of converting someone, they began with the Law. When its punishment had had its effect, they comforted the sinner. As soon as the hearers were struck with fear, the apostles did nothing but absolve them. Only then did they say, "Now you must show your gratitude to God." The apostles did not issue orders, they did not threaten the people when they failed to comply. On the contrary, they pleaded with them, they exhorted them by the mercies of God. True sanctification follows justification; true justification follows repentance.

Now I will give some examples to show how even sermon outlines can betray one's inability to distinguish properly between Law and Gospel. These are crude, but they make it easy to get the point. Luther often used such examples. Let me do what he did, for whatever good I have to offer I learned from him.

61

Wrong Sermon Outlines

1. Theme: The Way to Heaven. It consists I. of faith, II. of true repentance. This is genuine Antinomian and Herrnhut doctrine.

2. Theme: Good Works. I. Wherein they consist; II. they must be done in faith. In such an outline you have already said what good works are, before you have spoken about faith. In order to describe good works, I must describe them as flowing from faith. Otherwise you would have to judge good works by the Law, and that is wrong, for by the verdict of the Law every good work even of a Christian, no matter how good it looks, is a work subject to condemnation.

3. Theme: Concerning Prayer. True prayer consists I. in the certainty of being heard, II. in faith. In this sequence part I would turn out all wrong.

4. Theme: Promises and Threats of the Word of God. I. Promises, II. threats. First he comforts me and then pelts me with stones, so that I forget the comfort. The Law must first inflict its wounds, and then the Gospel with its promises must bind up the wounds. Closing the sermon with threats will go far toward making it unfruitful.

5. Theme: True Christianity. It consists I. in the Christian life, II. in true faith, III. in a blessed death. Gruesome!

6. Theme: What Must a Person Do to Become Sure of His Salvation? I. He must amend his life; II. he must be sorry for his sins; III. but he must also lay hold of Christ by faith. How can I amend my life if I do not yet abhor the sinful life? No. III is the worst [in position and wording]. For nothing makes me more certain than faith.

Thus it was surely wrong for the Pietists to say that the Sermon on the Mount describes the steps in the order of salvation. They were led to this view by Christ's opening statement: "Blessed are the poor in spirit, for theirs is the kingdom of heaven" [Matthew 5:3]. But here "poor in spirit" means having nothing to which the heart clings. Even a millionaire can be poor in spirit; for if his heart is not attached to money and earthly goods, he does not really possess them. On the contrary, a beggar who trusts in what little he has can be rich in spirit. The former is blessed but not the latter. The Pietists think that Christ's next statement: "Blessed are those who mourn, for they shall be comforted," refers to mourning over sin, as the second step in the order of salvation. But Christ means mourning and cross-bearing for God's sake in this life. Then Christ says: "Blessed are the meek, for they shall inherit the earth." Here the Pietists have no end of trouble, for faith and justification are not yet present, and this works havoc with their order of salvation. They resort to amazing acrobatics in their attempt to salvage their sequence of steps, but to no avail. Next Christ says: "Blessed are those who hunger and thirst for righteousness, for they shall be satisfied." This is supposed to be step four in the order of salvation! But does meekness really precede the others? Therefore if you ever plan to preach on the Beatitudes, be very careful that you do not copy the Pietistic preachers!

Luther was opposed by the Antinomians and had to come to grips with them. They taught that grace must be preached first, and then repentance. In fact, the Law should not be proclaimed in church at all; it belongs in the courthouse and on the gallows. Tell it to thieves and murderers, but not to respectable people, least of all to Christians.

Luther discusses this question in detail in his *Against the Antinomians,* 1539, *Luther's Works,* American Edition, Vol. 47, pp. 114 f. See also his comments on the Antinomians in his remarks on Genesis 21:15, 16, *Lectures on Genesis, Luther's Works,* American Edition, Vol. 4, pp. 49 ff.

"Therefore," says Luther, "let us learn that God hates all proud people; but those who have been humbled and have felt the power of the Law He comforts, if not through men, at least through an angel from heaven. For He does not permit such people to perish, just as He does not permit those who are smug to remain in Abraham's house. Moreover, a teacher in the church must be well informed and experienced in both respects, in order that he may be able to refute and crush the gainsayers and to comfort again those who have been refuted and crushed, lest they be devoured" (ibid., p. 51).

Twelfth Evening Lecture
(Dec. 12, 1884)

My friends, the chief fault in the sermons of our time is that they are mostly aimless; and this is true particularly of the sermons of believing preachers. While unbelieving or fanatical preachers pursue a very definite goal—though not the right one—believing preachers for the most part think they have done their official duty if what they have proclaimed has been the Word of God. But that is as if a professional hunter feels he has done his job as long as he simply loads his gun and shoots into the forest; or as if a soldier in the artillery thinks he is doing his duty simply by moving his cannon to the front and firing away. They would be useless hunters and soldiers. Just as bad and useless are preachers who have no plan in their sermons and pursue no goal. Their sermons may contain many fine thoughts, but they will have no effect. They may now and then hurl thunderbolts of the Law, but no lightning strikes. They may sprinkle the garden entrusted to them with the nourishing water of the Gospel, but they are not so much watering the plants as the garden path, and so all is lost.

Neither Christ nor the apostles preached like that. Every hearer knew, "He meant me!"—even though no specific person had been singled out. For example, when the Lord Christ had told the powerful and shattering parable of the murderous tenants in the vineyard, the chief priests and Pharisees themselves "perceived that He was speaking about them" (Matthew 21:45). When the holy apostle Paul had preached to that dissolute and unjust governor, Felix, "about justice and self-control and future judgment," Felix soon noticed, "He means me!" He "was alarmed," but because he did not want to be converted, he told Paul, "Go away for the present; when I have an opportunity I will summon you" (Acts 24:24-27). But he never did. Paul's well-aimed sermon had hit the mark.

Therefore, my friends, the reason why nearly everywhere in our native Germany unbelievers have gained the upper hand in Lutheran congregations is without doubt that the sermons of Christian preachers are aimless. Unbelievers increase in the congregations, while at the same time the number of Christian preachers has also increased, for there are now many more than in my youth. Why don't they accomplish anything? Oh, if only these fine men would have the humility to sit at Luther's feet and study his sermons, they would learn how to preach in order to make an impression! For the Word of God will never return empty if it is preached properly. Oh, when you begin your ministry, may God help you not to be aimless prattlers who must then complain about not getting anywhere. And that would be your own fault, because in the preparation of your sermons you did not have people with specific problems in mind. However, important as it is that the sermons have specific goals, it is just as important to have the *right goals*. If your sermons do not, all preaching is in vain, whether you proclaim the Law or the Gospel.

Thesis VIII

In the fourth place, God's Word is not rightly divided when the Law is preached to those who are already terrified because of their sins, or when the Gospel is preached to those who are secure in their sins.

In our first lecture we listed six differences between Law and Gospel. They differ: 1. in the manner of their revelation to mankind; 2. in their content; 3. in their promises; 4. in their threats; 5. in their function and effects; 6. in respect to the persons to whom the one or the other is to be proclaimed. This difference is usually listed last, but not because it is less important, for it is of supreme importance. The Gospel must be preached only to poor, crushed sinners, while the Law is to be addressed to secure sinners. Whoever reverses this confounds both and in the process mingles them in an extremely dangerous manner. We saw earlier, on the basis of 1 Timothy 1:8-10, that this is indeed the case.

Consider Isaiah 61:1-3. "Day of vengeance" does not refer to a judgment on human beings, for that would not be proclaiming "the year of the Lord's favor," but the Son of God wanted to take vengeance on Satan, who had plunged mankind into wretchedness. Therefore this is a glad and consoling message for us. If God had not taken vengeance on Satan, we would be lost. If Christ had not redeemed us from the devil, we could not be joyful but would have to remain sorrowful.

According to God's Word not one drop of evangelical comfort is to be offered those who live securely in their sins. Conversely, not one word of threat and punishment should be addressed to those who are broken-hearted, but only promises, consolation and grace, forgiveness and righteousness, life and salvation.

That is what our Lord Christ did. When that notorious sinful woman came to Him, knelt before Him in the presence of the self-righteous Pharisees, washed His feet with her hot tears, and wiped them with her hair (which she had probably used in the service of her vanity)—she was crushed and disconsolate, but turned to the Lord whom she had recognized as the Mercy Seat—what did the Lord do? Not one word about her secret sins—for she had undoubtedly lived in the vilest of sins, in fornication—not one word about that! He simply says: "Your sins are forgiven," and adds a short admonition: "Go, and do not sin again" [Luke 7:36-50; John 8:11).

So the Lord treats Zacchaeus, that disgraceful tax collector who had cheated the country and the people. He had, however, heard some things about the Lord and had come to the conclusion, "Things can't go on this way; there has to be a turn for the better." Now, when the Lord passes through Jericho, the tax collector climbs a sycamore tree, determined to get a glimpse of this holy Man, but he does not think the Lord would want to see him. What does the Lord do? He looks up and calls out: "Zacchaeus, make haste and come down; for I must stay at your house today." Zacchaeus probably thought that the Lord would rebuke him and tell him of his sins. But not a word about that. Rather, Jesus says: "Today salvation has come to this house, since he also is a son of Abraham." It is Zacchaeus who says: "Behold, Lord, the half of my goods I give to the poor; and if I have defrauded anyone of anything, I restore it fourfold." Not the Lord, but his own conscience, that had first been aroused and was now appeased, demands this of him [Luke 19:1-10].

The parable of the Prodigal Son teaches the same lesson. When he returns in disgrace, but comes to his father with a broken heart, what does the father do? Not one word of reproach comes out of his mouth. He hugs and kisses his son and exclaims: "Let us eat and make merry; for this my son was dead, and is alive again; he was lost, and is found." A great banquet is prepared, but not one word of reproach is heard [Luke 15:11-24].

And what about the Lord on the cross? Beside Him hangs an infamous criminal, but one who has been led through Christ's patient suffering to the confession: "We are receiving the due reward of our deeds; but this Man has done nothing wrong." Then, turning to Jesus, he says: "Remember me when You come into your kingdom." He thinks, "That is the Messiah!" And what does the Lord do? He does not say, "Why should I remember you who have been guilty of such crimes?" None of that. He simply says: "Today you will be with Me in Paradise" [Luke 23:39-43].

Thus the Lord shows us how to deal with a poor sinner who may have lived disgracefully down to the present day, but is now battered and crushed and terrified because of his sins. Then we must not utter one word of reproach and punishment but absolve him of his sins and comfort him. One who does that knows how to separate the Gospel from the Law.

That was the practice also of the holy apostles. Think only of the jailer at Philippi. . . . Trembling with fear, he falls down before Paul and Silas and asks: "Men, what must I do to be saved?" They do not tell him he must first do so and so, first feel truly sorry, but they say only: "Believe in the Lord Jesus, and you will be saved, you and your household." All they do is to invite him to accept grace, for faith is nothing but the act of accepting grace [Acts 16:23-34].

I call your attention to a passage in Luther's writings where he consoled a man who had sinned grievously. It is a letter he wrote to his friend George Spalatin . . . who had been party to the counsel given to a pastor to marry the stepmother of his deceased wife. . . . When Spalatin realized his error, he was disconsolate, feeling that he had forfeited all further comfort. When Luther heard of it, he wrote his friend, chiding him for doubting God's promises of forgiveness and applying the comfort of the Gospel in full measure. Here are some of his statements: "You must get into the habit of believing that Christ is a true Savior and that you are a true sinner. For God is not joking, and He does not deal with imaginary things. He was completely in earnest when He gave up His only Son for us all, Romans 8:32; John 3:16. These and similar words of consolation Satan has snatched out of your mind so that now, in your great anguish and depression, you can't remember them. Therefore, for God's sake, lend your ears and hear, brother, how I, your brother, sing cheerful songs, as one who stands outside of your sorrow and depression. I am strong precisely so that you who are weak and harassed by the devil can lean on me and get back on your feet. Then, when you have recovered, you will be able to defy the devil and sing confidently: 'I was pushed hard, so that I was falling, but the Lord helped me' "(Psalm 118:13). [Luther continues in the same vein. See the entire letter in St. Louis Edition, X, 1729 ff.]

I hope you will want to read this letter again and again. Remember it especially when someday a sorrowful and disconsolate sinner comes to you. Then read this letter and be prepared to deal with such a sinner in a truly evangelical way. Luther admitted that Spalatin had sinned, but he also knew that now, for God's sake, he must say nothing that might pierce the heart of poor Spalatin like a fiery dart.

I also direct you to a letter Luther wrote as early as 1516 to an Augustinian monk, George Spenlein, who could find no spiritual peace. [*Editorial note:* Walther cites the whole letter, in which Luther stresses the righteousness of Christ which covers all our sins (*Luther's Works,* American Edition, Vol. 48, pp. 11—14). Walther continues:]

This is the most beautiful Gospel I can possibly preach. It declares that Christ came for everyone, that He has borne every person's sin, that He calls everyone to come to Him, to believe in Him, rejoice in Him, and be certain that all His sins are forgiven and that he will die a blessed death.

Thirteenth Evening Lecture

(Jan. 9, 1885)

My friends, if a preacher is to accomplish anything worthwhile by his preaching, he must, first of all, preach the Word of God in truth and purity. Many preachers of our day omit certain teachings that are obnoxious to the world, convinced that they should not offend their hearers. But that is a big mistake. The only way to make a person a true Christian is not through eloquence, be it ever so lofty and impassioned, but through the Word of God alone. It alone produces repentance and faith and piety, and preserves people in them to the end.

However, a second requirement for the preacher to accomplish something is that he not only himself believes what he preaches to others, but that his soul is so filled with the truths he proclaims that he mounts his pulpit with the burning desire to pour out his heart before his hearers. He must be truly enthusiastic about his subject in the right sense of the word. Then it will seem as if his words shoot out of his mouth like flames from a soul that is on fire. This does not mean to say that it is a preacher's living faith which must first endow the Word of God with power and life, for the

Lord says expressly: My words "are spirit and life" (John 6:63), and the writer to the Hebrews says: "The Word of God is living and active, sharper than any two-edged sword, piercing to the division of soul and spirit, of joints and marrow, and discerning the thoughts and intentions of the heart" (Hebrews 4:12).

When a preacher gives expression to what he himself has often experienced in his heart, he will easily find the proper words to convince his hearers, words that will go to the heart because they come from the heart, according to the fine old proverb: "It is the heart that makes eloquent." And that does not mean an artificial, artistic oratorical performance, but the sane spiritual art of speaking in such a way that the words ignite a fire in the hearers' hearts. When hearers notice that the preacher is fully in earnest in his preaching, they will be drawn by an irresistible power so that they will give full attention to what his sermons say. For this reason many an unpretentious, less gifted, and less learned preacher achieves greater results than the most talented and learned men.

Therefore, my dear friends, I pray that you will be, first of all, genuinely alive, zealous Christians, aglow on behalf of the truth! This is the equipment for becoming a powerful preacher in due time, a preacher whose spirit the hearers cannot resist, as was the case with the apostles. The people did not know how it happened, but these simple men made such a powerful impression on them.

This is certainly not to say that outstanding talents and thorough theological scholarship should be disparaged. The very opposite is the case. For when great talents and thorough scholarship are added to a preacher's living faith, he will end up being a great and skilled instrument in God's hand; for all the natural endowments and all that we have acquired through natural diligence are not discarded by God when we enter His service, but He cleanses and purifies them and uses them in that service. As a result, where great talents and thorough scholarship were coupled with living faith, great things happened in the kingdom of God and great successes were achieved. I remind you of the apostle Paul, the only educated man among the apostles. As he himself said, he worked harder and accomplished more than all the others. I refer you also to the great Reformer, Luther. Had he been only a hero of faith and not also a man so highly gifted and so well educated, he would not have become the Reformer who so gloriously accomplished the greatest task of the time. Hence I urge you to strive day and night during your seminary days to reach the highest goal in all branches of theological knowledge. I hope this wish of mine may be fulfilled! Then your career will demonstrate the vital importance of both a living faith and natural talents coupled with faithfulness and diligence. Let this be enough on this point.

Don't think this was meant to be an introduction. It is only a foreword. I hope you will take it to heart, though I uttered it in weakness. May the Holy Spirit grant it! For so much, my friends, so much depends on your confronting the world not only as light-bearers but also as lights of the world, illuminated by God. Now let us get to our subject.

We have discussed the first part of Thesis VIII, namely that God's Word is not rightly divided when the Law is preached to those who are already terrified because of their sins. Now let us consider the second part, which says that God's Word is not rightly divided when the Gospel is proclaimed to secure sinners.

The one is as dangerous as the other. A preacher will do inestimable damage if he offers the comfort of the Gospel to a secure sinner, or at least preaches to the crowd in such a way that by his fault secure sinners think this evangelical comfort is meant for them. In this way the preacher can preach many people into hell instead of heaven. No, the Gospel is not for secure sinners. Of course, we cannot keep secure sinners from coming to our churches and hearing the Gospel. However, that is precisely the preacher's skill—to present the whole evangelical comfort in its full sweetness, but so that the secure sinners must notice, "This consolation is not meant for me." They must observe it from the whole way the preacher presents it. Listen to several proof passages from Scripture.

Matthew 7:6: We are not to give what is holy, that is, Christ's Word, to the dogs, the enemies of the Gospel; nor throw the pearls, namely the comfort of the Gospel, grace, righteousness, and salvation, to the swine, those who prefer to remain in their sins and seek their heaven and their bliss in the filth of their sin.

Isaiah 26:10: It is futile to "show favor to the wicked." He thinks he needs no grace, or already has all he needs. He imagines that his little sins have long been forgiven or forgotten. To such a one I must not preach the Gospel, for that is only showing him favor, and that will not help him. A godless person, who prefers to remain in his sins, whether gross or refined—for the devil can bind me not only through vile and repulsive sins, but also by means of very fine cords, like pride, envy, lovelessness, etc.— such a godless person "does not see the majesty of the Lord." Such people have no idea of the treasure offered to them. They have no understanding of the teaching of salvation by grace; either they do not want this grace, or they abuse it in a most disgraceful way.

They reason: "Well, if merely believing is enough for salvation, then my sins too have been forgiven. I will get to heaven even though I remain what I am; for I too believe in my Lord Jesus." The preacher who is responsible for such misuse of the Gospel by secure sinners assumes a great burden of guilt before God.

Proverbs 27:7: I can keep on offering honey to one who has already eaten his fill, but he will loathe it; but "to one who is hungry everything bitter is sweet." The Gospel, which is as sweet as honey, must therefore be offered only to hungry souls. Those who are not hungry must receive what is bitter, namely the Law.

Our first model is our dear Lord Jesus Christ. Observe Him in the gospels and you will discover: Whenever He confronted secure sinners, such as the self-righteous Pharisees surely were, He did not have a spark of comfort for them, but called them serpents and a brood of vipers and hurled a tenfold woe at them. He uncovered their abominable hypocrisy and assigned them to hell and eternal damnation, from which they could not escape. Even though Jesus knew that they would be the ones who would nail Him to the cross, He fearlessly told them the truth. Let preachers take note!

You must proclaim the Law in its full severity to secure and impious sinners, to enemies and hypocrites, even though you know in advance that you will get the same treatment the Lord received. This is not to suggest that we can bear what He bore, for we cannot drink the cup He drank. But we must experience the people's enmity. They will oppose us openly or agitate against us secretly. But no matter; if the preacher faces such people, he can preach nothing but the Law to them. And when he speaks to the crowd, such hearers must conclude: "He does not have us, but the pious ones, in mind; for the Gospel is intended for them."

To be sure, the Lord also says: "Come to Me, *all,*" but He adds immediately, "who labor and are heavy laden." In other words, He does not invite the secure sinners. They would only ridicule Him if He offered them his spiritual, heavenly treasure.

Once a rich young man came to Him and asked, "Good Teacher, what must I do to inherit eternal life?" [Mark 10:17 ff.]. Jesus first rejected the title, "Good Teacher," because the young man was self-righteous and thought he himself was a good teacher. He was not sincere. If he had regarded Christ as the Son of God and Savior of the world and believed in Him, and *for that reason* called Him "Good Teacher," all would have been well. But because He only wanted to flatter the Lord, the title was refused. What did the Lord do? He told the man, "You know the commandments: 'Do not kill, do not commit adultery, etc.'" Eagerly the young man replied: "All these I have observed from my youth." In other words, "If that is all, You are not a wise man; for I already knew all that. I had hoped to get other insights from You. What do I still lack?" [Matthew 19:20]. Did the Lord say, "You still lack faith"? By no means! He had before Him a wretched, secure, self-righteous man. Hence, not a word of Gospel. He must first lead the man to a knowledge of his own wretched state, although He knew in advance that all would be in vain. But God does many things out of love, so that one day man will have no excuse in the day of judgment. God will say: "Thus and so I did for you, but you would have none of it!" The Lord continued: "Go, sell what you have, and give to the poor, and you will have treasure in heaven; and come, follow Me." When the young man heard that, "he went away sorrowful; for he had great possessions." His conscience was struck. . . . It accused him, as the Lord intended. We do not know if he was converted later. Be that as it may. We see here how we must conduct ourselves over against sinners who are still secure and self-righteous. Here the sternest message of the Law is in place. We are not in a position to issue orders like Christ, the Lord of lords, but we have enough questions to ask them, so that they can draw the conclusion: "We are still completely immersed in sin and therefore lost."

The apostles followed the same practice. Whenever they preached, they first proclaimed the Law in a way that pierced the hearers' hearts. At Pentecost (Acts 2) Peter first condemned his hearers as murderers of Christ. Then, when they were afraid and asked: "What shall we do?" Peter said: "Repent, and be baptized every one of you in the name of Jesus Christ for the forgiveness of your sins." Thus he preached the Gospel and assured them that they, too, could have forgiveness of all their sins, even the most horrible. So everywhere the apostles preached repentance first and then faith; for they knew their hearers were mostly secure sinners who had not yet recognized their misery.

But they were also stern with those who pretended to be Christians but were secure in their sins. See 2 Corinthians 12:20—13:2 for a fine example of how to deal with secure sinners who pretend to be Christians.

When we preach, we must first preach our hearers into hell before we can preach them into heaven. First we must put our hearers to death by the Law, and only then can they be brought to life through the Gospel. First we must make them realize that they are sick unto death, and then we must heal them with evangelical comfort. First, we must expose their own righteousness through the Law and show what a filthy garment it is, and then they must be clothed with the righteousness of Christ through the Gospel. . . .

To be sure, we cannot prescribe the *degree* of repentance, for Scripture shows that it varies greatly in individuals. However, everyone must taste some of the bitterness of repentance, or else he will never savor the sweetness of the Gospel. When God has brought someone to faith without great anguish and terrors, that person will experience these later on. People must always be plunged by God into true sorrow over sin, or else they will fall away. So the Lord said of those who believe for a time: "They receive the Word with joy; but they have no root." The sweetness of the Gospel does them no good unless the rocky soil of their heart is pulverized.

However, we do observe that those who in the beginning experienced great and profound sorrow have become the best and most steadfast Christians. Those have also become the best pastors and theologians whom the Lord already in their youth plunged into the waters of anguish and trouble with regard to their salvation.

We may observe this in Luther, to whom had been entrusted the greatest task of his time, namely the Reformation. Without being aware of it, he was prepared by God, not by being made learned and a good judge of people, nor by receiving a clear knowledge of the Word of God—for he lacked this until the Holy Spirit enlightened him—but by being led by God to fall on his knees and wrestle with God, and to be filled with anguish and terror almost to the point of blasphemy. But that was the proper school for the training of a Reformer.

The same is true of men like Flacius and John Gerhard. In fact, the lives of all great theologians would demonstrate that they first became small before they became great, proceeding from contrition to faith in the Gospel.

It is bad for a young person to have come to "faith" in the Word of God merely by way of dry rational conviction. If he is intelligent, he can easily run into the danger of adopting various errors and becoming a heretic, for he has never experienced the proper spiritual anguish. But one who has experienced the power of the Word, one who has passed through a genuine and sincere repentance, will not be quick to follow the treacherous promptings of his heart, for he has come to know them and does not trust them. When, therefore, his reason speaks up, he clings to the Word and bids his reason be silent. God grant that you have not only listened to this, that you will not only make use of it in your future ministry, but that you experience it in your own soul.

See Luther's views in his *Lectures on Exodus,* St. Louis Edition, III 858 ff.

Further, in Luther's *On the Councils and the Church (Luther's Works,* American Edition, Vol. 41, pp. 113 f.) he writes:

> That is what my Antinomians, too, are doing today, who are teaching beautifully and (as I cannot but think) with real sincerity about Christ's

grace, about the forgiveness of sin and whatever else can be said about the doctrine of redemption. But they flee as if it were the very devil the consequence that they should tell the people about the third article, of sanctification, that is, of the new life in Christ. They think one should not frighten or trouble the people, but rather always preach comfortingly about grace and the forgiveness of sins in Christ, and under no circumstances use these or similar words, "Listen! You want to be a Christian and at the same time remain an adulterer, a whoremonger, a drunken swine, arrogant, covetous, a usurer, envious, vindictive, malicious, etc.!" Instead they say, "Listen! Though you are an adulterer, a whoremonger, a miser, or other kind of sinner, if you but believe, you are saved, and you need not fear the Law. Christ has fulfilled it all!"

For God's sake, therefore, beware! When you are about to preach the Gospel, be sure to put it in such a way that you will not make sinners secure and thus become a preacher and preserver of sin. Of course we must preach Christ as the Victor over sin, death, devil, and hell, but we must also say to the people, "You must repent, and then the Holy Spirit will come with His grace and comfort, enlighten, and sanctify you."

In his *Instructions for the Visitors of Parish Pators,* 1528 (*Luther's Works,* American Edition, Vol. 40, pp. 274 f.), Luther writes in the same vein.

Before Luther appeared, only the Law held sway. The poor people were terrified. When Luther had come to a knowledge of the Gospel, he preached this sweet message to these poor, battered souls. But many misunderstood this message and thought, "If we want to preach like Luther, we must preach every Sunday about faith and justification and righteousness without works." Luther labeled this a greater error than the former one. If a preacher speaks only of faith and is silent about the Law, he leads his hearers to the dreadful state where they think they no longer need repentance, so that finally they are beyond help. . . .

Fourteenth Evening Lecture

(Jan. 16, 1885)

In former times many Lutherans had extremely superficial views about the difference between Lutheran and Reformed teaching. . . . The unfaithful pastors of our church were to blame, for they shamefully neglected the people. Because of such ignorance it is no wonder that the poor Lutherans were at last willing to unite with the Reformed.

Lately, however, there has been a change, and it was caused by the very fact that in Prussia Lutherans and Reformed were compelled to unite. This led Lutheran people to rethink their position and its difference from the Reformed. In 1817, when the union was inaugurated, Claus Harms, preacher and professor in Kiel, issued a new set of 95 Theses for the Reformation Festival. No. 95 says: "They are now planning a marriage in order to enrich the Lutheran Church, this lowly maid. But beware of doing it over Luther's grave! His bones will come alive, and then woe to you!" This has happened. Now every Lutheran child of average training knows that the difference between Lutheran and Reformed is very great and affects the chief articles of the Christian faith.

Now Lutheran people know very well that Lutherans cling firmly to the eternally true word of Jesus Christ: "This is My body; this is My blood." Hence they firmly believe that Christ's body and blood are substantially and truly present and distributed in the Lord's Supper and are received by the communicants. The Reformed, however, interpret these transparently clear words differently and say: "This represents Christ's body; this represents Christ's blood," and they insist that in the Lord's Supper Christ's body and blood are as far away as heaven is from earth, for Christ is now enclosed in heaven and will not return to earth until judgment day.

Now all Lutherans know that according to Scripture, the book of eternal truth, Holy Baptism is a washing of regeneration, a means by which the Holy Spirit brings about regeneration, while the Reformed assert that Baptism is only a sign, a symbol, a representation of what has already been done in man before.

Now all Lutherans know that Christ's humanity, through its personal union with His deity, shares in the divine properties of omniscience, omnipotence, omnipresence, and the dignity of being worshiped, while the Reformed assert that there is only a difference in degree between the man Christ and other human beings; He indeed possesses higher gifts, but even the most exalted are only creaturely gifts.

Now all Lutherans know that according to Holy Scriptures the Father's grace, the Son's redemptive work, and the effective calling by the Holy Spirit through the Word are all-inclusive, while the Reformed teach particularism and insist that God has already created the majority of human beings for eternal damnation and therefore from eternity destined them to eternal death.

A dreadful, horrible teaching in the bright light of the most blessed precious Gospel! In short, every Lutheran now knows that the difference between the Lutheran and the Reformed Church is fundamental, not peripheral but central.

In spite of that, why is it that so many who want to be Lutheran allow themselves to be enmeshed in the net of the Union [between Lutherans and Reformed] and, while claiming to be Lutheran, calmly remain in that makeshift arrangement, in a church not founded by Christ but obey an earthly king—a church in which there is no agreement such as the apostle demands in 1 Corinthians 1:10, where the one faith, one Baptism, and one hope of Ephesians 4:4-6 is lacking? Why is that? Because people think that, in spite of the many and great errors in the Reformed Church, it is still essentially one with the Lutheran Church; it is a situation quite different from the relationship between the Lutheran and Roman Catholic Church. This may be true, but would to God the Reformed Church were united with us in the essentials! Then agreement in less important matters might soon be achieved. But just this is lacking in the Reformed Church, the correct answer to the question: "What must I do to be saved?" In justification, this cardinal teaching of the Lutheran Church, the Reformed do not agree with us and do not show the right way to grace and salvation. Nowadays very few realize this. All the Reformed and related sects say, "Indeed man is saved by grace alone." But in practice it soon becomes evident that, while they hold to the theory, they do not carry it out but point in the opposite direction. This is the subject of our next thesis.

Thesis IX

In the fifth place, God's Word is not rightly divided when sinners, struck and terrified by the Law, instead of being directed to Word and sacrament, are instructed to strive for the state of grace through prayer and struggles, that is, to keep on praying and wrestling until they feel that God has pardoned them.

This is the common teaching of all Reformed and related sects, including Baptists, Methodists, Episcopalians, and Presbyterians. All these are merely branches of the great Reformed church tree, and they all teach what our thesis condemns. They do not proclaim the pure evangelical doctrine as to how a poor, terrified sinner can come to the certainty that he has a gracious God.

However, to become divinely certain of the right way to divide God's Word in this respect, let us examine some Biblical examples. Let us observe the holy apostles, who were impelled and filled by the Holy Spirit and therefore without doubt divided the Word of God rightly and showed stricken sinners the right way to attain peace, rest, and certainty regarding their state of grace. And so that no doubt might remain, let us look at the greatest and crassest sinners and see how the apostles treated them.

On the first Pentecost (Acts 2) Peter told the assembled crowd: "Let all the house of Israel therefore know assuredly that God has made Him both Lord and Christ, this Jesus whom you crucified." Brief as these words were, this was a powerful preaching of the Law. Consequently: "When they heard this, they were cut to the heart." The Spirit of God led them to a realization of the great sin they had committed in crucifying their own Messiah, and they asked: "Brethren, what shall we do?" What did the apostle do? Did he tell them they must better themselves, become more contrite, fall on their knees and plead for mercy, and then perhaps God would help them? Not a word of it. He said: "Repent, and be baptized every one of you in the name of Jesus Christ for the forgiveness of your sins." *Metanoeesate,* "change your attitude," obviously refers to the second part of repentance, namely faith . . . for the Law had already done its work. The apostle Peter had no intention of seeking their salvation by driving them into even greater misery, anxiety, and terror. Now that their hearts had been pierced, it was enough; they were ready to hear the blessed Gospel and take it to heart. Hence the apostle only said, "Change your attitude; believe in the Gospel of this Crucified One; forsake all your errors and be baptized." And they were baptized, receiving the assurance of forgiveness. . . . Peter added: "And you shall receive the gift of the Holy Spirit." . . . The people were simply asked to accept the Word and be consoled by these sweet words of promise. There was no suggestion of such methods as the sects nowadays employ.

This was Peter's first sermon, right after he came forth from the Holy Spirit's forge, so to say. he was aglow with the faith and thus won 3,000 souls with a single sermon, and gave them peace and assurance of salvation. The account ends with the words: "And they devoted themselves to the apostles' teaching and fellowship, to the breaking of bread and the prayers." Thus Peter's preaching did not warm their hearts only for a moment, as is often the case with fanatics who travel around and conduct so-called revivals. No, Peter's words entered their hearts and completely changed them, imparted joy and comfort and the willingness to bear all the disgrace and persecution true Christians then had to endure.

Now let us hear of a pagan (Acts 16), a most ungodly pagan. . . . He was the jailer at Philippi, who brutally put Paul and Silas "into the inner prison and fastened their feet in the stocks." The treatment was inhuman! "But about midnight Paul and Silas were praying and singing hymns to God, and the prisoners were listening to them." No doubt the jailer heard them also and was profoundly affected by this experience. . . . When an earthquake followed and the prison doors were opened, the jailer was about to commit suicide, because he thought the prisoners had escaped. . . . Then Paul shouted, "Do not harm yourself, for we are all here!" and this in spite of the way he had treated them! . . . Trembling with fear he asked: "Men, what must I do to be saved?"

Now, if the apostles had been Enthusiasts, they would have said, "Not so fast, my friend! Before a godless and ruthless man like you can be saved, he must undergo a long cure, and we will prescribe it." Not a word of this! They saw that the poor man was ready for the Gospel. He was still godless and did not hate sin. He said nothing about that. All he wanted was deliverance from sin's punishment and a blessed lot beyond the grave. Nevertheless, he was told: "'Believe in the Lord Jesus, and you will be saved, you and your household.' And they spoke the Word of the Lord to him and to all that were in his house . . . and he was baptized at once, with all his family." In that very night he was converted and brought to faith and to certainty of grace and reconciliation with God. He became a beloved child of God. The apostles did nothing except to proclaim to him the unconditional Gospel. And always Baptism followed immediately without any long-term period of detailed instruction.

Now compare that with the practice observed today in the Reformed Church. I am referring to the sects that have come out of the Reformed Church. If they would observe a Lutheran preacher acting this way, they would exclaim, "What an ungodly and frivolous preacher! How can he? He should impress on the sinner that he must first feel grace in his heart. But he does not act thus. He comforts that person and even baptizes him!" But that is Biblical and Lutheran; for the Lutheran Church is none other than the Biblical church, a church that wants to remain faithful to God's Word and not depart from it, either by addition or subtraction. . . .

Take the example of the apostle Paul himself. He had been an abominable man, for he had horribly persecuted the Christians. How was he converted? He himself recounts this experience best of all in Acts 22:1-16. . . . Having been led blind to a certain house in Damascus, he was visited by a Christian named Ananias. . . . This man did not say to Paul, "First you must pray and feel grace!" No, "First be baptized, after you have come to know the Lord Jesus, and wash away your sins, and now call on the name of the Lord Jesus!" That is the correct sequence of grace: Not first praying for God's grace, for only after a person has received God's grace is he able to pray correctly.

This, then, is our Lord's own practice, and He ought to know how to deal with poor sinners. As soon as Saul was terrified, Ananias comforted him; he did not call for various emotions but simply proclaimed the Word of grace to him and sealed it with Holy Baptism. Here we learn how a true servant of Christ must proceed when he brings sinners shattered by the Law to the certainty of God's grace.

The sects do the very opposite. They, too, begin by preaching the Law in all its severity, and quite rightly. We do the same, as did the apostles and Christ Himself. However, it is wrong to paint the torments of hell in such lurid colors that they really only stimulate the imagination rather than penetrate to the depths of the heart. To be sure, they often preach the Law very well in its terrifying threats, but not according to its spiritual sense. Most sects fall short here. They do not make of people poor, lost, and condemned sinners who feel their lost condition, but they rather induce people to think how terrible it is that God issues such frightful threats because of sin. If one does not by means of the Law lead a person to shed the garment of his own righteousness and gain the conviction that he is a wretched, ungodly creature whose heart sins day and night with evil passions, evil thoughts, and evil desires, then one has not preached the Law properly. A preacher must get a person to despair of himself to his dying day and confess: "I am a wretched creature. The good that I do does not come from me but from God. I, however, am the one who corrupts and poisons the good that God wants to do through me." One whose heart is not in that condition is not yet properly prepared for the Gospel.

But failing to preach the Law properly is not the worst fault of the sects. When a person has been driven to despair and anguish, he does not yet receive the Gospel. By no means. They think it would be a great sin to comfort such a person at once. That poor sinner is told what he must do to obtain grace, how long he must pray and wrestle and cry until he can finally say, "Now I feel that I have the Holy Spirit and God's grace! Now I can shout Hallelujah!" To speed up the process, Methodist preachers will kneel around the sinner in a public gathering and plead with God to forgive him his sins. Sometimes there is no success. Sometimes it takes weeks and months. When someone honestly states that he feels nothing but helplessness and evil desires within himself, he is told, "Yes, you are still in a very bad condition. Keep on praying and wrestling!" Finally, when he has had an emotional experience, he is told, "Praise the Lord! You are rid of your sin! Now all is well. You have finished the battle of repentance. Now you are a child of God and His grace."

That is a false basis, however. That emotion might have had a different source. It may have been a physical reaction to the preacher's dramatic presentation, and not the witness of the Holy Spirit. For that reason many honest souls who have come to faith at times feel that they have the Lord Jesus, and then again, that they have lost Him; now they feel they are in the state of grace, and then again, that they have fallen from grace. Woe to such poor souls if in the hour of death they do not feel grace and conclude, "Alas, I am eternally lost and condemned!" How often that

78

may happen! However, we must not doubt that the Holy Spirit will come to the rescue of such mishandled souls, so that they will scuttle all their fighting and wrestling and working and fling themselves into the arms of God's free grace and thus die a blessed death. But that is not the good result of Methodist preaching; it is the achievement of the Holy Spirit in spite of Methodist preaching.

All this shows that such wrong practice rests on three great and dreadful errors.

First, the sects do not believe and teach a genuine and complete reconciliation of man with God. They treat God as a very hard man whose heart must first be softened up by bitter wailing and weeping. That, however, is nothing but a denial of Jesus Christ, who long ago softened God's heart and reconciled Him with the whole world. God does nothing by halves. In Christ God loves all sinners without exception; their sin has been wiped out and the entire debt has been paid. Now the poor sinner need be afraid of nothing when he comes to the heavenly Father, who has been propitiated through Jesus Christ.

Yet it is thought that since the Lord Christ has done His part it is now up to man to do his; through the combination of both efforts man is reconciled to God. The sects picture reconciliation thus: The Savior made God willing to save men, if man would also be willing to be reconciled. But that is an anti-Gospel! God *is* reconciled! Therefore Paul [2 Corinthians 5:14-21] calls out to us: "Be reconciled to God." That is to say: "God is reconciled to you through Jesus Christ. Therefore take the hand the heavenly Father holds out to you." Paul also says that since one has died for all, "therfore all have died." That means: If Christ has died for the sins of all people, it is the same as if all people had died and had atoned for their sins. Therefore nothing is necessary on man's part to reconcile God; He is already reconciled. Righteousness is already at hand; man does not first have to achieve it. If he wants to earn his way, he is committing an outrage, fighting against the grace, reconciliation, and complete salvation provided by the Son of God.

Second, the sects teach wrongly about the Gospel. They regard it as nothing but a guide for what man must do to earn God's favor, whereas the Gospel is God's proclamation: "You people have been redeemed from your sins and reconciled with God; your sins are forgiven." No preacher among the sects would dare say that openly. If it does happen occasionally, as in some sermons of Spurgeon, that bit of Lutheranism is the exception. And he was accused of "going too far."

Third, the sects are wrong about faith. They regard faith as a quality in man that improves man; and because it does so, it is regarded as being of extraordinary importance and benefit.

It is, of course, true that one who comes to true faith will become a completely different person. Faith inevitably begets love, as fire produces heat. But this characteristic is not the reason why faith justifies us and gives us what Christ has already won for us. The sects do not give the Scriptural answer to the question: "What must I do to be saved?"—namely: "Believe in the Lord Jesus Christ," that is: "Don't do anything; just accept what God has done for you. Then it is yours and you are saved." That is the precious teaching of the Word of God.

How supremely blessed we Lutherans are to have this teaching! It leads us directly to Christ without any detours. It opens heaven for us when we feel hell in our hearts. Because of this teaching we can receive grace every moment; for if we make all kinds of exertions—even with the best intention—we are wasting our time. We can approach Christ directly, just as we are, conscious of sin but knowing that He calls us to Him through His Gospel. This is the saving doctrine of the Evangelical Lutheran Church, which it has learned from Christ and the apostles.

Be sure to apply this teaching to yourselves. It would be dreadful if one of you would go to bed tonight thinking, "I don't know if God is gracious to me and if my sins are forgiven. I don't know if I would have a blessed death if God should summon me out of this life tonight." God grant that none of you will go to bed in that frame of mind, for then you would retire under God's wrath. As we picture God to ourselves, so He is for us. If we think and believe that God is gracious to us, He is gracious. But if we make of the loving God a bogey who is angry with us, then we will have a God who is not gracious, whose wrath rests on us. However, the God who is angry has been removed by our Savior; we have a God who will have mercy on all.

Furthermore, I wish that your heart will be filled with joy so that you will one day joyfully proclaim this most blessed teaching to your congregations. If you had only an arid moralism to offer, you might think, "What a drab business this is! It won't accomplish anything!" But if you have experienced in your own heart what it means to dispense the comfort of the Gospel and say to your hearers, "Even though you are lost and condemned sinners, just come and believe that you have been redeemed"—I say, if you believe that and keep it in mind, you can only look forward with joy to the day when you will face your congregation for the first time and can bring this blessed message. If you believe that with all your heart and keep it in mind, you will surely have to say, "I have chosen the most beautiful and glorious calling in the world!" For every messenger who brings good news is always welcome. God grant that it may be so with you!

Fifteenth Evening Lecture

(Jan. 23, 1885)

Beloved friends in the Lord! You know that the papists teach that even the pious will not enter heaven when they die but must first be cleansed of their remaining sins in the fires of Purgatory, before they can have the beatific vision of God. They teach furthermore that (with a few exceptions) no one, not even a godly person, can be sure already in this life that his sins are forgiven and that he will be saved. That is indeed a cheerless and thoroughly anti-Christian teaching.

As you know, our Lutheran Church teaches the exact opposite. But alas! While most Lutherans entertain a certain human hope that they have a gracious God who has forgiven their sins and will give them eternal salvation, they are not really sure. That is a most tragic phenomenon. It shows that these Lutherans do not understand the Lutheran teaching at all, let alone take it to heart. How could Christian doctrine be called Gospel, a joyful message, if those who have accepted it would always have to doubt that their sins are covered and that God has declared them righteous and saved? What, then, would be the difference between a Christian and a pagan, who is without God and without hope in this world, if even the Christian would not know how he stands with God and what his eternal destiny will be, damnation or salvation? Does not Scripture say that "faith is the *assurance* of things hoped for, the conviction of things not seen"? Does not our dear Lord Jesus Christ say: "Come to Me, all who labor and are heavy laden, and I will give you rest"? "Whoever drinks of the water that I shall give him will never thirst"? "My sheep hear My voice, and I know them, and they follow Me; and I give them eternal life, and they shall never perish, and no one shall snatch them out of My hand"?

Now, if that doctrine of doubt were correct, would not all these promises be an empty illusion, indeed, to put it bluntly, nothing but lies and deceit? Our Lord Jesus Christ asks His followers to fight against their flesh and blood, against the world and the devil, and to be faithful unto death. He asks them to renounce all they have, come to Him, take up His cross, deny themselves, and follow Him. He tells them in advance, "If you follow Me, the world will hate you, despise and persecute you." If, then, that doctrine of doubt were correct, who would care to go to Christ and follow Him in order to fight all those great battles of this life under His bloody banner? Who would have the strength to pursue godliness, if he would have to doubt whether he could reach the goal? Indeed, whoever has taken this doctrine of doubt into this heart is a miserable person and will remain a wretched slave of the Law. His conscience will constantly tell him, "Things are not right with you! Who knows what God thinks of you and what punishment is in store for you!"

Unquestionably this doctrine of doubt is the worst error to which a human being can succumb. It frustrates Christ and His redemption and the entire Gospel. Here is no room for joking!

Where is the root of this error? Nowhere else but in the confusion of Law and Gospel. How important, therefore, that an honest servant of God know how rightly to divide Law and Gospel.

Last week we saw that the only way to lead a person terrified by sins to certainty that his sins are forgiven and that he is redeemed is to preach God's Word, the Gospel, to him and invite him simply to believe it and apply it to himself, and not to doubt the truth of this heavenly message of grace. But then he must also be asked to be baptized, if still unbaptized, for the forgiveness of sins. From the conversion of the 3,000 at Pentecost, of the jailer at Philippi, and of the apostle Paul himself we learned that this is the only right way. But we saw that one false method is to give the stricken sinner all kinds of rules, how he must act, what he must do, how earnestly and how long he must pray and wrestle, until he finally hears an inner voice tell him that his sins are forgiven and he is a child of God. That is the conversion method of the Reformed and related groups.

Alas, this method is also found among Lutherans! First, that was the way of the Pietists. Some of their concerns were legitimate. The Lutheran Church had gone to sleep, and a spiritual death covered the church like a pall. The Pietists wanted to be helpful, but instead of going back to the pure Reformation church to learn how to bring the spiritually dead to life, they adopted the method of the Reformed, as may be seen from the example of Dr. John Philip Fresenius, of Frankfurt (1705—61). . . .

He wrote a number of rather fine devotional books. But I refer you particularly to his book on *Confession and Communion.* To show you how also Lutherans mingle Law and Gospel, I single out this book, because I myself had some unhappy experiences with it. When I entered the university I was not, indeed, an unbeliever in theory, for my parents were believing. But I left the parental home when I was only eight years old, and from then on I was constantly associated with unbelievers. All the professors with one exception were unbelievers. When I entered the university I could not recite the Ten Commandments and could not list the books of the Bible. My knowledge of the Bible was miserable, to say nothing of the true faith.

However, I had an older brother who went to the university before I did. He had come into contact with a group of converted people and joined their ranks. When I came, he at once introduced me to this circle of Christian students. I had no idea of the goal I was heading for, but I greatly respected my older brother, who invited me.

At first I was attracted by the friendly and loving attitude of these students toward me. I wasn't used to that, since behavior at the prep school was very crude. But I liked the manner of these students extremely well. So it was not the Word of God that first drew me. But I soon felt so happy in the company of these Christian students that I enjoyed going to their prayer meetings, and behold, God came and worked effectively in my soul through His Word, and in a short time I had become in truth a believer, although still with little understanding.

This lasted about half a year, when we were approached by an older candidate, a genuine Pietist, who had no prospects of ever receiving a parish in the territorial church. Rationalism held sway, and the other students thought we were crazy and avoided us like the plague. Well, this candidate came to us and said, "You think you are converted Christians? Not at all. You have not yet experienced a true struggle of repentance." For some time I resisted, because I thought he wanted to move us from the Gospel back to the Law. But he persisted, until finally I began to question our Christianity.

I had felt so happy in my faith in my Lord Jesus Christ, but now came a period of the most intense spiritual trials. I asked this candidate, "What must I do to be saved?" He prescribed various things and gave me several books, among them the one by Fresenius. The more I read it, the more I doubted whether I was a Christian. My heart kept telling me, "You haven't done enough to be a real Christian." On top of that, this candidate was more pietistic than Fresenius himself. In those days, whenever I read a book dealing with the order of salvation, I read only the part about repentance. When I came to the Gospel and faith, I closed the book, convinced that these did not apply to me. The less I tasted the sweetness of the Gospel, the darker it became in my heart. God knows I did not want to be deceived; I wanted to be saved. I always felt that the best books were those that came down on me very hard and offered nothing of God's grace. Finally I heard of a man who was said to be a true spiritual physician. [*Editorial note:* This was Martin Stephan (1777—1846), leader of the 1839 Saxon immigration.] I wrote to him, but decided that if he said anything about grace and Gospel, I would throw the letter into the fire. However, the letter was so consoling that I could not resist it, and I was freed from the state into which Fresenius had brought me.

How fortunate are those students who receive the pure, blessed and comforting doctrine of the Gospel right away! But, alas, experience shows that the richer the supply of the pure teaching of God's Word, the less it is appreciated!

[*Editorial note:* Walther cites Fresenius' division of communicants into nine different classes and goes into considerable detail in commenting on three rules Fresenius prescribes for one who is not yet converted but desires to be converted. His three rules were: 1. Pray for grace; 2. Keep watch over grace; 3. Study the Word of God in the right manner. Fresenius adds: "Whoever observes these rules faithfully will in a short time become a different person, and the grace of God will be so effective in him that he will ever more clearly discern in himself the marks of a new creature in Christ." Walther concludes:]

Now I ask you, where does Holy Scripture give such counsel? Whenever the apostles preached and were asked, "What must we do to be saved?" they had only one answer, "Believe in the Lord Jesus." That is also the only correct method for a preacher to use when he wants to lead his people to faith and to certainty of forgiveness and eternal life. Then he must also not neglect to say to those who in this way have come to certainty of their forgiveness and state of grace that they must now pray, fight and wrestle and always use God's Word in the right way. For from the fact that orthodox Lutherans bear witness in opposition to this false method one must not conclude that Lutherans are not in favor of a true, serious Christianity, of sincere and unceasing prayer, of serious fighting and constant watchfulness. By no means. Honest Lutherans are just as zealous about sanctification as they are about not letting anyone lead them to Christ by detours.

Sixteenth Evening Lecture

(Jan. 30, 1885)

No teaching of our Evangelical Lutheran Church is so offensive to the Reformed as this teaching that man obtains God's grace, forgiveness of sins, and eternal salvation through nothing but confident reliance on the written Word, on Baptism, Holy Communion, and absolution. The Reformed, especially a so-called theologian, will say: "That is such a mechanical way to heaven! What good is the dead letter? Doesn't the apostle Paul say that 'the written code kills, but the Spirit gives life' [2

Corinthians 3:6]? What good is a Baptism with water? The true Baptism is one 'with the Holy Spirit and with fire' [Luke 3:16]. What good is a meal where the natural body and blood of Christ are received? The true food that really satisfies spiritual hunger and thirst is the truth that has come down from heaven. What good is it if a sinful mortal, who cannot look into the heart, tells me, 'Your sins are forgiven?' My sins are not forgiven until God Himself says these words in my heart, so that I can feel them." This is the Reformed view. It is not Scriptural.

According to Scripture, the letter is not something dead. In the context of 2 Corinthians 3:6 it is not the written Word of God as such that is referred to, but the Law. It kills, but the Spirit or the Gospel gives life. Furthermore, the letter cannot itself be dead, for what is dead cannot kill. As for Baptism, passages like Acts 22:16, John 3:5, Galatians 3:27, and Titus 3:5-7 all assert its power. And according to Scripture the Lord's Supper is not an ordinary meal, but a heavenly meal on earth, full of promise and power, "given and shed *for you* for the forgiveness of sins." Finally, when a lowly preacher pronounces the absolution, it is not his own, but Christ's, for he absolves by the command of Christ, in His stead, and in His name (see John 20:21-23).

. . . The Reformed teach as they do because they do not know how man is to receive grace, forgiveness of sins, righteousness before God, and eternal salvation. They point to a different way. Spurning the means God has given, they have devised new methods, as we heard earlier. May the Holy Spirit strengthen us in our conviction and give us joy in our faith!

The ninth thesis is one of the most important; for the confusion of Law and Gospel among the sects consists in their directing the terrified sinner to prayer and wrestling for grace, instead of pointing him to Word and sacraments. It looks quite pious and Christian and can easily deceive the inexperienced. But, thank God, we have a Word that will not deceive us, one that we can trust and turn to as the light for our darkness. When death approaches us and says, "Come along!"—and we feel nothing—we may confidently follow and say, "I will go along gladly. Thank God for delivering me from this terrible prison! It is certain that I will be brought before the throne of a gracious God." Why? Not because of what I feel or what good works I have done, or because I have become a better person. All of that is sinking sand, for in the hour of death these pleasant feelings can easily forsake me. However, one who has learned to rely on the Word possesses the good staff that will help him when he must pass through the dark valley of death. May God equip you with that staff, so that in your ministry you will not beat the air but know, "This is the Word of the eternal and living God, and the devil in hell shall not negate it." When the Lord speaks, all must be silent. For He is Lord of all, and all must be subject to Him!

We have presented the Scriptural basis for this teaching. Today we want to see that this is not just my opinion but the teaching of our Lutheran Confessions. Before citing them, I make some reference to the positon of Zwingli, the grandfather of all the Reformed churches . . . although his crude theology was refined by Calvin. . . . In the fall of 1529 Zwingli subscribed the Marburg Articles, agreed upon by both Lutherans and Zwinglians where it states: "Eighth, that the Holy Spirit, ordinarily, gives such faith or his gift to no one without preaching or the oral word or the gospel of Christ preceding, but that through and by means of such oral word he effects and creates faith where and in whom it pleases him. . . . Ninth, that holy Baptism is a sacrament . . . through which we are regenerated to [eternal] life" (*Luther's Works,* American Edition, Vol. 38, p. 87). . . . A half year later Zwingli repudiated all of this.

In his own statement of faith sent to the emperor at Augsburg, 1530, Zwingli wrote: "I believe and know that the sacraments, far from conveying and imparting grace, do not even offer it." "Grace is effected by the Holy Spirit, and therefore this gift can only be imparted by the Holy Spirit." "The Spirit needs no vehicle, for He is Himself the Power and Conveyance, and He does not need to conveyed." "We read nowhere in Scripture that external things like the sacraments convey the Spirit, but if external things have ever come with the Spirit, it was the Spirit, not the external things, that did it." [There is much more along the same line.]

Now let us hear the testimony of our Symbolical Books. "We should and must constantly maintain," says Luther (Smalcald Articles, Part III, Art. VIII, par. 10; Tappert, p. 313), "that God will not deal with us except through his external Word and sacrament. Whatever is attributed to the Spirit apart from such Word and sacrament is of the devil." The Apology (Art. IV, par. 67; Tappert, p. 116) states: "But one cannot deal with God or grasp him except through the Word. Therefore justification takes place through the Word, as Paul says (Romans 1:16), 'The Gospel is the power of God for salvation to every one who has faith,' and (Romans 10:17) 'Faith comes from what is heard.' From this we can prove that faith justifies. For if justification takes place only through the Word, and the Word is received only by faith, then it follows that faith justifies."

This is highly important! It tells us that those who think little of the means of grace do not really believe that man is saved by grace alone. They think forgiveness of sins simply conveyed through Word, Baptism, Lord's Supper, or absolution is too easy. But, for goodness' sake, if we are really saved by grace alone, why should it be especially difficult? Precisely because we are saved by grace alone, God must have seen to it that we need nothing further than a means by which He gives us forgiveness of sins, grace, and salvation. God says to me: "Only believe! Take it, just trust Me! I am telling you the truth. Just come and lay hold of what I give you!" When I hear the Gospel, I must believe that it is God who is bringing me this good news through this person, and He tells me at the same time, "Why do you exert yourself with your works? Christ has won everything for you! Only believe, it's all yours; I do not lie!" That is what God says.

And what is true of the Word applies also to the sacraments, for they, too, are means of grace. They are the visible Word. The Word of God, the Gospel, is only audible; but the sacraments are also visible, for they are acts combined with things perceptible to the senses. It is therefore false to claim that the Word has a power all its own, that Baptism is a special remedy for other ills, and the Lord's Supper for still others.

Let us hear what our Confessions say about this. "As the Word enters through the ears to strike the heart, so the rite itself enters through the eyes to move the heart. The Word and the rite have the same effect, as Augustine said so well when he called the sacrament 'the visible Word,' for the rite is received by the eyes and is a sort of picture of the Word, signifying the same thing as the Word. Therefore both have the same effect" (Apology, Art. XIII, par. 5; Tappert, p. 212). . . .

In his commentary on Isaiah 20:2 Luther writes: "God, however, adds signs to the Word to arouse faith and fear and because He does not wish to give His Spirit except through some outward means." "The external thing, unless divinely ordained, of course accomplishes nothing. But what is divinely instituted cannot fail to produce results" (*Lectures on Isaiah, Luther's Works,* American Edition, Vol. 16, p. 168).

It is not our church's teaching that by the act of hearing or being dipped into the water we come to faith and grace; for then we would be saved by works! We must hear the voice of God addressed to us. To be baptized without faith does no good, even though we should be baptized ten times daily. Nor does the Lord's Supper benefit us without faith, though we should receive it every day. Our blindness and obduration, our darkness and hardness of heart would be all the worse, and our condemnation all the more severe. Word and sacrament exert their power when they produce in us the faith that appropriates the gifts they offer. That is the teaching of our church.

[*Editorial note:* Here Walther cites at length from a sermon Luther preached on Deuteronomy 4:28 in 1529, shortly before his meeting with Zwingli at Marburg (St. Louis Edition, III, 1691 ff.). In the sermon Luther castigates the "sects and fanatics" who disparage the Gospel and the sacraments as means of grace. "No heresy," says Luther, "can put up with the grace of God." The "enthusiasts," Luther continues, do indeed speak of God, the forgiveness of sins, and the grace of God, and also of Christ's death. But with regard to obtaining Christ and grace, they say that the Spirit must do it alone, that the external Word, Baptism, and the Lord's Supper profit nothing. They deny that God has arranged to have His treasure offered and imparted through Baptism, the Lord's Supper, and the external Word. Walther comments:]

I must confess to you that this bothered me for a long time, when I was a student. It seemed too simple. Surely, that could not be the right way! Finally, when I was in great distress, I realized, "That is the only way!" By God's great grace I have continued in that faith. By God's grace, for no one can come to it and remain with it by his own strength. By nature we are all more inclined to take any wrong way rather than the right way. But in the end also those in the sects who are of God will turn to the right way, at least in the hour of death, even though they will not imagine they are becoming Lutherans. That does not matter, for I can be called Lutheran and yet go to the devil. But unconsciously they will discard everything they relied on and surrender to God's mercy. The same is true of people in the papal church. God's goodness and grace are wonderful. A man may have despised God's grace for 80 years and be burdened with millions of sins, disgusting sins, but if he then collapses and cries, "God, be merciful to me, a sinner!" God will still accept him. However, let no one abuse God's mercy by thinking that he can keep on sinning and then say, in the last hour, "God, be merciful to me, a sinner!" Whoever thinks thus is on the way to hardness of heart, and God may snatch him away in a moment when he will have no opportunity to have a pious thought, and now he is suddenly in the presence of the Judge!

But this is enough for today. This is an extremely important discussion. A week from today we want to continue it, for it is too important for us to end it here. This I owe you, for I bear a heavy responsibility. Soon I will stand before God's throne, where I must give account of the many precious souls to whom one day thousands of people will be entrusted. Then God will ask me, "Have you faithfully discharged your office?" Therefore I must tell you these things whether you like them or not. But I am sure you like them, because you have had the precious Word of God from childhood on. I hope you will already have had some experiences that have taught you that nothing will give you real comfort in your trials but the Word of God, if you want to be sure of your salvation.

Seventeenth Evening Lecture

(Feb. 6, 1885)

When Philip of Hesse arranged the colloquy at Marburg between Luther and Zwingli in 1529, it looked as though the desired goal of brotherly and ecclesiastical union might be achieved. The Swiss yielded in point after point until they came to the Lord's Supper. While the Swiss declared that for the sake of peace they were willing to use Luther's language about a substantial presence of the true body and blood in the Lord's Supper, they had a *spiritual* presence in mind. Earnestly and tearfully they begged the Lutherans not to reject them from fraternal and ecclesiastical fellowship because of this one point of difference.

Luther, however, had soon perceived that the Swiss were not quite honest. His suspicions were confirmed a half year later when Zwingli repudiated all the concessions he had made. Luther told him, "You have a different spirit!" This famous statement struck Zwingli like a bolt of lightning, as he wrote a friend. As often as he repeated these words to himself they had a searing effect. Why? It was because Zwingli and his cohorts knew themelves defeated; because they knew they were unmasked and would now have to reveal their dishonest plan to introduce a merely external union.

Saying that the Swiss had a different spirit, Luther undoubtedly meant to say . . . that they lacked the kind of spirit the Lord had in mind when He told His disciples: "Truly, I say to you, unless you turn and become like children, you will never enter the kingdom of heaven" (Matthew 18:3). Yes, my friends, the spirit of childlike simplicity that takes the Father at His Word is still lacking in all who follow in Zwingli's footsteps. They have the spirit of rationalism, of doubt, of uncertainty that leads people, whenever they are confronted by the mysteries of Scripture, to say with the unenlightened and unregenerate Nicodemus, "How can this be? I cannot understand that; it is contrary to my reason." Hence such people, even when they make concessions, are never quite sure, and they cannot really be trusted. This is clear from the fact that they enter unions with people who teach the opposite of what they teach. They also create the impression that they are ashamed of their religion and are unwilling to concede as much with their mouth as they must concede in their heart.

By contrast, the spirit of Luther and the true Lutheran Church is the spirit of childlike simplicity, the spirit of faith, of submission to the Word of God, of taking reason captive under divine wisdom. It is the spirit that says: "This word remains forever true, and there is naught Thou canst not do; For Thou, Lord, art almighty" *(The Lutheran Hymnal,* 306:4).

Whoever cannot say this is no Lutheran but an enthusiast. "Unconditional surrender to the Word of God" is the hallmark of our church, while the teachers in all sects are constantly tossed about and show that they are not standing on the rock of God's Word. But no church can be trusted that lacks the spirit of childlike simplicity, even though it confesses the truth with the mouth. That is truly a dreadful accusation, but one that is not without foundation, as you have already heard. Let us today see some more proof for it.

Many Protestant churches . . . reject the absolution spoken by the pastor as part of the liturgy. They believe that Lutherans are not sufficiently reformed, but retain much papistic leaven, such as clerical vestments, Communion wafers, the crucifix, candles, chanting, the sign of the cross, bowing at the mention of the name of Jesus. All these are innocent ceremonies which the Lutheran Church does not consider necessary to salvation; but neither does it condemn them as sin. No creature is permitted to declare something to be sinful if God has not declared it sinful in His Word. What God has neither commanded nor forbidden is in the area of freedom. However, many Protestants go further and say that the most horrible relic of papal practice in the Lutheran Church is the absolution.

They make this accusation, first of all, because they do not even know what we teach about absolution. They do not take the trouble to ask us how we understand it. Behind our backs they call us papists who want to lead their poor people back to Rome. Usually they think we teach that through ordination a man is equipped with a special secret power to forgive sins, that absolution is a privileged preserve of preachers, and that the preacher's word, "Your sins are forgiven," is effective, while it is without force when spoken by a layperson. However, that is Roman doctrine, not ours. Even our Small Catechism teaches that the Office of the Keys is a "peculiar church power which Christ has given to His church on earth, to forgive the sins of penitent sinners, but to retain the sins of the impenitent, as long as they do not repent." Hence absolution is a power given to the church, not to preachers. These are not the church, but only servants of the church. If they are Christians, they are members of the church. If they are not Christians, they do not belong to the church but are hewers of wood and drawers of water, like the Gibeonites in the Old Testament [Joshua 9:21]. If they are Christians, the Office of the Keys is theirs also. It does not belong only to the preachers, however, but to the church and to every member, even the lowliest laborer, as much as to the most esteemed church president. That is the clear teaching of our church: "So in an emergency even a layman absolves and becomes the minister and pastor of another. It is like the example which Augustine relates of two Christians in a ship, one of whom baptized the other (a catechumen), and the latter, after his Baptism, absolved the former" (Treatise on the Power and Primacy of the Pope, par. 67; Tappert, p. 331). . . . Both the Baptism and the absolution were subsequently declared to be valid.

What, then, is the doctrinal basis of absolution? Lutherans teach the following:

1. Christ, the Son of God, took upon Himself all sins of all sinners and had them imputed to Him. Therefore John the Baptizer pointed to Him and said: "Behold, the Lamb of God, who takes away the sin of the world!" (John 1:29).

2. Through His lowly life, His suffering, crucifixion, and death Christ atoned for the sins of all people and won forgiveness for them. No one is excluded, from Adam down to the last person who will be born in this world, for St. Paul writes: "For our sake God made Him to be sin who knew no sin, so that in Him we might become the righteousness of God" (2 Corinthians 5:21). Already Isaiah said: "He was wounded for our transgressions, He was bruised for our iniquities; upon Him was the chastisement that made us whole, and with His stripes we are healed" (Isaiah 53:5). In prophecy the Messiah sighs: "I must pay for what I have not robbed" (Psalm 69:4 [Luther's translation]).

3. By the resurrection of His Son Jesus Christ from the dead God the Father has affirmed and sealed the work of reconciliation and redemption which Christ accomplished on the cross. God has publicly attested before heaven and earth, before angels and men: "This My beloved Son has said on the cross, 'It is finished!'—and herewith I declare that it *is* finished. You sinners have been redeemed. Here is forgiveness of sins for everyone! It is already there! You need not first acquire it."

4. By the command to preach the Gospel to every creature Christ at the same time commanded that forgiveness of sins be proclaimed to all, that is, the good news: "All that is necessary for your salvation has already been done! If you ask, 'What must we do to be saved?' remember that all has already been done. There is nothing left to do. Just believe what has happened, and you will be saved."

5. Christ not only issued the general order to His apostles and their successors in office to preach the Gospel, the message of the forgiveness of sins, but He also ordered them to speak this comfort to every individual who desires it: "You are reconciled to God!" For if forgiveness has been won for *all,* it has also been won for *every individual.* If I can offer it to all, I can also offer it to each individual. I not only can do so, but I must do so. If I do not, I am a servant of Moses and not a servant of Christ.

91

Concordia Seminary in 1883, where Walther served as professor and president to the end of his life (courtesy Concordia Publishing House Archives).

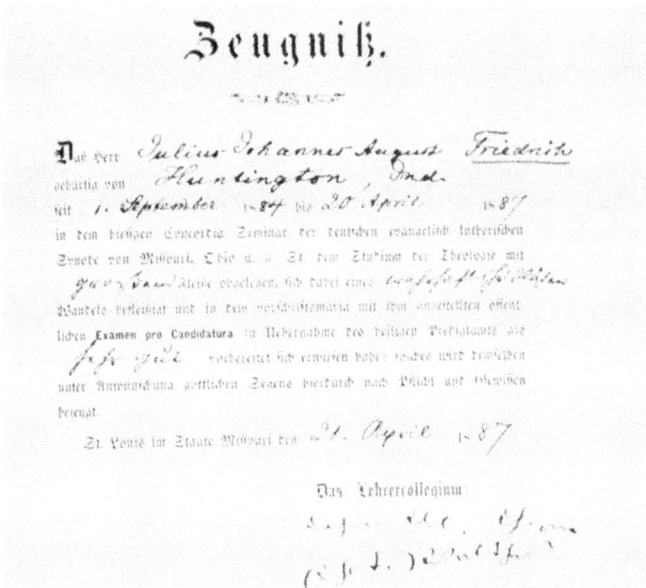

The last diploma signed by Walther as seminary president on April 21, 1887, for graduate Julius Friedrich (courtesy Concordia Publishing House Library).

Another view of Walther's study, where many of his works were produced (courtesy Concordia Historical Institute).

The faculty of Concordia Seminary, St. Louis, taken sometime between 1887 and 1892. Sitting (from left): C. H. R. Lange, M. Guenther; standing: G. Stoeckhardt, F. Pieper, A. L. Graebner (courtesy Concordia Publishing House Archives).

Since forgiveness of sins has been won, not only the preacher (with his special mandate) can proclaim it, but every Christian, male or female, yes, every child. And the child's absolution is just as certain as that of St. Peter; yes (what am I saying?), as certain as that of Jesus Christ—as if He stood before us in person and said: "Your sins are forgiven!" There is no difference. For, as indicated, the question is not, "What can man do?" but "What has Christ done?"

Imagine that a whole city has rebelled and even murdered the king's son, in a conspiracy of the whole community against their sovereign lord and has thus become subject to the death penalty. In the story we cannot say that the murdered son took the people's part, but we can say that another son moved his father to pardon the rebels, to prepare a document of amnesty and sign it; then he should go or send messengers to the rebels and inform them; then they would again become good and grateful citizens and loyal subjects.

Now if the king would yield to his son, but calmly remaining in his castle would send out messengers with the document, who would then proclaim it in all the streets: "You have been pardoned!"—while the rebels had been trembling with fear at having been defeated and were expecting to be promptly executed, what kind of people would that be who would say, "We don't believe it; the king himself must come in person, else we won't believe it"? That would be impudence without equal. In this case no one would be so impudent; every one would be glad to see the document of amnesty with the king's signature, stating: "Herewith I pardon all rebels. May they just accept this pardon and become good citizens again!"

Now suppose these messengers would be unable to reach all the people, but others who heard the message of pardon would go everywhere and spread the news. That would be just as valid a pardon as that proclaimed by the messengers. Not because they had special authority to offer the pardon, but because the pardon had already been decreed, signed and sealed, and made public: "The king has expressly commanded this pardon to be proclaimed."

So it is with us, too. We are the rebels; God is the King against whom we have rebelled, and the Son of God is the One who has done everything necessary to induce our heavenly King to pardon us all. All that has been done.

Now, then, what does a Lutheran preacher do when he proclaims forgiveness of sins and absolves? He does nothing but inform the people: "So it is with you. Christ has taken your part, and God accepts you by grace." And the preacher does so in obedience to a specific command of Christ.

If someone asks me to tell this or that person that I forgive him, and I carry out that assignment, the pardon is just as valid and effective as if that man came in person and said, "I forgive you." Or if you had a friend in Germany who had seriously offended you, and you learned that he was now tormented by remorse, afraid of dying without mercy—would you have to travel there yourself? No, you could write a letter or commission an acquaintance who was going there: "Tell my friend that I have forgiven him long ago, and he should no longer worry. I have been reconciled!" The friend would accept this message as fully valid. So it is with absolution.

Now I ask you, does this have anything papistic in it? Certainly not. The papists teach that a priest's power of absolution derives from his ordination. And for those who have been absolved the power of the absolution consists in their contrition, their confession, and their works of satisfaction. First of all, a complete confession: If something is omitted, the entire confession and absolution is without effect. Second, the penitent must experience complete contrition in his heart, or else the keys will not unlock heaven for him. Third, he must perform the works of penance prescribed by the priest. Of all that there is nothing in our teaching. We say: The efficacy of absolution does not depend on ordination or on the preacher, but 1. on the completeness of Christ's work of reconciliation and redemption, and 2. on Christ's command to preach the Gospel to every creature. That is to say, "You must absolve all people and assure them of forgiveness."

Now a few testimonies from our Confessions and from Luther. "The people are carefully instructed concerning the consolation of the Word of absolution so that they may esteem absolution as a great and precious thing. It is not the voice or word of the man who speaks it, but it is the Word of God, who forgives sin" (Augsburg Confession, Art. XXV, par. 2-3.; cf. 4-5; Tappert, pp. 61 f. See also Apology, Art. XII, par. 39; Tappert, p. 187. Also Large Catechism, Lord's Prayer, par. 88; Tappert, p. 432).

[*Editorial note:* Walther also introduces a number of passages from Luther's sermons which emphasize that Christ's work of redemption is all-inclusive and is presented to all people as a gift that needs only to be accepted, and that human beings have been authorized and commanded to convey this gift. All enthusiasts and fanatics are ignorant of how sins are forgiven. The whole papal system rests on the teaching that grace is infused into man through a secret operation; whoever desires to share in it must be contrite, confess, and do works of penance. Walther comments that all sects are guilty of the same error, teaching that whoever wants to be forgiven must pray and fight and wrestle until he feels the infusion of grace.

(See St. Louis Edition, XII, 1586; XI, 1104; XIIIa, 978 ff.) Walther continues:]

But grace cannot be infused, for it is God's gracious attitude outside of us; it can only be proclaimed to us. Therefore we can have true peace only through the Word, as we hear it or read it. We can derive absolution from every chapter of the Bible, for there is none that does not contain the truth that "your sins are forgiven!" Every consoling statement about God's mercy is an absolution. For that reason Luther says that a true evangelical preacher cannot open his mouth without speaking the absolution. And that is true. Remember, a true evangelical preacher! A preacher of the Law like Moses cannot do it, for he brings the people to despair and hell, while the evangelical preacher snatches them, even the greatest sinners, out of hell. . . .

But our time is up. I believe the subject is important enough that we should return to it once more and compare a few more beautiful quotations. Then, if we have time, we want to consider in detail the words of our thesis: "until they feel that God has pardoned them." We have not yet spoken about that. And yet it is important. You need it here more than the pastors in Germany, because in this country there are so many sects. When our people observe their great show of sanctity, they are easily led astray. . . .

Eighteenth Evening Lecture
(Feb. 13, 1885)

A condemned criminal, hearing a vague rumor that he will be pardoned but unable to be sure, is doubtless, my friends, in a bad situation. Every sound indicating that the door is being opened causes him to start, for he does not know whether he will hear words of his pardon or be led to the place of execution. Only a completely insensitive and godless man could still be joking in such a situation.

Every person is spiritually in a similar state by nature . . . under God's sentence of temporal and eternal death. While he may have heard a dim rumor that God would pardon him, he cannot become sure. As often as he is seriously ill or in trouble or anxiety, he feels the doors of eternity opening before him, but the poor man does not know whether that will lead to eternal death or eternal life. Now all laughter will flee him, even though he may formerly have made fun of what is sacred.

Well now, has not the kind, gracious, and merciful God done anything to make us certain about the forgiveness of sins and an eternity of peace and rest? Has God done nothing to deliver us from this wretched situation? Unthinkable! Of course God has acted! Do not His great deeds surpass all human understanding? He sent His only Son into this world, let Him become a human being like us, burdened Him with our sins, and delivered Him up to death on the cross for our redemption. And He should then leave us in a lifelong state of doubt as to whether He is still our enemy? Impossible! As soon as the eternal Son of God had come to this earth, God's chief messenger came down and announced to the Bethlehem shepherds, to us, and to all the world: "Behold, I bring you good news of a great joy which will come to all the people; for to you is born this day in the city of David a Savior, who is Christ the Lord." And when Christ had finished His great work and God the Father had raised Him from the dead, and thus had vindicated Him and in Him justified and absolved us all, Christ commanded His disciples: "Go into all the world and preach the Gospel"—the joyful message of redemption—"to the whole creation." Furthermore: "Lo, I am with you always, to the close of the age," thereby guaranteeing that this joyful message will sound forth in all the world until the last day.

Oh, how blessed and highly favored we are! Who can give expression to our bliss! Heaven and earth are full of the goodness of the Lord our God! At every turn we are told: "Your sins are forgiven. Heaven's door stands open. Only believe, believe it, and you have it!"

But alas, this unspeakable pleasure of highly favored humanity is greatly spoiled by false teachers, as we have seen in the last three evening hours. We now want to gain further conviction on this matter. This is to serve a twofold purpose: 1. We want nothing to spoil the cup of inexpressible joy which our heavenly Father has filled for us; and 2. When you enter the ministry of reconciliation, you will be careful not to rob poor sinners of what God gave them long ago, in fact, planned for them from eternity.

We are still discussing Thesis IX. It is really the central thesis in the whole cycle. Whoever understands it correctly knows how to distinguish Law and Gospel; but whoever does not understand this thesis will never learn the distinction by means of any other rules. Recall what it says: "In the fifth place, God's Word is not rightly divided when sinners, struck and terrified by the Law, instead of being directed to the Word and sacrament, are instructed to strive for the state of grace through prayer and struggles, that is, to keep on praying and wrestling *until they feel that God has pardoned them.*"

As we have seen, the inability of enthusiasts to distinguish Law and Gospel becomes apparent especially in their rejection of absolution. Not only do they have a completely wrong conception of what absolution is and what we teach about it, but they also think our absolution is the same as the doctrine of the papists, because the outward action seems to resemble it. But even though the papists also speak the precious words of absolution, they have emptied them of their content. We retain the precious words but are also concerned about preserving the substance as we offer absolution to those who desire it.

In the Gospel for the 19th Sunday after Trinity we are told of the healing of the paralytic [Matthew 9:1-8]. "The crowds . . . glorified God, who had given such authority [to forgive sins] *to men.*" They were not mistaken. God really gave men the authority to forgive sins, and they rejoiced in the Messiah.

It is always so. People led to withered pastures where the comfort of the Gospel has been withheld are like famished sheep. But when they are fed the lush green grass of the pure Gospel, how avidly they devour it! This may be seen in Germany. The churches of rationalist preachers are empty, but where a preacher speaks "in demonstration of the Spirit and of power," the church is full. People still have their Bible, their catechism, and their old hymnbook. They stick to the Bible passages they have learned and they enjoy their old devotional books. When a live preacher comes and brings them the Gospel, they are beside themselves with joy.

Unfortunately, there are also preachers who are believers but preach over their hearers' heads, and so the hearers remain spiritually dead. One must not only proclaim the truth but also speak so simply that even the uneducated can understand it. We must preach so that it is as clear to everyone as the noonday sun: "That is the only way to salvation." It would not be surprising if God would hurl bolts of lightning at preachers who have high-flown language in their manuscript in order to show off their oratorical skills. . . .

[*Editorial note:* Here follows a large portion of Luther's sermon on Matthew 9:1-8 (St. Louis Edition, XIIIa, 917 f.), interspersed with Walther's comments. Luther rebukes the Anabaptists, who disparage water Baptism, and the Sacramentarians, who say there is nothing but bread and wine in the Lord's Supper, which can therefore not impart forgiveness of sins. In general, Luther attacks all who in any way question the validity and power of the absolution pronounced by men, and who deny that one can be sure of his forgiveness. Here are some of Walther's comments:]

In Baptism it is, of course, not the water that does anything. It is water like all other water, with no special powers, but here it is combined with God's Word: "He who believes and is baptized will be saved." When these words come to the baptismal water they make it more precious than heaven and earth and all earthly treasures. . . .

To gain certainty about the forgiveness of sins, we must know what God has to say to us. Just because you feel good or because God showers His gifts upon you, you cannot conclude that God has forgiven you, for "He makes His sun rise on the evil and on the good, and sends rain on the just and on the unjust." You can gain certainty only when God Himself *tells* you. There is no other way to certainty.

But where does God tell us that He wants to forgive us? In His Word, in the Gospel, in Baptism, in the Lord's Supper, in the absolution. In the Lord's Supper the real gift of grace is not so much the body and blood of Christ as it is the promise of forgiveness which Christ has attached thereto, saying: "Given and shed for you for the forgiveness of sins." Christ's body and blood are only the royal seal impressed on the Savior's words. In short, the Word is primary in all that God does to assure us of His grace.

This is true also of the absolution. It is the Word that matters. We must not wait for an angel from heaven to come and tell us: "Your sins are forgiven." We could wait a long time. God has not promised anything like that. If He had, we could confidently pray for it. Although we are poor sinners, God wants to give us the best gifts. If He has made a promise, He will keep it. Be of good cheer! "Open your mouth wide, and I will fill it" (Psalm 81:10). God has promised us forgiveness of sins, and if we believe it, we will have it. . . .

Calvin was not satisfied with Zwingli's teaching on the Lord's Supper, but his own teaching is not correct either. He said that one does not receive Christ's body and blood with the bread and wine, but by being lifted up to heaven through faith. Then the holy Spirit would cause one to receive Christ's body and blood. But that was pure fantasy that originated in Calvin's head. So people demonstrate that they are unwilling to believe that God loves us poor sinners so much that He comes to us. They think we must rise up to Him. But He has already come down to us. . . .

[*Editorial note:* Walther now quotes from a sermon of Luther's on John 20:21-23 (St. Louis Edition, XI, 731 f.). Luther emphasizes that the power to forgive sins does not rest on the authority of priests or pastors, but entirely on the divine majesty. When Christ says: "If you forgive the sins of any, they are forgiven," what is established here is not the power of the one who speaks the absolution, but the power of those who believe. Walther comments:]

If Christ had not risen, we would be unable to absolve anyone. On what would we base the absolution? Only after God the Father had acknowledged Christ's work of reconciliation and redemption and by the resurrection had absolved Christ [who had taken upon Himself the sins of the world], and in Him all people, could we say to one another: "Be of good cheer, all your sins are forgiven and wiped out. Just believe it!" This is based on the fact that God the Father has glorifed Christ, our Substitute, and thereby declared before heaven and earth: "Yes, you human beings have been redeemed; you have been reconciled. Your sins are forgiven."

Sad to say, when I returned to Germany the first time, I heard with my own ears an eminent believing preacher say, "Indeed, a layman can speak many a consoling truth to you, but he cannot absolve you. That is a privilege which God has given to the servants called and ordained by the church." What must that man have thought of absolution? It can have been nothing other than the papistic conception. That was by the way, more than 30 years ago. I argued with him, but he refused to budge.

No, the point is not that the pastor possesses a mysterious power to remove sins, but that Christ has already removed them and that now everyone should tell everyone else. Especially the preachers should do this, not because of special powers but because of God's order that they should administer the means of grace, Word and sacrament. But from an emergency situation one can see that a layman can do it as well as an official.

This shows that our teaching is the direct opposite of the papistic teaching. The pope anathematizes our teaching, saying that no one can be certain of his salvation or of being justified. A leading Roman theologian, Bellarmine, writes (*On Justification,* ch. 3): "In this life people can have no certainty of faith with regard to their righteousness with the exception of those to whom God deigns to give a special revelation." . . . Is that not terrible? . . . How cruel!

The absolution I give is valid, not because I speak it but because faith saves. Even though I were a perfect saint or even an archangel, this would not help in the least to make the absolution I give valid. But when I speak the Word of the Gospel, without which no one can be saved, that Word is efficacious.

Let me also call your attention to an incomparable writing of Luther's, *The Keys (Luther's Works,* American Edition, Vol. 40, pp. 325 ff.—see especially pp. 364—67). From it I first learned what the Gospel is, even though I thought at the time that I already knew it. God be eternally praised for this writing! When I first came to Christianity, I became involved with the Pietists. Then I read Luther's writings, including this one.

[*Editorial note:* Walther gives some information about the history of this writing, in which Luther says, in a long section quoted by Walther, that "the keys or the forgiveness of sins are not based on our own repentance or worthiness." Walther comments:]

Do not misunderstand our good Luther. Contrition is necessary. Luther did not offer the comfort of the Gospel to carnally secure sinners. But to a contrite person longing for forgiveness Luther said: "There, take it, it's yours!" You must not worry whether your contrition is adequate, but just the opposite; thank God for receiving the absolution, for then your contrition is also satisfactory. Absolution should not be based on contrition, but vice versa. . . . From the Word of God we know that God has absolved the whole world. Therefore it is certain that all sins are forgiven.

But if a godless rogue receives the absolution, it will benefit him nothing, because he refuses to accept it. If he believed the Holy Spirit, he would desist from his crimes. . . . Yet the absolution itself remains valid. Even if Judas had been absolved, his sins would have been forgiven in the sight of God, but he did not accept the absolution. This treasure involves two persons, one who offers it and one who receives it. But an impenitent sinner does not accept it. . . .

Luther uses the illustration of a king giving you a castle, which you refuse to accept. That does not invalidate the king's gift; it is your own fault that you do not receive it. So it is with absolution. . . .

Nineteenth Evening Lecture
(Feb. 20, 1885)

Among many differences between the so-called Pietists and the orthodox Lutherans during the first half of the 18th century, one of the most important was this: The Pietists, especially the followers of Spener, A. H. Francke, and J. J. Rambach—although not the really faithful disciples of these men—taught that those who cannot name the precise day and hour in which they were converted are not true Christians, and may not be regarded as such by themselves or by others. The orthodox denied this.

Now, it is indeed true that conversion does not take place in the course of a day or an hour, but in a moment. According to Scripture conversion is nothing but being raised from spiritual death to spiritual life, nothing but a return from the broad way leading below to the narrow way that leads upward; it is nothing but being transferred from Satan's kingdom to the kingdom of Jesus Christ, the Son of God. Just as there is no intermediate state between death and life, just as there is no middle way between the narrow way that leads upward and the broad way that leads downward, just as there is no kingdom between Satan's kingdom and Christ's kingdom, so every human being is either spiritually dead or spiritually alive, he is either on the narrow way or the broad way, he is either in the kingdom of Christ or that of the devil. Hence a person is either converted or not converted. There is no third possiblity.

To be sure, Scripture tells us of instances of people who could in fact give the day and hour when they were converted to God and received His grace. . . .

However, many did not have the same experience. Church history teaches us that in the 1,800 years of the church's existence millions upon millions who were reared in the church could not name the day and hour of their conversion and yet knew and could prove that they had become different people and through the Holy Spirit had been led to a living faith in Christ, to grace and righteousness, and to the hope of eternal life.

Where, do you suppose, did these well-meaning Pietists get the idea that one who could not pinpoint the day and hour of his conversion could not be a Christian? They believed one must suddenly experience a heavenly thrill of joy when an inner voice would tell them: "You have found favor with God and are now His child!" Hence they felt compelled to teach: "If that is the way one is converted to God, then one must also be able to say in what day and hour he was converted, when he became a different person, had his sins forgiven, and was clothed with the garment of Christ's righteousness."

But that is a great, fateful, dangerous error, as we have already noted in part. Today we shall consider the last part of Thesis IX, which treats of this matter specifically. Here it is stated that God's Word is not rightly divided when people who are struck and terrified by the Law are instructed to wrestle for the state of grace through prayer and struggles, and keep on praying and struggling until they *feel* God has pardoned them.

That is also the system of our Methodists. But before we proceed, we must clear up a misunderstanding about the teaching that a person should under no circumstances base his salvation and state of grace on his feelings. This teaching, too, is dreadfully misused by many people. There are those who consider themselves good Christians and yet are spiritually dead. They have never experienced any real terror because of their sins; they have never dreaded hell, which they have well deserved; they have never been on their knees making a tearful confession to God that they are horrible and condemned sinners; and much less have they ever wept sweet tears of joy and thanked God for having had mercy on them. They read and hear God's Word, but they experience nothing. They go to church and receive absolution, but they are not refreshed, and they come to Holy Communion but remain ice-cold and unfeeling.

Yet if they do feel ill at ease because they are so indifferent with regard to their salvation and have no taste for the Word of God, they seek to quiet their conscience by saying: "Well, the Lutheran Church teaches that nothing depends on one's feelings. So if I have felt nothing, it does not matter. I can still be a good Christian for, after all, I believe." However, that is a dreadful case of self-delusion. A person in such a state has nothing but a dead intellectual faith, only a sham faith or, to put it bluntly, a mouth-faith *(Maulglauben)*. He may say, "I believe," but his heart is uninvolved. No, God's Word calls out to us: "O taste and see that the Lord is good!" [Psalm 34:8]. One who has never experienced this must not think that he has true faith. And the apostle Paul says: "The Spirit Himself bears witness with our spirit that we are children of God" (Romans 8:16). How can the Holy Spirit make this witness to us unless we can feel it? A witness must speak loud enough for the judge to hear him. . . .

The apostle Paul says, futhermore, that "since we are justified by faith, we have peace with God through our Lord Jesus Christ" (Romans 5:1). Objective peace is already there before our justification, for Christ has made peace through His blood. Hence this must refer to a peace that can be felt and experienced. Again, the apostle writes: "The kingdom of God is . . . righteousness and peace and joy in the Holy Spirit" (Romans 14:17). One who has tasted worldly and carnal joy but never spiritual joy is simply dead.

The example of the saints in the Bible also demonstrates this truth. They are constantly aglow with praise to God for all that He has done for them. This surely presupposes that their heart was conscious of His mercies. If David had been ignorant of them, would he have exclaimed: "Bless the Lord, O my soul, and all that is within me, bless His holy name! Bless the Lord, O my soul, and forget not all His benefits, who forgives all your iniquity, who heals all your diseases" [Psalm 103:1-3]? By no means. He felt a warm glow in his heart. Finally, ask any person who has all the earmarks of being a genuine, live Christian, "Have you ever experienced what you are talking about?" He will say, "Certainly I have experienced it. I have felt the terror of God that descends upon a sinner whom God desires to save. But then I have also experienced the sweetness of God's grace in Christ Jesus. As often as I think of the love of my Savior, my heart melts within me. Again, even though I know that I have found grace, I am still beset by anguish and fear whenever I look at the Law." Please note, therefore, when we say that no one should base his salvation and his being in the state of grace on his feelings, we do not mean to say that a person need have no feelings at all in matters of his religion and can still be a good Christian. That is not what we teach.

Luther was certainly no sentimentalist like Melanchthon, who relied much on his feelings. Luther clung to the Word, no matter how he felt. Yet on the words: "Because you are sons, God has sent the Spirit of His Son into our hearts, crying, 'Abba, Father!'" [Galatians 4:6], Luther commented in his *Church Postil:* "Here everyone must examine himself to discern whether he also feels the Holy Spirit and senses His voice in his heart. St. Paul says that where the Spirit is in the heart, He cries, 'Abba, Father!'" [*Editorial note:* Walther brings several pages from this sermon of Luther's, in which he emphasizes that genuine faith is certain of forgiveness and God's love and will therefore hear the voice of the Spirit (St. Louis Edition, XII, 239 ff.; cf. *Lectures on Galatians,* 1535, *Luther's Works,* American Edition, Vol. 26, p. 389).]

Such faith is seldom found in our day. Either the people are spiritually dead and therefore carefree and confident that they will get to heaven somehow, or they are uncertain and anxious. How many approach death wondering what will happen to them, whether they will go to heaven or not. That is a horrendous faith, a sham faith. Faith must be certain.

As you know, the Roman church not only denies that one *can* become certain but also teaches that one *should not* come to certainty. According to Rome it would be presumptuous for a person who had received no special revelation from God to say: "I know and am certain that I will be saved." But that is an inverted Gospel. In fact, the whole papacy is nothing but a tragic perversion of the Gospel into Law, especially the laws of the church.

People will say they know that Christ has redeemed the whole world, but they wonder whether they too have been redeemed. Such people know nothing of either Law of Gospel. One who has learned to know the Gospel is sure that "since God's Son has redeemed the whole world, I too have been redeemed. But if I am redeemed, God wants me to believe it. He does not deter me, He does not, like the Pietists, warn me against coming to faith too early." It is impossible to believe too soon, for when the Gospel is preached to us we must believe it, as we value our salvation, or we will incur God's wrath. But if we do not cling to the Word, we cannot be certain. There will be daily and even hourly wavering. One moment we feel we are Christians, and the next moment we think we were mistaken and are not Christians.

There must be true confidence, and this confidence can exist even while we quake and tremble. We may be terrified at the chasm gaping before us, but there is a protective railing on both sides, so that we can safely cross the abyss. That is the marvelous paradox in a Christian: He trembles and yet is certain at the same time.

St. Paul does not say that the Spirit bears witness in general, but He bears witness with our spirit [Romans 8:16]. Hence our spirit must receive this witness spiritually; and when we hear this witness, that is our feeling. When a Christian begins to have doubts, he hears another voice speaking within him: "Christ died for you, didn't He? Then you don't need to lose courage and despair. You belong to the redeemed of the Lord and are an heir of heaven. Be of good cheer!" This voice, which speaks without our prompting, is the testimony of the Holy Spirit. It is heard particularly when the Christian is in spiritual anxiety. One does not listen to a witness every day, but summons the witness when one has been accused. So it is also in spiritual matters. Just when the Christian is in the greatest trouble, the Holy Spirit calls: "Do not lose courage!"

But beside the Holy Spirit's witness there is also the outcry of the devil, even for one who is sure of his state of grace. While he is certain of God's grace, a secret voice whispers: "But you are not yet rid of your sins! Remember your evil thoughts and desires and words of this day! And the good you did was only pretense." Those are the fiery darts of the devil. But then the Spirit will take our side and bear witness for us, if we are Christians.

Now we shall take up that part of our thesis which lies before us today, the part that says it is a dreadful mingling of Law and Gospel to teach that if you want to become sure of the forgiveness of your sins you must keep on praying, struggling, and wrestling until you get a joyful feeling that whispers: "Cheer up, your sins are forgiven." "Now," they say, "grace will be in your heart." Strictly speaking, grace cannot be in my heart, for it is in God's heart. No, first you must *believe* and *then feel*. The feeling arises from faith, not vice versa. One whose faith rises out of his feelings does not have the true faith, for faith requires a divine promise. But you may be sure that those have the right faith who can say: "I look at nothing in the whole world but the Gospel. On it I rest my faith." Then let the devil come and frighten and torment them. Even though they may not at once have sweet feelings, they will say:

> Though "No!" my heart should ever cry,
> Still on Thy Word I shall rely.
> (Cf. *The Lutheran Hymnal,* 226:8)

This teaching is based especially on 1 John 3:19-20: "By this we shall know that we are of the truth, and reassure our hearts before Him whenever our hearts condemn us; for God is greater than our hearts, and

He knows everything." When a Christian whose heart or conscience condemns him seeks comfort and a voice within him condemns him and denies that he is a child of God, he must listen to John, who says: "Whenever our hearts condemn us, God is greater than our hearts." We should think: "When my heart judges me, I appeal to a higher court; and God, the supreme Judge, acquits me of my sins." . . . Oh, blessed is everyone who can believe that with all his heart! For such a person hell is closed and heaven opened wide. Let the devil and all his crew roar that I am condemned, I can retort: "On the contrary, I am eternally saved, for God says so!" And the proper feelings will come in due time. Just when a Christian thinks: "Alas, I feel nothing! I am so cold and so dead! God's Word tastes like rotten wood! The absolution does not refresh me!"—then suddenly some great joy will revive his heart. God will not forsake him.

To be sure, we cannot dictate to God. There is a great difference among Christians. Some experience the great grace of moving through life calmly and with pleasant feelings and without serious conflicts. . . . Others, however, are led by God through darkness and anguish, through grave doubts and troubles. But we must distinguish whether such a person is spiritually dead or is caught in severe trials. This is not difficult. When I am anxious about not feeling anything, and would so much like to experience some emotions, this is a good sign that I am a true Christian. One who wants to believe is already a believer. How could a person possibly want to believe something he regards as untrue? Nobody wants to be deceived. As soon as I want to believe something, I already believe it in secret.

Pastors, please take note! Often good church members will come and say, "Pastor, I just can't believe, and I feel very bad about it." "Would you like to believe?" "Oh, yes!" Then let the pastor console the member: "You are already a believer. Just cheer up and wait patiently until God lets the hour of trial pass. Then you will see your faith burst forth full of power and joy."

Thomas refused to believe that Christ rose from the dead unless he could "place his finger in the mark of the nails." Mercifully Christ granted him this great grace . . . but then said to him: "Blessed are those who have not seen and yet believe" (John 20:24-29). But basically "seeing" is the same as "experiencing." . . . We must first believe and then see, not the other way around. It is equally certain that we must not first want to feel. We must, rather, believe and then wait for God to give us the sweet feeling that He has taken away our sins.

Hebrews 11:1 offers a definition of faith. It is "the assurance of things hoped for, the conviction of things not seen." But in that case faith cannot rest on seeing, feeling, or experiencing; for then it will rest on sand and soon the entire structure will collapse. Woe to those who have become accustomed to considering themselves pardoned only when they have pleasant feelings! As a rule, such feelings vanish in the hour of death. Blessed are they who can say:

> I cling to what my Savior taught,
> And trust it whether felt or not.

But woe to those who think in the hour of death: "I feel nothing at all. Now I must die and Jesus is no longer in my heart. O wretched man that I am!" How many people in the enthusiastic sects may have been lost because in the end they let go of the Lord Jesus in the opinion that they had no permission to cling to Him! They all think that it is only the feeling that gives them permission to come to Jesus and receive His consolation. Therefore they often ask a brother, "How do you feel?" [*Editorial note:* Walther gives these four words in English.] If he answers, "I feel nothing," they say, "Oh, you poor man! Come, let us pray and wrestle until you get the feeling." Then he will get some sort of feeling, but often it is only a sensory emotion and not awareness of the Holy Spirit. . . .

[*Editorial note:* In a sermon from his *Church Postil* Luther speaks of those who grope for God like a blind man and want to feel Him and grasp Him so that He will not get away. This is not true faith. Real faith is exemplified by the ten lepers, who had no previous feeling or guarantee that Christ would hear them. They simply took the cheerful risk of entrusting themselves to His unfelt, untried, unknown goodness. (St. Louis Edition, XI, 1577 f.). Walther comments:]

This is what faith is really like. It does not demand advance guarantees, but it believes as soon as the Word is proclaimed, and then comes the guarantee, sooner or later. It is the general experience that when a person has become a Christian he soon has pleasant feelings. God deals with His spiritual infants the way an earthly father deals with his little ones. He gives them baby food and sweets. So God at the beginning gives His Christians the sweets of pleasant feelings. But when they have had much experience and have exercised their faith, God takes the sweets away and offers them black bread, which is often quite hard and heavy. God reasons: "You have had sufficient experience in your Christianity, and so this will not tax you too severely. If I would give this bread to the little ones, they would be unable to digest it." In trials Christians often reminisce: "Oh, what a blessed person I once was! How I reveled in sweet feelings, in the joyful certainty that I have a gracious God in heaven. . . .

Now the Christian is able to digest even the hard rye bread. A beginner, however, from whom God might withdraw comfort would say:

"What a wretched person I am! Preachers always talk about how wonderful the Christian life is, but now I find that a Christian is the most unhappy person, with nothing but anxiety, trouble, and fear."

What a loving Father God is to His Christians! He does not at once lay heavy burdens upon them. He puts them through a training period and only gradually withdraws feelings of comfort, so that they may learn to cling to God in the dark. Hence no one should think that a reduction in pleasant sensations indicates a fall from grace or that one no longer has the first love. The love of a mature, experienced Christian for his Savior may not taste quite as sweet, but it is far purer, because many impurities have been burned off.

When I have prayed a Lord's Prayer with all due devotion (which indeed is rarely done), I may speak the Amen with joy, even though during the prayer I did not sense the moving power of the Holy Spirit. But I prayed in the midst of struggles, and my prayer was heard.

[*Editorial note:* See also a sermon of Luther's on the Gospel for the First Sunday After Epiphany (St. Louis Edition, XI, 453 f.). Here Luther rejects all reliance on feeling and asserts that God may be found only where His Word is. Walther comments:]

There you have an indictment of all enthusiastic sects. They all share this error: They do not rely exclusively on Christ and His Word but primarily on something going on inside them. They usually think that all is well with them because they have converted themselves. As if that were a guarantee of getting to heaven! No, we must not look back to our conversion and rely on that. On the contrary, every day I must return to my Savior as though I were not yet converted. A previous conversion is of no benefit if I now become secure. I must approach the throne of grace every day; otherwise my previous conversion is of no avail. Yes, I can make my own conversion my savior. But that is dreadful! That would really be making myself my own savior.

Twentieth Evening Lecture
(Feb. 27, 1885)

When a Lutheran ministerial candidate is finally given an assignment where he is to conduct his office as a Lutheran preacher, that place should be to him the most precious and beautiful on earth. He should not want to exchange it for any kingdom; it should be to him a little paradise, whether it be urban or rural, whether open prairie or virgin forest, whether a well-established community or sparsely settled. The holy angels with great joy come down from heaven to serve those who shall inherit salvation [Hebrews 1:14]. How eagerly ought *we* pursue our fellow-sinners so that we may bring them to salvation, too!

But the newly called pastor must approach his parish with a seriousness equal to his joy. He must resolve: "I want to do everything possible so that every soul entrusted to me will be saved." Hence, when he discovers that most of his members—as often seems to be the case—are still blind and dead and unconverted, he must not allow that to irritate or discourage him, but rather drive him to the ardent desire: "I want to rouse them all from their spiritual death and through God's means of grace turn them into live Christians. I will not let the devil stop me, but approach the task in faith." Or perhaps he discovers that some members of his new parish are living in open shame and vice. Let him not despair but rather think: "I have a potent Word, and by means of it I will try to free these slaves of sin." Or he notices that his congregation is still on a very low level of spiritual understanding, of knowing what the Gospel is all about. Then let him resolve: "I will cheerfully go to work and patiently and diligently instruct these poor, ignorant people, so that they see the light." Or he may find that there are upright souls in his parish who are, however, pietistic in their attitude and as a result are legalistic and regard as sin what is not sin. Then let him resolve: "I will refrain from doing what I may lawfully do, for I know there are souls who consider it sin. I do not want to give them offense." Or the opposite may be the case. There may be people with a more antinomian attitude, more inclined to go too far in Christian liberty, people who were never accustomed to having the Law preached to them in its severity. Then the preacher must not at once think: "I must oppose these people with all my might. For the next year I will give them nothing but the most incisive preaching of the Law." Not so. You must go after these people and only gradually increase the application of the Law; for the apostle Paul says of himself what every servant of Christ should take to heart: "I have become all things to all men, that I might by all means save some" [1 Corinthians 9:22]. That is to say: "I cannot be satisfied merely with proclaiming the truth, but I must proclaim it in such a way that it meets the needs of all the people. I must refrain from saying things that must be postponed until later when the people will trust me and my teaching. Then I can speak freely to them and do not have to fear that they will be repelled."

In short, if the preacher discovers that his congregation is still a dark wasteland, he must think: "Very well, by the grace of God I will turn this parish into a blooming garden of God." Or if he notes with great joy that most of his members are mature, experienced, believing, active Christians, with only a few who appear to be unconverted, let him resolve: "Very well, I must attempt, first of all, to bring the unconverted to Christ." At the same time, of course, he must resolve to give the well-grounded members the strong food they need.

How much to be pitied is the young preacher who enters the office thinking: "The time of hard work and toil is now past. My ship has come into the harbor of rest and peace. I'm going to enjoy it. Now I am my own boss, and nobody in the world is going to order me around!" But equally to be pitied is the preacher who looks on his call as just a job in which to make a living, with the attitude: "Now I'm going to make this into an attractive, relaxed, and comfortable parish. I'm going to avoid making enemies and do all I can to keep all the members as my good friends." Unhappy man! Both of them want to utilize the spiritual in order to gain physical rewards! Such men are not servants of Christ! One day He will say to them: "I never knew you; depart from Me, you evildoers" (Matthew 7:23).

But blessed is that preacher who from the first day of his ministry firmly resolves: "As God grants me grace, I will do all I can so that not one soul in this congregation will be lost through my fault. By God's grace I will do what I can so that, when I must put down my shepherd's staff, I can say to Christ: "Here am I and those whom You have given me. I have lost none of them!"—as Christ could say to His Father [John 17:12]. "The blood of these people, including those on the left [Matthew 25:33], does not cling to my hands."

Now the question arises: "What must a preacher do above all in order to reach that glorious goal?" He must come to God every day in fervent prayer and intercession for his congregation and zealously speak God's pure Word in public and in private, rightly dividing the Word of truth.

This is the topic before us in this school year, namely the proper distinction between Law and Gospel, the two cardinal doctrines of all of Scripture. Of every Bible passage, even of every historical fact recorded in Scripture, we may say: "This is Law, and this is Gospel." No one should leave a theological institution who is unable to say: "This is Law, and this is Gospel," or: "The protasis is Law and the final clause is Gospel," or vice versa. Much could still be said about the ninth thesis, but we cannot spend any more time on it; otherwise we will not get to the end.

Thesis X

In the sixth place, God's Word is not rightly divided when faith is pictured either as if merely regarding something as true would justify and save in spite of mortal sins, or as if faith justifies and saves for the sake of the love and renewal it effects.

Today we do not want to go beyond the first part of the thesis. The mingling of Law and Gospel mentioned there is found primarily in the papacy. It is chiefly because of this error that the papists will have nothing to do with Luther and his teaching. They have heard and read that he taught good works do not save, but only faith apart from good works. Therefore they conclude that Luther must have been an ungodly man, for he told his followers: "Simply believe. You do not have to do any good works; you will get to heaven."

However, that is by no means Luther's teaching, but the direct opposite. To be sure, he did not say: "One must have faith, but with it also good works and love," but rather: "We must have the kind of faith that of itself produces love and is fruitful in good works." But then faith does not justify for the sake of love; rather faith, created by the Holy Spirit and unable to do otherwise than be active in good works, justifies because it clings to the promises of grace and lays hold of Christ. It does not justify because it is fruitful in good works; on the contrary, because it is true faith it produces good works. Faith does not need to be told to do good works; it does them spontaneously. Faith acts in this way, not because it thinks: "You are obligated to do good works, since God has forgiven your sins," but because it cannot do otherwise. It is altogether impossible for true faith to be in the heart and not manifest itself in love and good works.

Of this the papists have no idea. They think people can be in the true faith while they live in mortal sins. For that reason they tell us: "Your teaching of salvation by faith alone is some religion! It is the most horrible that has ever been invented!" That is what they say of Luther. But Luther never dreamed of teaching a faith that only believes what the church believes. Yet that is what the papists connect with faith, saying: "Faith is the conviction that the church's teaching is correct. Whoever has this conviction has the true faith." But they add immediately that such a person will not thereby be saved. Consequently among them one may be a fornicator, adulterer, drunkard, or a thief and still be counted among the faithful.

Galatians 5:6 speaks of "faith working through love." If faith is not active in love, it is ineffective—not because it has no love, but because it is no genuine faith at all. Love must not be added to faith, but love must flow from faith. A fruitful tree does not produce fruit because it is ordered to do so, but it will bring forth fruit of its own accord as long as it is alive. Faith is such a tree. It will produce good fruit, and as long as it does, it is evident that it has not withered. But if there is no fruit, it is dead, for it will bring forth good fruit as long as it is alive. So it is with the sun. It will continue to

111

shine until the end of time without being told to do so. Faith, too, is such a sun.

God "cleansed their hearts by faith" (Acts 15:9). One who says: "Oh, I have a firm faith and will not depart from it," but does not have a clean heart must be told: "You are in deep darkness, for you have no faith. You may regard all truths proclaimed in the Lutheran Church as true—but if your heart is still full of love for sin, if you willfully continue to act contrary to your conscience, then your faith is pure illusion. That is not the true faith which the Holy Spirit has in mind when He speaks of faith in Scripture."

Jesus passes the dreadful judgment on His enemies: "How can you believe, who receive glory from one another and do not seek the glory that comes from the only God?" (John 5:44). There the Savior says in so many words: "If anyone seeks honor, he has no faith." As soon as the true faith has been planted in the heart, it will produce the fruit of giving all glory to God. And if one nevertheless receives honor from others, one will say in his heart: "You have not deserved it." He will say to his God:

> Whate'er of good this life of mine
> Has shown, is altogether Thine.

[*Editorial note:* Walther reproves the pride which a young preacher may feel when people compliment him on his sermon, he speaks against pride in general, and he cites 1 John 5:4 and James 2:1 for further descriptions of genuine faith. Then he continues:]

Any preaching that speaks of faith as if mere mechanical acceptance justified and saved, even in the presence of mortal sin, turns faith into a work that man can himself produce, so that even in the midst of mortal sin he can say: "True, I have sinned; but I will believe, and then I will get to heaven." In that case what is faith but a good work that man can himself produce and preserve? But faith is a treasure which only the Holy Spirit can impart.

[*Editorial note:* Walther speaks against the Roman doctrine that those living in mortal sin can still have faith. He continues:]

It is hard to believe, but the Calvinists are caught in the same error, but from a different angle. Because of their doctrine of predestination they teach that the elect may "interrupt the exercise of faith" by heinous sins "and occasionally lose the consciousness of their faith for a season." Because of His decree of predestination God "does not permit the elect to lapse to a point where they would fall from the grace of adoption to sonship and from the state of being justified." They "do not entirely fall from faith and grace nor remain in their fall till the end and are not lost" (cf. Synod of Dort, V, 3-8).

That is indeed a dreadful teaching. If people believe that they cannot lose faith and grace, they will not be concerned about repentance when they have fallen into gross sins, including adultery and murder. The story is told of Oliver Cromwell, that wretched person, who had his king and many others throughout England put to death, that on his deathbed he became worried about his spiritual condition. He called for his chaplain and asked whether one who was once in the faith could ever lose it. The wretched chaplain said no. Cromwell said: "Then all is well; for I know that I once had the faith." On that he based his confidence.

[*Editorial Note:* Walther cites the Confessions (Smalcald Articles, Part III, Art. iii, par. 42-45; Tappert, pp. 309 f.) to the effect that when believers fall into mortal sin they lose the Holy Spirit. He goes on to declare that temporary loss of faith happens oftener than we think, citing the examples of David and Peter. He then cites a theological opinion of Luther's regarding a commentary a certain pastor had submitted for review. The author maintained that the elect do not lose the Holy Spirit even though they knowingly become guilty of gross sins and vices, but Luther stated that anyone willfully living in sin could not possibly have faith (St. Louis Edition, IX, 1706 ff.). Walther continues:]

How can I dare to approach God with an evil conscience and thank Him for forgiveness? . . . Only an insane person would say, "Forgive me for what I have done, but I intend to keep on doing it; I will insult you whenever I see you, but please forgive me." Yet that is the way people act who want to take comfort in God's grace and still continue in their sin. . . .

What matters is not the external enormity of the sin but the attitude of my heart in connection with that sin. A sudden sin of passion or temper does not extinguish faith, for I sinned without wanting to do it. I can remain in grace. But where there is persistence in sin against conscience and better knowledge, faith departs, one cannot pray to God, the Holy Spirit moves out of the heart, and another spirit moves in.

A Christian realizes that if he consents to sin in only a small measure, his confidence in God has diminished. He notices that unless he turns back at once, sin will rule over him and make him incapable of faith. Then he may fall on his knees and tearfully say to God: "Lord, You know that I do not want to sin!" As Peter once said to Jesus: "Lord, You know everything; You know that I love You" [John 21:17]. So a Christian should be able to speak to God and say: "My God, You know that I do not want to sin, and yet I do sin. But You know that I have become an enemy of sin."

What Paul expects of every Christian is "love that issues from a pure heart and a good conscience and sincere faith" (1 Timothy 1:5). Faith and a good conscience must always be together. Where there is faith, there is also a good conscience. But a person without a good conscience certainly has no faith either, for the two belong together. Such people "have made shipwreck of their faith" (1 Timothy 1:19).

All sins are great sins. Even the so-called sins of weakness, of which the justified cannot rid themselves, are no trifle. Even though faith is not extinguished thereby, they are no joking matter.

And let no one find security in the thought that he is one of the elect and therefore bound to be saved, regardless of what he does. If you live in your sins and persist in them, that is a sign that you are not among the elect. Not as though God really did not want you, but He foresaw that you are such a disgraceful scoundrel and that you abuse His grace. No indeed, if you are that kind of person, you are not in the state of grace, and if you persist in this condition you will be damned! No one can deny that Adam and Eve were among the elect. Yet they fell and lost God's image, the Holy Spirit, their holiness, everything. But they repented and thus returned to the state of grace.

As soon as I lose faith because of a mortal sin, I also lose God's grace and become a child of death and damnation. I may return to faith later on, but in the interim I am a child of death, thoroughly wretched and lost.

Twenty-first Evening Lecture
(March 6, 1885)

When, my friends, the unbelieving world hears that in the Christian religion all depends on faith if a person wants to be saved, it regards this as impossible and incredible. To the world this is an obvious folly and an indication that even the Christian religion amounts to deception, just like all other allegedly supernatural religions. For also the Brahmans demand faith in their Vedas, the holy books of Hinduism. And Muhammad, though recognized as a lying prophet, demands faith in his Koran as the holy book of Islam, as containing the only true and saving religion. Similarly, they say, Christianity, which also claims to be a supernaturally revealed religion, demands faith above all and makes faith dependent on it. But, so the objection goes, what difference should it make to God what I believe or don't believe? True religion can't be anything but leading an honorable life of virtue and good works. How can it be a sin not to believe something that completely contradicts my reason, which after all is also a gift of God? If there is a God and a final judgment, God cannot ask me what I believed, but rather what I did and how I lived.

Others try to go into the matter a little more deeply and assert that if faith is especially pleasing to God because it is such a splendid work and so beautiful a virtue, why in all the world shouldn't God take just as much pleasure in other virtues, like love, patience, courage, uprightness, impartiality, truthfulness, and the like?

Now, what is the reason for these objections to the teaching of Christianity about faith? Without a doubt the first source is ignorance. People do not know what, according to Scripture, faith is. According to Christian teaching a justifying and saving faith is anything but a mechanical acceptance of the doctrines of the religion, the way faith is viewed by Hindus and Muhammadans. On the contrary, the Christian religion teaches that a mere rigid act of regarding the teachings of Scripture as true is futile and the direct way to hell. Such reliance is built on sand. Again, Christian teaching is far from extolling faith because of its being so splendid a work and so beautiful a virtue. On the contrary, Christianity teaches that faith justifies and saves, not because it is such a good work, but for the sake of the redemption in Christ, which faith appropriates.

This brings us back once more today to our tenth thesis. . . . This evening we want to discuss the second part of this thesis, which states that *God's Word is not rightly divided when faith is pictured . . . as if faith justifies and saves for the sake of the love and renewal it effects.*

Scripture affirms unmistakably that there can be no true faith without love, without renewal, without sanctification, no true faith that does not make the person who has it rich in good works. At the same time Scripture is equally insistent that this renewal, this love, these good works which faith produces are by no means the reason why faith justifies and saves. Countless Bible passages affirm this. We cite the chief ones.

Romans 4:16: "That is why it depends on faith, in order that the promise may rest on grace." We teach justification by faith, says Paul, just because we teach that human beings are saved entirely by grace. . . . The fact that faith is a good quality plays no role in justification. The point is exclusively that Jesus Christ has already redeemed the whole world, has done and endured everything we human beings should have done and suffered, and that we simply accept this. Hence the way to salvation is that we do nothing at all, but that Jesus Christ has already done everything, and that we cling to this, trust in it, and put our confidence in it. . . .

Philippians 3:8-9: "I count everything as loss because of the surpassing worth of knowing Christ Jesus my Lord. For His sake I have suffered the loss of all things . . . in order that I may gain Christ and be found in Him, not having a righteousness of my own, based on law, but that which is through faith in Christ, the righteousness from God that depends on faith."

A precious passage! A true sun for learning the correct essence of the Gospel. Here Paul claims to be righteous, not by his own righteousness, but by Christ's righteousness. Hence, being justified by faith is becoming righteous by Another's righteousness. We have not earned it, and we have contributed nothing. If we had added love and were justified because of it, our righteousness would not be entirely outside of us, but only something that supplemented our own efforts.

Romans 4:5: "To one who does not work but trusts Him who justifies the ungodly, his faith is reckoned as righteousness." If a person is justified, he was formerly ungodly. He was not a pious person whose faith made him holy and for that reason justified him. . . . God says to the believer: "I see no righteousness in you, but I cover you with the righteousness of My Son, and now I see nothing but righteousness." Indeed, whoever does not come to Christ as an ungodly person does not come to Christ at all.

Ephesians 2:8-9: "By grace you have been saved through faith; and this is not your own doing, it is the gift of God—not because of works, lest any man should boast." That sounds as though the apostle kept thinking: "You still haven't said enough to keep your readers from self-righteousness.". . .

Romans 11:6: "If it is by grace, it is no longer on the basis of works; otherwise grace would no longer be grace." It is either grace or works; it cannot be both. There is nothing left for you but to believe that you have become righteous by the pure, eternal mercy of God, through faith. And even if your faith produces good fruits, this happens only after you already have everything. A person must first be saved and then become godly; he must first "get to heaven," and then he will become a different person.

That is the remarkable nature of the Christian religion. He is lost who first wants to do everything to get to heaven. No, first you must "get to heaven" and be saved, and then you will begin to thank God. Therefore Luther says that the Christian religion is, in a word, a religion of gratitude. Whatever good we do is not for the purpose of earning anything. We wouldn't know how to go about it, for all has already been given to us: righteousness, our eternal inheritance, our salvation. Now there is room only for gratitude.

Of course, God is so kind as to bestow extra glory in eternity on those who have been especially faithful in this life. And that is no trifle. When God bestows gifts, He does so lavishly. Hence there will be a big difference among Christians in eternity. For even the least "more" is something extraordinarly great in eternity. Why? Just because it is eternal.

Therefore, after we have received eternal life, we should be truly thankful to God for all that we are and have. These manifestations of gratitude are the only proper works.

Even in the world, when someone is very obliging to another person and it later turns out that he did it only because he hoped to get something out of it, that person will be regarded as a miserable wretch. What was thought to be an act of love turns out to be selfish greed. We abhor such people. When they are disappointed in their expectations, they turn against you.

Therefore those works that we do out of gratitude to God are the proper good works. One who has the true faith will give no thought to selfish gain. He can do no other than gratefully show his love and good works. His heart has been changed, has become soft, through the riches of God's love. And God is so gracious that He rewards the works which He Himself performs in us; for the good works a Christian does are God's works. Some insist that in sanctification a person must do something too. But man never initiates anything good. First God must incite him and give him the desire and power to do good. Hence, when we appear to be doing good, it is God's power and God's work.

Papists, too, will say that man is justified and saved through faith. But they immediately add that this is so only if love is added to faith. We also believe that where there is no love, there is no faith, as Scripture teaches. But the papists maintain that one may have the true faith kindled by the Holy Spirit, but unless love is added, such faith avails nothing. For that reason they say that "love is the form of justifying faith," that is, love makes faith what it is. They say that if love is not added to faith, it may be true faith but it will not justify, for it is love that makes faith a justifying faith. This is called "formed faith." Without love it is "unformed faith."

"For faith, unless hope and charity be added to it, neither unites man perfectly with Christ nor makes him a living member of His body" *(Canons and Decrees of the Council of Trent,* Session 6, ch. VII; Schroeder, p. 34). They do not say: "faith which does not produce love." That would be quite correct. For if faith does not produce love, it is no faith; then it is only the shadow of a faith. But no, they say that you might have a proper faith and yet not be justified unless love is added. It is not that love must flow from faith—according to their teaching that is impossible, for they understand faith to be simply a mechanical acceptance of the church's dogmas—but love must be added, and then faith will justify. In other words, it is love and works that justify!

[*Editorial note:* Walther discusses the story of the rich young ruler. He continues:]

At times, the papists speak very clearly. Canon 28 of the Council of

Trent states: "If anyone says that with the loss of grace through sin faith is also lost with it, or that the faith which remains is not true faith, though it is not a living one, or that he who has faith without charity is not a Christian, let him be anathema" (Schroeder, p. 45). . . . Faith, in their view, is a lovely container that has no other value than that something is stored in it, and love is that treasure. Thereby the container greatly increases in value. . . . Hence faith justifies only insofar as it has love. . . .

For Luther's analysis and verdict on the scholastic concept of "formed" and "unformed" faith, see his *Lectures on Galatians,* on Galatians 3:11 *(Luther's Works,* American Edition, Vol. 26, pp. 268 ff.) and 2:19 (ibid., p. 161). In support of their view of the place of love in justification, the scholastics cited Galatians 5:6: "For in Christ Jesus neither circumcision nor uncircumcision is of any avail, but faith working through love." Luther comments that they "completely transfer justification from faith and attribute it solely to love" and declares that Paul does not say that faith justifies through love, but that faith works through love. In other words, the "works are done on the basis of faith through love," and Paul does not say "that a man is justified through love" (ibid., Vol. 27, pp. 28 f.).

The papists teach this error in principle, but it is much in evidence also within the so-called Protestant churches. Having stated that everything is by grace and is obtained by faith, they are afraid that this might be offensive to people and so they add that, of course, faith must produce good works. But by that addition they have falsified and ruined the whole proclamation, and all preaching about grace and faith is in vain. They make it sound as if faith were not enough but must be supplemented by love. To put it correctly you would have to say: "Of course, one who has no love must realize that he has no faith either; hence he cannot be righteous before God"—not as though love justified before God, but because only that is true faith which is created by God the Holy Spirit, who pours out love to God and the neighbor.

Twenty-second Evening Lecture

(March 13, 1885)

It cannot be denied that there are today many more believing theologians than 50 years ago, when I was a youth. At that time not only the church's administrative positions but nearly all pulpits were occupied by crass rationalists. The few believing theologians were tolerated, but only when they kept quiet, did not seriously affirm their faith, and above all did not zealously oppose unbelief.

What a change has taken place since then in the so-called Protestant church! The crass rationalists who turned the Bible into a mere book on ethics and labeled the specifically Christian teachings oriental pictures and fables that have some value only for the morals they inculcated, they have apparently had their day and are now bankrupt. Today those wishing to be considered intelligent do not want to be associated with crass rationalism. The attempt of the so-called Protestant Society to reintroduce such rationalism has failed. Even the leading spokesmen declare that it is out of date. Anyone wanting to rate as a person with brains today must acknowledge that Christianity is a religion of supernatural revelation and the Bible is indeed the Word of God in a certain sense—that it contains the Word of God.

But how did these modern believers arrive at this faith? By being vividly conscious of their own misery of sin? By being acutely aware of their lost estate and their need of redemption? Unfortunately there is very little of that. One cannot escape the impression that they have arrived at their faith by way of rational speculation. For that reason nearly all of them reject the verbal inspiration of Scripture and criticize all Biblical books as only enemies can, without being conscious of their enmity. They have transformed the Christian religion into a philosophy of religion.

Modern theology in its essential aspects is totally different from the theology of former times. It does not want to be a system of faith but of scholarship. By means of human principles of knowledge it aims to demonstrate as absolute truth what the common people believe.

Consequently, modern theologians do not evince the fear that animated David when he said: "My flesh trembles for fear of Thee, and I am afraid of Thy judgments" (Psalm 119:120). Such respect for Scripture is hardly found anywhere. Nearly everywhere Scripture is treated like Aesop's fables. I am telling you the truth. As you compare the older theologians with the modern, you will see that I have spoken the truth. Scholarship has been enthroned, and theology sits at its feet, ready to do the bidding of philosophy. For that reason any time a person accomplishes something in a branch of scholarship not hitherto cultivated, he is at once made a "doctor of theology," as if scholarship, learning, and theology were one and the same.

Ah, my dear friends, if you will not preserve the light of the pure Gospel in this Western land visited by God, Judgment Day will surely come quickly. We are living in the last days. God help us to remain faithful as long as the world still stands—at least in this last part of the world to which the sound of the Gospel has come! Don't forget, there is only one way to true faith. God has not provided two or more ways, one for the scholars and one for the uneducated. No, if the scholar desires to come to faith and be saved, he must get down and sit in the pew of the sinners just like the unlearned, yes, even like the cowherd. God plays no favorites. There is no other way to faith than the way of acknowledging one's sin and lost condition, of having a broken and contrite heart. Whoever does not come to faith in this way is not a believing Christian, let alone a theologian. However, when I say that this is the only road to faith, this must not be misunderstood. Otherwise it can easily lead to a horrible mingling of Law and Gospel. That brings us to the eleventh thesis of our so-called "Luther Hours."

Thesis XI

In the seventh place, God's Word is not rightly divided if one wants to offer the comfort of the Gospel only to those who, through the Law, experience contrition not out of fear of God's wrath but out of love to God.

This is primarily the way of the papist church, but it is to be found also in the so-called Protestant church, among all enthusiasts and Pietists. There when a person is shaken because of his sins and feels contrition, he is asked, "What is the source of your contrition? Is it only the realization that these sins will bring you to hell and damnation, and you sense God's wrath and the gaping abyss below?" "If so, that is not enough," say the papists and also the enthusiasts; "true contrition must flow from love to God. Then you will be ready for the Gospel."

That is surely a terrible error. I hope I won't have to prove to you that it is a horrendous mingling of Law and Gospel. It is obvious. The Law has no other function than to bring us to a knowledge of our sins, but it has no power to renew us. Only the Gospel can do that. Only faith is active through love; we do not become active through love, through our sorrow over our sins. On the contrary, as long as we do not know that through Christ God is our reconciled God and Father, we will hate Him. And if a person who is not yet converted says he loves God, this is not true. He is a hypocrite, though perhaps without realizing it. Only faith and the Gospel produce the new birth. One who does not yet have faith cannot love God. And whoever commands a poor sinner to be terrified by his sins and rue them out of love to God is a wretched perverter of the Law and the Gospel.

This is the correct Biblical teaching: The sinner must come to Jesus just as he is, even though he must confess, "My heart is full of hatred toward God. But whither shall I turn? How can I be saved?" Then a true evangelical preacher will tell him: "That's very easy. Have you come to

120

know yourself as a lost and condemned sinner? You are looking for help but don't know where to find it. Well, then, come to Jesus with your evil heart. Come with your hatred against the Law and against God. Go to Jesus; He will accept you as you are. He has the reputation, 'Jesus receives sinners!' You must not *first* become different, *first* be cleansed, *first* amend your life. The only One who can make you better is your Lord Jesus. And He will do it, if only you will believe in Him."

Romans 3:20: "Through the Law comes knowledge of sin." There the apostle states that the Law's proper function is not to produce love but to lead to a knowledge of sin, and I can well have this knowledge without having love to God.

Romans 5:20: "Law came in, to increase the trespass; but where sin increased, grace abounded all the more." One who does not know the Law is at ease regarding his sins. But when the Law is powerfully proclaimed and it strikes that person's conscience like lightning, he will not get better but worse. He will begin to rebel against God. "What? I am to be eternally damned? I know I am God's enemy, but I can't help it." This is the effect of the Law. It drives a person to despair. But good for the person who has come that far! He has taken a long step on the way to his salvation. He will receive the Gospel with joy, while one who has never had this experience will yawn and think that it is easy to get to heaven. But a poor sinner on the brink of despair knows what a joyful message the Gospel is and accepts it with gladness. See also Romans 4:15; Romans 7:7-8; Galatians 3:21 for further statements regarding the Law's proper function.

2 Corinthians 3:6: "The written code kills, but the Spirit gives life." This precious passage is horribly twisted by many. They say: "It is all wrong to insist on the letter of Scripture. One must lay hold of the spirit, the general ideas drawn from Scripture. But to act like Luther at Marburg, when he kept the words, 'This is My body' in view, that is not Christian." However, though it is indeed contrary to the teaching in the United Church [which advocates union between Lutherans and Reformed] it is genuinely Christian. The meaning of these words is that the Law kills, while the Gospel makes alive. We don't have time now to explain this in more detail, but your further reading will show you that "the written code" denotes the Law, and "the Spirit" denotes the Gospel.

These Bible passages are illustrated by excellent Biblical examples. They all show that contrition does not flow from love to God.

At the first Pentecost the apostle Peter told the assembled crowd that they were guilty of the murder of the Messiah, Jesus of Nazareth. "When they heard this, they were cut to the heart," an effect produced by the Holy Spirit. They thought: "If that is what we have done, we are all lost! What will God say when we appear before His judgment seat? He will say to us, 'You have killed your Messiah!'" We do not read that they said they were sorry they had offended the faithful God. No, it was not love to God that impelled them, but fear and terror, and they cried, "What shall we do?" Now, did Peter ask them, "What is the nature of your contrition? Does it flow from love of God or from fear of punishment and hell?" None of that. The apostle answered at once, "Repent, and be baptized every one of you in the name of Jesus Christ for the forgiveness of your sins" [Acts 2:36-38]. Here repentance is not to be taken as referring to the first part, namely contrition, but to the second part, faith, for they were already terrified and at once received Baptism. Their repentance consisted in this, that they no longer wanted to murder Jesus but to believe in Him. Thus the apostles received them, and they were added to the number of those who were being saved.

The account of the jailer at Philippi, which I have so often mentioned, demonstrates the same truth. . . . His question about salvation came from fear and terror, not from a prior love to God, and the apostles said immediately: "Believe in the Lord Jesus, and you will be saved" (Acts 16:30-31).

So it was also with Saul, the rabid persecutor of Christians. On the Damascus road the Lord Himself appeared to him and struck him down. That was all. Jesus added: "It hurts you to kick against the goads" (Acts 26:14). Then, when the Gospel with its heavenly power entered his heart, the wretched man was snatched out of his misery. And the Lord gave him no other assignment than that he, the terrified but now comforted sinner, should confess Him instead of persecuting Him. He was to be baptized and receive the seal of the forgiveness of his sins.

When you preach, do not be stingy with the Gospel. Bring the comfort of the Gospel to all, even the greatest sinners. If only they are terrified of God's wrath and hell, they are ready to receive the Gospel. That is indeed contrary to our reason, for we think it strange that such scoundrels should be consoled at once, rather than being made to suffer the pangs of conscience for a while. And that is the way of the fanatics. But a genuine Biblical theologian thinks: "God has prepared that person through the Law, and to him I must now preach the Gospel and faith in Jesus Christ."

What Paul says about the "godly grief" that "produces a repentance that leads to salvation" (2 Corinthians 7:10) is often misunderstood. It is thought that the godly grief is the contrition that flows from love to God. However, that is not the case. The apostle means the grief that is not self-induced but produced by God through His Word. . . . It is a great perversion of Christian teaching to tell the sinner, "You must first have contrition." If he asks, "How should I go about that?" he is told, "You must sit down and reflect and seek to elicit contrition from your heart." So the papists teach. But that is pure hypocrisy. No person in the world can give himself contrition. Though he toils to the point of tears to elicit contrition, it is nothing but hypocrisy. A *godly* grief is necessary, because faith is necessary. God desires to produce this grief in us and terrify us. Contrition is not a good work we do but something that God does. With the hammer of His Law God strikes the soul. One who wants to make himself sad would like to make himself even sadder. But one who has the true sorrow would like to be rid of it. He is tormented day and night, perhaps attempting to drown his sorrow in drink, but to no avail. He may put on a bold front before his comrades, but when he is home alone, his conscience condemns him and tells him he will be lost, if he should die in that condition. That is godly grief, not produced by man but by God. God wants nothing to do with man's wretched contrivance.

Here are two testimonies from the Apology. [*Editorial note:* We omit these quotations (Art. XII, par. 8 f. and par. 29, 32-34; Tappert, pp. 183 and 185 f.). Walther comments:]

Learned theologians often speak like a blind person about color, for they have never experienced a wholesome fear over their sins. When a poor sinner comes to such a theologian, and the theologian asks, "What kind of contrition is it that frightens you?" the poor man may not know what kind of contrition it is but may only say, "I don't know, but I am very frightened." Then the learned gentleman says, "My good man, go to the barber and let him bleed you; your blood is too thick. Then you will feel better." Those are the highly enlightened theologians. God have mercy!

When our theologians wrote our Confessions, they did not sit down and devise a system, but they sat down as true Christians. They knew by what means a poor human being comes to peace and the consolation of salvation. Melanchthon spoke like a simple Christian. This Confession is all the more precious because everything is spoken on the basis of Scripture and out of experience.

In the Preface to his Latin writings (1545) Luther relates the state of his heart before he was enlightened by the Gospel. He confesses how terrified he was when he read Paul's words that the righteousness of God is revealed in the Gospel (Romans 1:17). The Law had already condemned him, and now, as he understood it, the Gospel also condemned him! We cannot thank and praise God enough that Luther found the time before his death to recall the spiritual experiences that prepared him to become the Reformer. Luther said that before he understood that righteousness is God's gift to be received by faith, "I did not love, yes, I hated the righteous

God who punishes sinners, and secretely, if not blasphemously, certainly murmuring greatly, I was angry with God." [For the entire account see *Luther's Works,* American Edition, Vol. 34, pp. 336—38.]

Just ask a modern theologian if he loved God before he was converted. He will say, "Of course, who wouldn't love God? We have always been taught to love God." But that is blindness. It was different with Luther. Before he understood the Gospel, he hated God. . . . But when he saw the light, he could say, "Here I felt that I was altogether born again and had entered paradise itself through open gates."

The same man who had hated God and murmured against God is suddenly filled with overwhelming joy and now loves God with all his heart, having received this most blessed message: "Christ, the Son of God, has acquired righteousness for all the world. Just believe it!" God grant all of you, as He did Luther, such an open door to paradise! Then your congregations will share in that blessing and you will be protected against a dead orthodoxy.

[*Editorial note:* We omit a quotation from Huelsemann and Walther's comments about the difference between "godly grief" and "worldly grief" (2 Corinthians 7:10).]

Twenty-third Evening Lecture
(March 20, 1885)

Of the various functions and official acts of a servant of the church, the work of preaching is the most important. If a pastor's sermons accomplish little or nothing, there is no substitute. All other endeavors will produce little or no positive result. . . .

When Christ was about to return to the glory He had with the Father before the foundation of the world was laid, He gave His disciples His instructions, commanding them: "Go into all the world and *preach* the Gospel to the whole creation" (Mark 16:16) and *"teach* [KJV] all nations" (Matthew 28:19). Only then Jesus adds, "baptizing them in the name of the Father and of the Son and of the Holy Spirit." And the final words of the instructions were, "teaching them to observe all that I have commanded you." Note, then, that the first and the last, the Alpha and the Omega of the apostolic or pastoral ministry is preaching and teaching.

Yet the work of preaching is also the most difficult given to a servant of the church. Those preachers who think: "Oh, preaching is easy for me and gets easier the longer I'm in office; as long as I stick to the pure Word of

God and avoid heresy, that should be sufficient"—such preachers are caught in a great and terrible, extremely dangerous and destructive error. Merely spouting pious phrases without aim or order is not proper preaching. Only the Holy Spirit bestows a proper sermon through the Word. Hence a good sermon comes into being for a truly believing preacher only by the expenditure of all spiritual and mental powers, by fervent prayer, by getting rid of all earthly cares and vain desires. That is difficult! Proper baptizing is easy; anyone can do it. Proper absolving is also very easy; anyone, even a child, can do it. Properly distributing Holy Communion is also very easy; any intelligent Christian can do it. But to preach properly is difficult. Hence a student of theology should make proper preaching his chief objective. If he is unable to do that, he has no business in the ministry. For in our orthodox church the servant of God is a servant of Jesus Christ. His worth does not consist in "something" bestowed on him at his ordination, something other people do not have, something to make him such a sacrosanct special person. By no means. The true worth of a good servant of the church consists in his ability to preach properly. If he can't do that, he has no business in the pulpit, for it is there for preaching. The sermon is the central point of every worship service.

What is the preacher to effect by his preaching? Remember: He must alarm the secure sinners and rouse them from their sleep of sin; then he must bring the terrified to faith; then he must lead the faithful to certainty with regard to their state of grace and their salvation; those made certain he must then bring to sanctification; and he must strengthen the sanctified in their holy and blessed estate and preserve them in it until the end. What a task!

Above all, however, we must not forget: The performance of this task requires especially that the Word of truth be rightly divided, as the apostle says, that is, that Law and Gospel be properly distinguished. Whoever does not understand this, and mingles and confuses both, preaches in vain. Even more, his sermons are destructive and lead souls astray, bring them to a false faith, false hope, false contrition, produce hypocrites and often also drive people to despair.

But to distinguish properly between Law and Gospel is an exceedingly difficult task. Here all must remain pupils as long as they live, as Luther says. Nevertheless, even a young theologian must be able to recite the first lesson in this curriculum. He must know the goal and be on the way to reaching it. We have already noted how difficult the distinction between Law and Gospel is. Now we present further evidence.

Thesis XII

In the eighth place, God's Word is not rightly divided if the impression is given that contrition is a cause of the forgiveness of sins alongside of faith.

There is no doubt that contrition because of sin is necessary to receive forgiveness. The Lord Jesus began His public ministry with the words: "Repent, and believe in the Gospel" [Mark 1:15]. The first thing He mentions is repentance, which, placed over against the Gospel, is nothing but contrition. The last time Christ assembled the holy apostles before He ascended into heaven and withdrew His visible presence from the church, He said to them: "Thus it is written, that the Christ should suffer and on the third day rise from the dead, and that repentance and forgiveness of sins should be preached in His name to all nations" [Luke 24:46-47]. Repentance must be there as well as faith.

Why is this? Our Lord tells us: "Those who are well have no need of a physician, but those who are sick. . . . For I came not to call the righteous, but sinners" [Matthew 9:12-13]. That is why contrition is absolutely necessary, for without it no one can be brought to faith. Such a person is surfeited and will therefore not come to the heavenly wedding feast. Already Solomon had said: "He who is sated loathes honey" (Proverbs 27:7). Where there is no hunger and thirst, the Lord Jesus is not welcomed. Where a person has not become a poor, lost, and condemned sinner, he will not be seriously interested in a Savior from sin.

At the same time you must not forget that contrition is not a cause of the forgiveness of sins. Contrition is not necessary for the sake of forgiveness at all, but for the sake of the faith which lays hold of forgiveness. Why, then, is it a mingling of Law and Gospel to give the impression that contrition is a cause of forgiveness?

1. Because contrition is effected exclusively by the Law. Making contrition a cause of forgiveness turns the Law into a message of grace and the Gospel into Law. And that is a horrible confusion of Law and Gospel which destroys Christianity entirely.

2. Contrition is not even a good work. The contrition which precedes faith is only something suffered by man. It is anxiety, pain, torment, a being crushed that is produced by God through the hammer of His law. It is not a fear that man has produced for himself; it is a fear he would like to be rid of but cannot, for God has come upon him with His holy law, from which there is no escape. One who sits down to meditate and to induce contrition will never come to genuine contrition in this way. Those who want to produce it for themselves become wretched hypocrites. They try finally to convince themselves that they have contrition, but it is not true;

they do not have it. Only God grants true contrition, when His law is preached in its severity and when man does not wilfully resist.

Now, a so-called Lutheran pastor will not be quick to say: "Contrition is a cause of the forgiveness of sins." Only the papists say it, but not a Protestant preacher who has the pure doctrine in some measure. And yet, unfortunately, it happens all too often that preachers who want to be genuinely Lutheran confuse Law and Gospel by presenting contrition as if it were a cause of forgiveness. They do this in a twofold way: Either by demanding too little of contrition, or too much.

In their inexperience many preachers shy away from driving the people to despair. They may preach that contrition must precede faith, but they are afraid that if they do not add something, the one or the other member might be led to despair. Therefore they add: "Even if you do not feel such great pain, if only you desire contrition, God will accept that." But by means of this comfort contrition is actually presented as a cause of forgiveness of sins. And that is false comfort. God is not satisfied because I wish to have contrition, but because by my contrition I have been prepared as a poor, lost sinner to believe the Gospel when it is preached to me. We would have to say: "What is necessary for you is to get to the point of hungering and thirsting after God's grace. But God does not demand contrition as a penance for your sins; for that He does not demand contrition at all. But He demands it so that you, a secure sinner, might be aroused and led to ask, 'What must I do to be saved?'"

That is why Luther said that the first time he correctly understood the concept of repentance, no word seemed so sweet to him. Now he knew that he need not do penance for his sins, but only be terrified by his sins so that he would desire God's grace. Thus for Luther this was not something dreadful but a word of true Gospel. Now he realized: "God has brought you to the point of regarding yourself as a poor, lost sinner. Now you are the right one for Jesus. Now go to Him! He will accept you with all your sins, all your grief, all your sorrow! He will accept you as you are."

Do not ask: "Do I have sufficient contrition? May I come to Jesus?" By asking such questions you show that you want to come to Him; then you long for Him. But if you have such longing to come to Jesus, you will also have true contrition, even though you do not feel it. It is the same as with faith. One can have contrition and not feel it, as I myself experienced. For years I was in the state of true contrition and stood at the brink of despair because I did not feel the sweet emotion of a heart dissolved in sorrow for having so grievously offended God. All I had was the acute feeling of being a lost sinner. Then I turned to a man of more experience, and he clarified the matter for me in a few moments. Thus, in saying that

God will be satisfied with a mere desire for contrition, we show that we are mingling Law and Gospel by regarding contrition as something meritorious for the sake of which God is gracious and forgives our sins.

This becomes apparent also when we are satisfied if someone has only a little contrition. There are wicked people who spend their years in sin and shame. Suddenly their conscience is aroused and accuses them, for instance, of perjury. They quake and tremble. Or their conscience charges them with having stained their hands with another's blood. However, they are not terrified because they are poor sinners, but only because this one deed frightens them. Otherwise they think they have a good heart. I observed such a case in Germany, where a godless man committed perjury. He did not admit it, but when people talked to him, he began to tremble. Once when I came to him, he had to hold on to the table so as not to tremble so much. Nevertheless, he could not be induced to confess his sin. Therefore the Gospel could not be preached to him.

There are many such wicked knaves who have already heard their verdict of death. They may say to the preacher: "I admit it, I have done so and so that was wrong. But otherwise, pastor, you can believe me, I have a good heart. I did that one bad thing, but I couldn't help it." One who is satisfied with such a partial contrition conceives of it as something of merit, whereas it is nothing but the bursting of an ulcer. It has not yet been drained, and therefore I cannot apply the healing salve of the Gospel.

On the other hand, some demand too much, when they tell their poor hearers: "Contrition is necessary, as Scripture emphasizes, and even your own reason tells you that God cannot forgive you if you are unconcerned about your sin. You must have contrition, and now I will show you what it must be like." Then they will read passages like Psalm 38:6-8 or Psalm 6:6-7. Legalistic preachers will then ask: "Can you say that? Have you ever been 'utterly bowed down and prostrate' and did you 'go about mourning all the day'? Were your 'loins filled with burning'? Can you say that 'there is no soundness in my flesh' and 'I groan because of the tumult of my heart'? As long as you have not had this experience, you have not had true repentance."

That is all wrong. Such, indeed, was David's repentance, but where does it say that everybody has to experience it to the same degree? Nowhere. We find the very opposite, as the examples of the hearers at the first Pentecost and the jailer at Philippi demonstrate. We see it even in David's case. He had been impenitent for a whole year. Then Nathan confronted him with his terrible sins. David was crushed and cried, "I have sinned against the Lord"; nothing further. And the prophet Nathan assured him, "The Lord also has put away your sin" [2 Samuel 12:13].

Pietists claim there must be a long period of repentance before one is permitted to believe. They even warned against believing too soon, saying that one must first be worked over by the Holy Spirit. One cannot be converted in 14 days, but it might take as many months and even years for God to get a person ready. What a dreadful teaching! Such preachers have not stopped to realize the awful burden of responsibility they have assumed. If they warn a person in this way, what will happen if he dies during that time?

I have personally experienced how dreadful this teaching is. A pietistic candidate had given me these intructions. I did everything to achieve a true repentance and fell into despair. I went to him and he said, "Yes, now you must believe." But I did not believe him, because I thought he was deceiving me, for his advice did not jibe with the marks of repentance he had previously given me. Therefore I said to him, "If you knew the condition I am in, you would not comfort me. I want to have rules for my further conduct." He gave them to me, but that was all useless.

No, for God's sake, do not hesitate to preach the full Gospel to anyone of whom you may humanly assume that he is rid of his self-righteousness and wants to receive salvation by grace alone. It is not too soon. It is impossible to come to Jesus too soon. What is often lacking is that people do not really go to Jesus. They call themselves poor beggars. But one whom God has granted the grace of crushing him so that he finds no more comfort in himself and has become utterly despondent—such a one asks, "Where can I find comfort?" He is truly contrite, and we must preach the Gospel to him; we must not warn him against coming to Jesus too soon. That is an abominable teaching. I must rather say to him: "You not only may come to Jesus, but you must do so! Just go and don't think it is too soon. Just go, for this night God may require your soul of you!" Wouldn't it be terrible if I had deprived him of this comfort, and he would die this night? Then God would hold me responsible for this sinner's soul.

One basic reason why so many mingle Law and Gospel at this point is that they confuse daily repentance with the repentance that precedes faith. Psalm 51 describes daily repentance. David calls it a sacrifice that is acceptable to God. Hence he is not referring to the repentance prior to faith, but to repentance after faith. Most sincere Christians who have the pure doctrine are much more conscious of contrition after faith than before faith. If they have proper preachers, these will have directed them to Jesus without detours, and so they are now with Him. Afterwards, though they are often crushed, the old self-righteousness returns again and again. Then God must again and again smite the poor Christian with the Law and humiliate him anew.

We see this also in David. He had come to faith in a moment, but think of all the trouble he had later on! A prophet had spoken the Word of the Lord's forgiveness to him, but to his dying day he bore much anxiety and grief and misery in his heart. Also, God no longer let him enjoy his former successes, but one misfortune after another struck him, until finally God delivered him through death. But then he had contrition together with faith, and that is indeed a sacrifice acceptable to God.

This kind of contrition is not exclusively the work of the Law, involving only the Law, but it is at the same time a work of the Gospel. The Gospel brings love to God into the heart. This contrition proceeding from love to God is indeed a truly sweet pain and acceptable to God. For we can do God no greater honor than to prostrate ourselves in the dust before Him and confess, "Thou, Lord, art righteous and I am a poor sinner! Have mercy on me for Jesus' sake!"

I now refer you to a precious passage from the Smalcald Articles, a veritable pearl among our Confessions. No sect has the true teaching regarding contrition. Only our Lutheran Church has it, and Luther himself here presents it. We bless him for having left us this heritage. God "allows no one to justify himself. He drives all together into terror and despair. . . . This is what the beginning of true repentance is like. Here man must hear such a judgment as this: 'You are all of no account. Whether you are manifest sinners or saints, you must all become other than you now are and do otherwise than you now do, no matter who you are and no matter how great, wise, mighty, and holy you may think yourselves. Here no one is godly,' etc. To this office of the law the New Testament immediately adds the consoling promise of grace in the Gospel" (Smalcald Articles, Part III, Art. iii, par. 2-4. See the whole article on Penitence, Tappert, pp. 303—10).

When Luther wrote these words, he was undoubtedly thinking of himself. When he exercised himself in penitence, he surely thought it no joking matter but took it so seriously that he often lost consciousness from sheer dread. Sometimes he shut himself up in his room for several days to perform penitential exercises. When others broke into the room, they found him lying unconscious, the result of his terrible anguish. The devil's spirit of sorrow had overwhelmed him, so that no comfort reached him. Music gave him some relief, and for that reason he esteemed music so highly. It is true, music can exercise an extraordinary influence on people's moods.

Twenty-fourth Evening Lecture

(April 10, 1885)

Some 120 years ago, my friends, rationalism became predominant in the so-called Protestant church of Germany. It was both the time of the deepest disgrace and humiliation the nation ever experienced and the most complete apostasy from the Gospel of Christ. The most superficial minds and the emptiest heads, who had no real learning, were looked upon as great lights who were ahead of their time. To achieve such a reputation nothing more was required than that a so-called theologian had the courage, or rather the audacity, to label all the mysteries of Christianity errors of earlier, darker, less enlightened times, and to say at the same time that the teachings about God, virtue, and immortality were the real core of the whole Christian religion.

What a wretched time that was! It got so bad that rationalistic preachers, eager to demonstrate that they were not yet superfluous but still served a useful function in the world, used their pulpits to treat themes such as these: "Intelligent Agriculture," "Profit in Raising Potatoes," "The Necessity of Planting Trees," "The Importance and Proper Character of Sanitation." You can easily check this in rationalistic sermon books, where such topics were handled with a great deal of pathos.

Some rationalists, however, were embarrassed by these products of genuine rationalism. In 1772 a certain Joachim Spalding published a book with the title *Concerning the Usefulness of the Ministry, Written for the Consolation of My Colleagues.* The author stated that such themes are not entirely fit for the pulpit. His own view was that if sermons are to be useful, they must never begin with doctrines of faith, for that only confuses the people. Only topics of practical ethics should be considered. No wonder that in those days many people who were still concerned about the question of their salvation abandoned our ravaged church and either took refuge with the Moravians or even turned to the Roman Catholic Church.

But, thanks be to God, that dreadful time is gone forever! Especially since the successful conclusion of the so-called wars of liberation against Napoleon I, that monster, a breath of spring moved across all of Germany. Great masses, including many preachers, experienced a truly miraculous awakening from the sleep of death caused by rationalistic unbelief. Since then many preachers have again undertaken to lay aside the arid, comfortless, and powerless pagan rationalistic morality and to preach Christ and faith in Him as the only way to salvation and to true peace of the heart already in this life.

131

If only that had always been done correctly and were still being done correctly! But, alas, it cannot be denied that well-meaning preachers are still mingling Law and Gospel and thus doing great harm to their hearers. May God by His grace preserve you from this error when you become pastor of a congregation, with which you, as much as in you lies, must appear before the throne of God and give an account as to whether you have kept faithful watch and have given this congregation the true Bread of life, and not bad food that caused sickness and even death. May the study of our 13th thesis help you toward this goal.

Thesis XIII

In the ninth place, God's Word is not rightly divided when faith is demanded in such a way as if a person could give it to himself, or at least contribute something toward it instead of seeking to preach faith into the heart by presenting the promises of the Gospel.

This thesis does not call it wrong to demand faith of one's hearers. All the prophets and apostles, as well as our Lord Jesus Christ Himself, did this. When we demand faith, this is no way a legalistic demand, but the sweetest invitation that says only this: "Come, for all is now ready!" When we say to a half-starved person, "Come, you poor man, and eat your fill; sit down at my table and eat whatever you like," he will surely not say, "What? You have no right to give me orders!" In the same way, when I demand faith, this is not a legalistic demand but rather an evangelical invitation.

What is here considered false is the idea that a person could give himself faith. As soon as that is done, faith is turned into a human work and the demand for faith becomes a legalistic one. Then it is obvious that the Law is being mixed in with the Gospel. A preacher should so preach that even if he does not refer to faith his hearers will still hear a true Gospel sermon. Using the word "faith" is of no importance. What matters is speaking in such a way that every poor sinner has the desire to lay the burden of his sin before his Lord Jesus Christ and say, "Thou art mine and I am Thine." Here Luther was especially great. He rarely says, "Believe! Believe!" But when he proclaims Christ's work, salvation by grace, the riches of God's mercies through Jesus Christ, everyone realizes: "Here I must only take what is offered and rest in the bosom of divine grace."

That is the great art you must seek to acquire, that every one of your hearers will think: "Well, if that is true, then I too am a blessed person and my anguish and unrest have been in vain. I am completely redeemed; I am also reconciled with God; I am one of the rescued, one of those upon whom God looks with pure grace." As soon as a person thinks thus, he has come to faith.

132

Suppose you were preaching to a group of Indians, picturing Jesus Christ as the Son of God who came down from heaven to redeem all people from their sins by taking God's wrath upon Himself and overcoming death, devil, and hell in their stead in order to open heaven to all, and telling them that now anyone can be saved simply by accepting what this our Lord Jesus Christ has brought us. Then suppose that in that moment you would be fatally shot by a hostile Indian from ambush. It would be possible that you left behind a small Indian congregation, even though you had not said a word about faith. For whoever did not impiously and wilfully resist would have to think, "I, too, have been redeemed." On the other hand, you could spend a lot of time and keep on repeating, "You must believe in order to be saved," and create the impression in the hearers that something has been demanded of them. Then they might worry whether they could do it, and if they could, if it really is what you demanded. Thus you might have preached much about faith and yet not have a sermon of faith. Whoever has come to realize: "Here it is a matter of taking," he has faith. To be saved by faith means simply to accept the gift of salvation.

I do not mean to say that you should not preach about faith. True knowledge of faith is greatly lacking, especially in our time. The best preachers think they have accomplished much when they have drilled into their hearers that faith alone saves. But they preached in such a way that the hearers were led to think: "If only I had this faith! It must be something very difficult, for I have not achieved it," and the poor hearers leave church in sadness. The word "faith" rings in their ears but gives them no comfort. Luther already complains that many preach about faith but do not show what that means and how one comes to faith. Such a preacher can toil for years and his congregation remains asleep. For that reason one hears many people talk in such a way that one can notice immediately that they are not sure of their salvation, but teeter and waver back and forth. If they are told, "Today you must die!" they are in extreme fear and anguish. And whose fault is it? The preacher's, who preaches so wrongly about faith.

When we say that faith should be demanded, we do not say that a person can give himself this faith. In Scripture everything is demanded of man. In all commandments there is the demand: "Do this, and you will live." Scripture demands: "Purify your hearts" [James 4:8] and "Awake, O sleeper, and arise from the dead, and Christ shall give you light" [Ephesians 5:14]. From this it does not follow, however, that man is able to do what is demanded. When a creditor demands: "You must pay me," it does not follow that the debtor is able to pay. A creditor may go to his debtor and demand payment, even though he knows the man can't do it.

133

But perhaps he sees how irresponsible the debtor is and even acts haughty and arrogant. So the creditor wants to remind him of his debt to humble him.

So God deals with us. When God shows me what I owe Him, when He makes demands, I realize that I can't do what God demands, or I try to do it but fail. Then when God has thus humbled me, He approaches me with the Gospel. This is what is lacking nowadays. When people say, "I can't believe," they are told, "Oh yes, you can. Just have the desire to believe! You can get rid of your sins, if only you will fight against them." But that is a disgraceful way to preach!

The synergists have poisoned the Gospel, denied the Lord Christ, and emptied His grace of its content. Melanchthon, as is known, is the father of synergism. . . . In his book *Concordia concors,* a history of the Formula of Concord, Leonard Hutter shows that Melanchthon was the principal reason why Article II, "Free Will," was written. . . . Melanchthon had said:

1. "There is and must be a cause in man why some are elected to salvation and others are rejected and condemned."

2. "Since the promises of grace are universal and there is no contradictory will in God, there must necessarily be in us some reason for the difference, why one is saved and another is rejected, that is, each one must act differently."

3. "The cause why some assent to the promise of grace while others do not lies in us."

4. "In conversion there are three concurring causes: The Word of God, the Holy Spirit, whom the Father and the Son send to kindle our hearts, and our will that assents to the Word of God and does not resist it."

All of these statements ascribe to natural man an ability to cooperate with God and thus teach work-righteousness, a teaching that vitiates the Gospel. In his *Loci,* his work in dogmatics, Melanchthon offers further statements which clearly manifest his synergism. [*Editorial note:* For reasons of space, we have greatly condensed Walther's comments on Melanchthon's statements.]

Twenty-fifth Evening Lecture

(April 24, 1885)

Among the many difficult tasks of a servant of Jesus Christ the hardest one undoubtedly is that he must not only proclaim the pure doctrine of the Gospel of Christ but also discuss and refute teachings that oppose the Gospel. When he does this, he experiences the truth of the old maxim: "Truth begets hatred."

If faithful Athanasius had only presented his teaching that Jesus Christ is true God, born of the Father from eternity, and also true man, born of the Virgin Mary, and had not earnestly attacked the Arians who denied these truths, he would without a doubt have led a life of acclaim as a highly talented man and enjoyed peace to the end. If Luther had acted like Staupitz and taught the pure Gospel to the brothers of his order without attacking the abominations of the papacy, nobody would have opposed him; for it had often happened that monks had come to the truth of the Gospel and also given expression to it, but did not do so in public nor oppose the errors of the papacy, and no one bothered them, as long as they continued to be loyal to the pope, the central point of the Roman Catholic Church.

The world and all false Christians can but attack those who believe and teach otherwise and regard them as disturbers of the peace, as contentious and malicious people. In their blindness these poor people do not realize that the most courageous soldiers of Christ would just as soon have kept peace with all people and remained silent, that it was extremely hard for them to appear in public and thus become the objects of hatred, slander, and vituperation, and even of persecution. But they, too, could not do otherwise. They not only had to confess the truth but also oppose error. Their conscience compelled them. Why? Because the Word of God demands this.

They remembered that Jesus Christ had said to His disciples not only: "You are the light of the world," but also: "You are the salt of the earth." [Matthew 5:13-14]. That is to say: "You must not only proclaim the truth but also apply biting salt to the world with its sins and errors, so that the world will not decay." They remembered Christ's emphatic words: "Do not think that I have come to bring peace on earth; I have not come to bring peace, but a sword" (Matthew 10:34). Not as though the Lord took pleasure in war and had come into the world to create disunity and strife. But the Lord's meaning is: "My teaching is of such a nature that there cannot possibly be peace among people where the teaching is correctly proclaimed in its positive and negative aspects. . . ."

A faithful preacher also knows that he is a shepherd. But what good is it if the shepherd leads the flock to green pastures but flees as soon as the wolf comes? The shepherd must stand his ground against the ravenous wolf, and that is what it means to "fight" in the kingdom of God. A true preacher also knows that he must be a good farmer. But what good is it if he sows good seed but then calmly permits another to sow the weeds of false doctrine among the wheat? It won't be long and the weeds will gain the upper hand and choke the wheat.

Please, dear friend, take this to heart! If you want to be faithful servants of Christ, you cannot accomplish that without warfare against false doctrine, false gospel, and false faith. Then your lot in the world will indeed not be a particularly attractive one. Already wise old Sirach said: "If you come forward to serve the Lord, prepare yourself for temptation" (Ecclesiasticus 2:1). He is saying that it cannot be otherwise. If you want to be the Lord's servant, you will be assailed. . . .

At the same time, let this be your comfort. As indicated, your cause will be maligned as evil unless you go along with what others think; but your cause will shine all the more brightly in heaven. God will say to you: "Well done, good and faithful servant; you have been faithful for a little, I will set you over much; enter into the joy of your master"(Matthew 25:21). Then we shall be truly refreshed. . . .

Remember also this, however: The more covert an error is, the more dangerous it is, and the more necessary it is to unmask it and oppose it. We are reminded of this by our 14th thesis.

Thesis XIV

In the 10th place, God's Word is not rightly divided when faith is demanded as a condition of justification and salvation, as though a person becomes righteous before God and is saved not only through faith, but also because of faith, for the sake of faith, and in view of faith.

Many think that as long as a preacher proclaims that a person is justified before God and saved through faith in Christ, he must obviously be a genuine evangelical preacher. What more could one ask? Surely that is the inmost core of the Gospel and the Word of God. Yes, if that is done in truth, that is indeed correct. But to be such a preacher requires more than saying the words: "Man is justified before God and saved through faith alone." He must also take these words in their proper sense and understand faith as the Bible does. Here much is lacking. Many take faith in a sense altogether different from that of the prophets, apostles, and our Lord Christ.

I won't even talk about the rationalists. They said that, of course, man is saved by faith. But in their view faith is nothing more than acceptance of the ethical teachings proclaimed by Jesus. If one accepts these teachings, one is a true disciple of the Lord and is justified and saved. Just look at random into a radical rationalistic book of the times and you will see that this was the preaching of crass rationalism.

Even papists are not averse to saying that faith saves and makes one righteous before God. If pressed, they might even go so far as to say that faith alone saves. But what is their understanding of faith? Only the so-called "formed" faith, that is, faith supplemented by love. Thus they can say many fine things about faith and yet mean the exact opposite of what Scripture teaches about faith.

Also all modern theologians present this teaching in their sermon books and devotional books: "Man is saved and made righteous before God through faith." But what do they mean? Faith to them is something man gives himself and produces on his own. They understand faith to be a product of human power and human resolve, thus again upsetting the whole Gospel.

But when God's Word says: "Man becomes righteous and is saved through faith alone," Scripture means to say: "Man is not saved by his own efforts, but *exclusively* through the work and suffering of his Lord and Savior Jesus Christ, the Redeemer of the whole world." Modern theologians, on the contrary, affirm: "There are two kinds of works. In the first place, something has to be done by God. He must accomplish the most difficult part, the work of redemption. But now something is also demanded of man. He cannot get to heaven without further ado. He must do his part, and that is something big—he must believe." But this again destroys the Gospel. How beautifully they often preach! But upon analysis it turns out to be something totally different. Scripture teaches clearly that man is saved not by something he himself does and accomplishes, but by what God does and accomplishes.

Luthardt [a prominent German Lutheran theologian] writes: "On the other side, repentance and faith are demanded of man as his achievement on all levels of salvation history. The person called should and can quickly meet the demand for repentance, and faith is the free obedience which man offers" *(Compendium,* p. 202).

Note the word "achievement." What is an achievement? It is an obligation I must discharge in order to get something in return. But faith is not an achievement. Then it would be a condition set up by God, as if He were saying: "I have done my part; now you do yours. I am not asking much of you, but I do demand repentance and faith." But is that a gift if I say, "This is my gift to you, but you must do something to get it"? No, that is no gift. If I make a gift to someone only because he fulfills certain conditions, it is no longer a gift.

Here in America many gifts are considered invalid. For that reason, if someone wants to make a gift without having to fear that the law will nullify it, he accepts the token payment of a dollar. Then the law cannot undo it. Why not? Because according to concept of "purchase" it is really a purchase, even though the property involved is worth millions. So the law is circumvented. But it clearly shows that there is an essential difference between giving and selling. Just as soon as God demands that I achieve something, though it may not be very difficult—although it would be immeasurably difficult if God Himself did not accomplish it—but suppose the demand were easy, it would not be a gift. Then God would not have *given* us His Son, but offered Him to us only under certain conditions. That is not the case. The apostle Paul says: "They are justified by His grace as a gift, through the redemption which is in Christ Jesus"(Romans 3:24). "As a gift," hence without the least contribution on our part.

Therefore, praise be to God, we poor sinners have a refuge where we may take shelter, even though we come as lost people who can pay nothing, as poverty-stricken, not having the least strength to offer God any product of our own efforts. How blessed we are that we have a Gospel which tells us: "Here is a refuge for sinners!" Jesus Christ is the faithful Savior; to Him we all can flee. We must not offer Him anything but our sins. If in response to his question whether I have anything else to offer I say, "Nothing but my sins," He will say "Well and good, you are the right one for me." As soon as someone tries to offer something, he denies the Lord Jesus. "There is salvation in no one else, for there is no other name under heaven given among men by which we must be saved"(Acts 4:12), except the precious name of Jesus. Please note, therefore: It is a great and terrible perversion of the Gospel if faith is demanded as a condition of justification and salvation.

When a beggar comes to you and asks for alms, will you say, "Yes, I will give you something under certain conditions"? He would ask what they are, and you would say, "On condition that you take what I give you." He would think you were joking and would laughingly reply, "Sure, I will gladly do that; and the more you give, the more joyfully I will take it."

But if I make faith a condition, I horribly pervert the Gospel. To be sure, if you refuse to believe, there is no help for you. But you are not to be in a position to say someday, "God indeed offered me grace, but on certain conditions that were too difficult." Not so. God has offered you His grace unconditionally. He held it out before you and said, "There it is; just take it!" . . .

How easily one can err in this matter can be seen in the present controversy on predestination. . . . Our opponents, hiding behind the old dogmaticians, teach that God elected people "in view of faith," and this is said to be the reason why some are elected and not others. Our opponents interpret "in view of faith" as if it meant "in view of man's conduct," something the old Lutheran dogmaticians did not have in mind. John

Gerhard, for example, wrote in his *Loci theologici* ("Concerning the Gospel," par. 26): "We hold that . . . the promises of the Law are conditional, for they demand complete obedience and require the condition of complete fulfillment. . . . But the promises of the Gospel are promises of grace and given in the manner of a gift."

You see, our thesis is appropriate here. Whoever says: "Faith is a condition set by the Gospel" turns the promises of the Gospel into conditional ones. That is where the Law is distinguished from the Gospel. The Law promises nothing good except on condition that what it demands is completely fulfilled, whereas the Gospel promises everything unconditionally, as a free gift. In short, the promises of grace demand nothing of man. For when the Lord says: "Believe!" He is making no demands. He only invites: "Accept this gift which I gladly give you. I want nothing for it. Just take it and make it your own." When God gives me a gift, there is nothing for me to contribute. But I must accept it. If I do not accept it, I do not have it, but not because God had attached a condition.

If faith is called an achievement, a condition is established; for if it is man's achievement, it is man's work. Therefore the statement of Luthardt (cited earlier) is a dreadful error that poisons his whole theology. [*Editorial note:* Walther again cites Gerhard, and also other Lutheran theologians of the past, such as Adam Osiander, John Olearius, Heerbrand, and Calov in support of his thesis that faith is not a condition of justification. More of Walther's own observations follow:]

If faith is an act of obedience it is a work of the Law. Then the apostle Paul was all wrong in saying that man "is justified by faith apart from works of law" (Romans 3:28). However, he is not wrong; but the modern theologians are. Faith is only a passive instrument. It is only the hand into which I lay a coin. The beggar receives the coin if he does not withdraw his hand. Otherwise there is nothing for him to do. What helps him is the coin laid in his hand, not his act of holding it out. If he should go to a miser and stretch out his hand, he would get nothing. The miser might even set his dogs on him.

In a certain sense it is correct to say that faith is our activity, for it is we who believe, not God. Nevertheless, faith is not my achievement. God alone works faith in me; I contribute nothing. Faith is not a condition but a means.

It was risky for the old dogmaticians to speak of faith as an "instrumental cause." But you can read the Bible from beginning to end and you will not find a single passage which says that man is made righteous *for the sake of* his faith. When the relationship of faith to righteousness is discussed, the language makes clear that faith is an instrument, not a cause.

It seems to me that is proof enough as to what is Biblical teaching. There is no alternative: Either you lay the Bible aside and choose another calling; or if you don't want to do that, because God has taken hold of you, then go strictly according to God's Word.

2 Corinthians 5:14 is a golden passage, brilliant like the sun even in Scripture. Since Christ has died His atoning death for all, it is just as though all had died an atoning death. From this it follows that I must not harbor the least doubt, but affirm with full confidence: "I *am* redeemed, I *am* reconciled, salvation has already been won *for me.*"

Twenty-sixth Evening Lecture
(May 1, 1885)

Only one thing is absolutely necessary to be a true Christian, namely to have true faith. But to be a proper preacher it is not enough for me to have true faith. I must also be able to express in proper words what must be believed. Therefore the holy apostle Paul so earnestly exhorts his helper Timothy: "Follow the pattern of the sound words which you have heard from me, in the faith and love which are in Christ Jesus" (2 Timothy 1:13). Presenting the truth in sound, unmistakable, adequate words is indispensable. Let those young theologians take note who were not trained, like Timothy, in the use of sound words of faith, but perhaps heard only rationalistic preachers, or at least believing preachers of the modern type. It may well be that some thoroughly erroneous expressions stuck in their minds and are used by them in their sermons to the injury of their hearers.

You know how the rationalists preached about repentance and conversion. They called it amendment of life. When they preached on sanctification, they called it the path of virtue. God's wrath they called His earnestness, at most. They referred to predestination as the "fate" hanging over man. Instead of using the word "Gospel," they spoke of the teaching of Jesus. One who has heard that kind of language from childhood can easily adopt such dangerous rationalistic expressions, even though he may not himself be in error.

But also believing theologians of the modern type often shrink from using such churchly and Biblical technical terms because they fear those might be offensive to their hearers. In their sermons they hesitate to speak about original sin, God's wrath over sinners, the blindness of natural man, the spiritual death in which all people are by nature. They hesitate to talk about the devil and his prowling around like a roaring lion, seeking someone to devour—for then they might spoil it with their hearers. They do not like to talk about hellfire, about eternal torment and punishment—on the contrary, they grope for terms that do not strike their hearers as so strange, mistaken, and offensive. They substitute words that are more appropriate "to the religious feeling of an enlightened people."

There is no doubt that these men, too, desire to convert people, but they use the wrong terms. They think they will convert people by not talking about certain subjects or by presenting everything in a way the natural man will find attractive. They are just like those poor doctors who hate to prescribe strong medicine for their delicate patients, but when they note that such medicine is required, they prescribe it but have it mixed with so much sugar that there is no taste of the bitter pill. And the result? It does no good. Therefore those who do not clearly and unmistakably proclaim the Gospel which the world finds offensive are not faithful in their office and do many souls great harm. . . .

Church history shows how dangerous it is when an otherwise admittedly orthodox theologian uses expressions that can easily be misunderstood. And the result? The most reprehensible heretics by a show of piety appealed to expressions used by such theologians. Why condemn them for using terms that orthodox men had used? What they did was to use the wrong terms, which orthodox men understood correctly, to cover their own heresy. Yet a certain amount of guilt rests on those who did not avoid such terms and were of the opinion that their language was clear enough. Thus Arius, Nestorius, and all scholastics appealed to admittedly orthodox theologians and thereby created the impression that they were continuing in the teaching of the ancient church and that those who opposed them must be false teachers.

Please take heed, my dear friends, and remember: As servants of the Gospel it is not only your duty to *believe* as the church believes, but you must also *speak* the language of the Christian church. Therefore, before you memorize your sermons and deliver them, you must subject your manuscripts to a critical review, not only to determine whether everything is according to the analogy of faith, but also whether you have always picked the proper expressions, so that you will not unwittingly destroy rather than build. This is extremely important. Therefore our Lutheran Church has from the beginning asked its preachers not "to depart in any way at all" from the doctrine taught in Scripture and the Confessions, "either in content or in formulation" (Preface, *Book of Concord;* Tappert, p. 13). They were held to conform not only to the subject matter but also to the manner of teaching it.

That is a large task and requires great diligence! But in three years much can be accomplished, and those among you who study faithfully will after three years not only know the true doctrine, but will also know how to present it. There will be differences. It will be harder for those who heard false teachings even in late adolescence. Their sermons quickly betray that they were not trained in the sound words of faith. Yet one should use the right words, as the apostle Paul admonishes the whole church at Corinth "that all of you agree" and "that you be united in the same mind and the same judgment" (1 Corinthians 1:10). It is of no use to have the same teaching if it is not taught in the same mind and judgment. So it goes in the United Church. Even though they speak as we do, they do not do so in the same mind and judgment. But both must be there: the same teaching and language, and the same mind and judgment.

In the 15th thesis we have an example of how harmful it is to use the wrong expressions.

Thesis XV

In the 11th place, the Word of God is not rightly divided when the Gospel is turned into a preaching of repentance.

For a correct understanding of these words you must remember that the word "Gospel" is used in a way similar to the word "repentance." In Scripture itself the word "repentance" is used in a twofold way, in a broader and a narrower sense. In the former sense it denotes all of conversion, namely knowledge of sin, contrition, and faith. So, for example, in Acts 2:38: "Repent, and be baptized." The apostle does not say, "Repent and believe." Hence he means all of conversion, including faith. How could he tell them first to be contrite and then be baptized? He must have thought of contrition in connection with faith. Therefore he meant to say: "If you acknowledge your sin and believe in the Gospel I have just preached to you, then be baptized for the forgiveness of sins."

Again, the word "repentance" is used in the narrower sense, referring only to knowledge of sin and a contrite and remorseful heart. "Repent, and believe in the Gospel" (Mark 1:15). Here Jesus certainly did not include faith in the concept of repentance, else He would have been redundant. (See also Acts 20:21; Matthew 21:32.)

The same is true of the word "Gospel"; it is used in both a wider and a narrower sense. The latter is the proper sense, while the former is used by way of synecdoche to denote all that Jesus preached, including the Law, which He preached in its severity, as we see from the Sermon on the Mount. In fact, the Lord preached the Law whenever He faced evil men.

Furthermore, the word "Gospel" is used as the opposite of "Old

Testament," which is often used to refer only to the teaching of the Law.

When Paul says that God will judge "according to my Gospel" (Romans 2:16), he cannot refer to the Gospel in the narrower sense, for that has nothing to do with judgment. Scripture says that "he who believes . . . is not condemned" [John 3:18], "he does not come into judgment" [John 5:24]. In the cited passage Paul uses "Gospel" in the sense of his teaching, which has both Law and Gospel.

Without a doubt the word "Gospel" is used in a narrower sense when Paul says of the Gospel of Christ that "it is the power of God for salvation to everyone who has faith" (Romans 1:16). This is not what the Law demands of us; it demands obedience. Here Paul speaks of the gift of Jesus Christ to the world, and we are asked to believe. Hence this is Gospel in the narrower sense, and it excludes the Law. (See also Ephesians 6:15.)

Our Confessions also use the Word "Gospel" in a twofold sense. This explains why we find this expression: "The Gospel proclaims repentance." This is very important, for if the Gospel of Christ, that is, the Gospel in the narrower sense, is turned into a preaching of penitence, Law and Gospel are being mingled in a horrible way.

"The sum of the proclamation of the Gospel is to denounce sin, to offer the forgiveness of sins and righteousness for Christ's sake, to grant the Holy Spirit and eternal life, and to lead us as regenerated men to do good" (Apology, Art. XII, par. 29; Tappert, pp. 185 f.). It is obvious that Melanchthon is here using the word "Gospel" in its broader sense, just as Luther often speaks of the Gospel as punishing sin. But when Luther comes to preach the Gospel in its real essence, he offers nothing but comfort, grace, and forgiveness, in short, the Gospel in the narrower sense.

The same is true of Melanchthon, as may be seen from this passage: "These are the two chief works of God in men, to terrify and to justify and quicken the terrified. One or the other of these works is spoken of throughout Scripture. One part is the law, which reveals, denounces, and condemns sin. The other part is the Gospel, that is, the promise of grace granted in Christ" (Apology, Art. XII, par. 53; Tappert, p. 189). . . .

However, it is not only extremely dangerous but also destructive of souls to preach in such a way that the people are led to think that the preacher regards the Gospel in its proper and narrower sense as a proclamation of the Law, as penitential preaching that reveals God's wrath because of sin. One who is not careful here will make a very serious mistake, even though his own faith is sound. Therefore Lutherans have from the beginning insisted on distinguishing between Gospel in the wider and in the narrower sense. . . . And even though heresy lies in the subject matter, and not in words, the proper choice of words is not a matter of indifference, for words are the expression of our thoughts. Thus when we use words that do not adequately express our thought, we are indeed not heretics, but we are careless. . . .

The first Lutheran to stray at this point was John Agricola, the antinomian fighter against the Law. He was thoroughly untrustworthy and misused the Gospel. At one time during a very severe illness he said frivolously, "You can't get rid of weeds." Though he was learned, he was exceedingly proud. He wanted to be a person of importance. When Luther proclaimed the Law with greater severity than formerly, Agricola—that miserable man—accused him of apostasy from his teaching. However, not Luther, but his audience, had changed. Then Agricola decided to be the reformer and anonymously published 18 "Propositions Spread Among Brethren." Thesis 18 read: "The Gospel of Christ proclaims God's wrath from heaven and at the same time the righteousness that avails before God, Romans 1:17. For a preaching of penitence has been attached to the promise, something reason does not understand by nature, but by divine revelation." (See the St. Louis Edition of Luther's Works, XX, 1624 ff.)

Agricola missed the point. In Romans 1:18 Paul begins a new section. Having announced his theme, he proclaims nothing but the Law in the rest of ch. 1, all of ch. 2, and the first part of ch. 3. He begins this teaching with: "For the wrath of God is revealed," etc. (Romans 1:18). Only after this section is finished does the apostle turn to the Gospel. Agricola presents the matter as if Paul referred to the Gospel in the narrower sense as the proclamation of God's wrath. . . .

Later the Philippists, appealing to Melanchthon's inadequate expressions, insisted that these presented the correct teaching. The worst was Caspar Cruciger Jr. In an essay on justification (1570) he wrote: "In this office of the Gospel God wants to terrify through the preaching of repentance, which punishes both the remaining sins revealed by the Law and the worst sin of all, which is revealed by the Gospel, namely ignorance and contempt of the Son of God." In other words, the Gospel lays bare the greatest sin. Some felt that Cruciger was not entiely wrong. "After all," they thought, "the Law knows nothing of justifying faith; hence the sin of unbelief must be revealed by the Gospel."

But it only seems so. The Gospel is a message of consolation. And even though despising the Gospel is the most terrible sin, the Gospel does not teach this; it is only a consequence. One thing is sure: If I turn it around, I can turn the most consoling doctrine into a most hopeless teaching. No, the Law also condemns unbelief—in the First Commandment: "We should fear, love, and trust in God above all things." Of course the Law does not know when that happens. That is something learned from the Gospel.

144

When God says to me: "Believe in My grace, trust My promise," it is the Law that commands me to believe and to trust God. The Gospel demands nothing of me. It is a joyful message. Thus also unbelief is forbidden in the First Commandment, no matter where it arises. If by unbelief I commit a sin, it is because the Law commands me to believe. But the Gospel did not come into the world to reveal the sin of unbelief; that was already done through the Law. You must bear this in mind, for otherwise you will not be able to cope with such fighters against the Law.

[Others among the Lutherans who promoted this error were Pezel and Paul Crell.] Such people may have meant well. They were pharisaic people who wanted to be of service to the world. Poor, blind people! They did not help the world, but deprived it of the only means of salvation.

Hear what our Confessions say. There had been much confusion on this matter, and the Formula of Concord restored harmony also on this point. [See especially Epitome, Art. VI, Affirmative Theses 6-7 and par. 11; Tappert, pp. 478 f. The latter reads:] "Hence we reject and deem it as false and detrimental when men teach that the Gospel, strictly speaking, is a proclamation of conviction and reproof and not exclusively a proclamation of grace. Thereby the Gospel is again changed into a teaching of the law, the merit of Christ and the Holy Scriptures are obscured, Christians are robbed of their true comfort, and the doors are again opened to the papacy." . . .

But our time is up. Next time we will try to become clear as to which Scripture passages speak of the Gospel in the narrower sense. The matter is of some importance, especially for young preachers, so that they will express themselves properly.

Twenty-seventh Evening Lecture

(May 8, 1885)

Mankind consists of three divinely established estates, teaching, nurturing, and defending *(Lehrstand, Naehrstand, Wehrstand)*. None of these should be disparaged, for "full of honor and majesty is His work" (Psalm 111:3). In each of these estates every human being can walk the way to heaven, please God and the children of God, and serve God and his neighbor. What more do you want? In the estate of teaching are those who teach in church and school; in the estate of nurturing are farmers, artisans, artists, and scholars; in the estate of defending there are rulers, government officials, jurists, and the armed forces.

Now, though the estate of teaching is the one most despised and hated by the world, it is and remains the most glorious estate, for seven simple reasons: The estate of teaching has

1. the most glorious subject to deal with, namely the human being, insofar as he has an immortal soul and is destined for eternal life, for only to that extent is the theologian concerned with man;

2. the most salutary means and instrument, namely the Word of the living God;

3. the most salutary and glorious goal, namely to make man truly happy here on earth and eternally blessed in heaven;

4. the most salutary occupation, one that fully satisfies the preacher's spirit and is conducive to his own salvation;

5. the most precious fruit, namely man's salvation; and with it

6. the most glorious promise, namely the promise that the Lord will work with him, so that his work shall never be entirely futile and lost;

7. the most glorious reward of grace, consisting of glory in the world to come, a glory that is unutterably great beyond all that we may ask or think.

Ah, if only people would think of this, they would be as eager for the holy ministry of preaching and teaching as they are for political offices that bestow prestige and provide much income. Parents would regard it as the highest honor and favor to see their sons prepare for this holy office. Young theologians would feel compelled every day to fall on their knees and praise God for the great things He has done for them, destining them from eternity for this exalted office. I might even say that if the holy angels, confirmed in their holiness, were capable of envy, they would without a doubt, even in their heavenly bliss, be envious of every teacher of the Gospel. . . .

However, the more glorious this office is, the more faithfully a preacher and teacher must be involved with the doctrine, the more he must take care to present his teaching pure and in such a way that the poor hearers will recognize their misery and God's rich goodness, come to faith, and be preserved in faith until they finally come to the place where they may see God and bless and praise Him forever.

We have already seen that the chief thing is rightly to divide the Word of truth, and not act like a carpenter, who lets the shavings fall and then throws them into the fire, but rather like a goldsmith, who works with gold and therefore is careful to save the least particle that might fall from his bench. May the Lord richly grant you His Holy Spirit so that when you begin your ministry you will faithfully watch over the immeasurable treasures entrusted to you, and properly look after the precious souls whom the Lord has given you, so that one day it may be said also of you: "Their works follow them." Then you will surely not regret the many inconveniences you had to put up with, already here at the seminary and then in your ministry. You will praise God when you see that, out of pure grace, He permits you to shine like the brightness of the firmament and like the stars of God for ever and ever [Daniel 12:3]. . . .

Here are two objections to Thesis XV. It is said that Scripture itself calls the Gospel a law; why, then, may we not call the Gospel a preaching of repentance? For it is the purpose of the Law to bring people to repentance. They appeal to Romans 3:27: "Then what becomes of our boasting? It is excluded. On what principle? On the principle of works? No, but on the principle [KJV: law] of faith." But that is not valid. The apostle uses a device known as antanaclasis, that is, he uses the opponent's word, but uses it in a different sense, in order to refute the opponent all the more forcefully.

For example, when the Jews self-righteously asked Christ, "What must we do, to be doing the works of God?" the Lord answered, "This is the work of God, that you believe in Him whom He has sent" (John 6:28-29). They used the expression "works of God" in the sense of what men do to please God. Christ retained the expression but in a completely different sense. He meant to say: "Works do not save. One must not do any works to earn something, but trust completely in Christ the Redeemer and His grace. Thus one is justified before God by receiving."

This figure of speech is used also in everyday life. When a son has botched his work and then asks his father to give him what he has coming, the father says, "Very well, I'll give you what you have coming to you, but with the whip." Even quite simple people often use such an antanaclasis.

So, too, when death is called "the wages of sin." Actually death is not a premium God has put on sin. . . . Consequently, one cannot prove from Romans 3:27 that the Gospel is a preaching of repentance. Only one who is ignorant of rhetoric can make this mistake. But to understand Holy Scripture one must also know the rules of rhetoric, for Scripture uses many rhetorical devices and figures of speech.

[*Editorial note:* We omit a quotation from Quenstedt.]

The opponents also cite Romans 10:16: "But they have not all heeded [KJV: obeyed] the Gospel." "Hence," they say, "the Gospel is not only a message of joy but also an improved Law, for it is really the Law that demands obedience." But this is all wrong. We must be obedient not only to God's legal will *(Gesetzeswille),* but also to His gracious will *(Gnadenwille).* According to His gracious will God offers and gives us everything. And our acceptance is called obedience. It is because of God's goodness that He calls it obedience. And, indeed, we do also keep the First Commandment in that way. Faith is demanded in the Law, but not in the Gospel. For "Gospel" means "joyful message"; but a message that commands me to do something is not a joyful message. Rather, that is a joyful message which tells me to put aside all fear because God comes to me in a friendly manner.

[*Editorial note:* We omit a quotation from Gerhard.]

We have heard that Luther called faith a return to the First Commandment. It is, indeed, the highest form of keeping the First Commandment if I accept God's grace as soon as it is offered to me, if I take comfort in it and thank Him for it, and if I do not have the audacity to try to earn what God offers me by grace as a gift.

Listen to testimony from Luther's *Preface to the New Testament.* Here Luther speaks in detail about the meaning of the Gospel in the narrower sense. [*Editorial note:* We omit Walther's long quotation from Luther's *Preface (Luther's Works,* American Edition, Vol. 35, pp. 357—62). Walther comments:]

Occasionally Luther used the word "Gospel" synecdochically to denote that which reproves man. But it is noteworthy that while the Gospel is often called Law, the Law is never called Gospel. Scripture never does so.

Learn of Luther to be very meticulous in your speaking of the Gospel so that you mingle nothing of the Law into it. We must preach the Law forcefully and let thunder and lightning fall from our pulpits. But as soon as we turn to the Gospel, the Law must be completely silent. Moses built a barrier around Sinai, but Christ and the apostles erected none around Golgotha. There everyone has free access. Whoever comes to the God of the Law must be righteous; whoever comes to the God of reconciliation on Golgotha may come as he is; in fact, he is welcome just because he is a sinner, if only he comes.

The Gospel is not a teaching that shows us what we must do to become worthy of God, but what we are to receive. Luther even used the expression that every person is already objectively justified. Now, if God justifies him and he refuses to accept this, then he is not justified but is and remains a damned sinner. And just this will one day be his hell, that he knows: "I was redeemed, reconciled, and righteous, but because I refused to accept this truth, I am now here in the place of torment."

You must bring your congregation the joyful message: "You have been redeemed, reconciled, and justified. Yes, you are blessed people. Salvation has been acquired for you. Just believe it!" But what good is it to you if someone gives you millions and you don't think it worth your while to hold out your hand? Then you will continue to be poor until death. Thus

148

countless people remain in their condemnation in spite of the complete redemption achieved by Christ and offered them in the Gospel.

Luther speaks of faith as accepting the Gospel as true. There is some justification for saying that regarding the Gospel as true is not, in itself, justifying faith. But Luther has in mind a faith that the message of the Gospel concerns the believer personally. One who does not regard himself as redeemed will not regard the Gospel as true either. It is a message God delivers to every single human being in the world: "You enjoy God's favor; He is no longer angry with you. His Son has taken away all your sins; you have only to accept this for yourself."

Be sure to adopt this as your basic principle: When you come to your parish, you will constantly greet it with this joyful message, so that the poor congregation will rejoice in having a pastor who is really an evangelist. Do not, whatever you do, follow your reason and think such preaching will make the people secure. Not so. When the grace and glory of the Gospel are properly proclaimed, the people will be stirred up and become joyful to do good works, and a heavenly fire is kindled in their hearts. It cannot be otherwise. One who handles fire will burn; and one who handles the fire of divine love will also be inflamed with love to God and the neighbor. Of course it is self-evident that the Law must also continue to be preached; for when people are surfeited, the Gospel will not help them.

Be sure to have the conviction that the Lutheran Church differs from all others in that it teaches a complete redemption and therefore makes of faith not a work but simply an act of acceptance, and invites all sinners, no matter how vile, if they are terrified because of sin: "Come; for all is now ready!" The teaching of our church on the sacraments has the same root, namely the true doctrine of salvation by grace alone. . . .

In a Lutheran parish the truly precious Gospel must be preached. A Lutheran congregation must be pervaded by this spirit. There the people are not constantly terrified by the Law, but they are made joyful through the Gospel. When we preach the Law, we do so not to make our people saints but sinners.

In justification human works have no place at all. But for the sake of our fellow human beings good works are necessary, for the Christian to manifest his faith, so that people may see his good works and glorify the Father in heaven and thus accept Him. Faith cannot possibly be without good works. Examine yourselves! Faith cannot be restrained. It is like a sea that can be channeled. If only a proper opening is made, the waters will rush forth and cannot be held back. Just so, a person cannot keep his faith bottled up inside him. He is ready to serve everyone, wherever he can. He cannot help confessing the Gospel, even though he knows in advance that he will reap nothing but scorn and mockery. He will even be prepared to risk his life. He knows that if he is unwilling to do this, he must relinquish Christ. The light of his faith will be extinguished the moment he denies Christ. Nor does he confess only because Christ said: "Every one who acknowledges Me before men, I also will acknowledge before My Father who is in heaven" (Matthew 10:32), but also because he cannot do otherwise. . . .

Now we get to the Bible passages that speak of the Gospel in its narrower sense. How this may be discerned is demonstrated in five cases.

1. When the Gospel is placed in opposition to the Law, it surely cannot be taken in the wider sense, but must be understood in the narrower sense. (See Ephesians 2:14-17.) . . .

2. When the Gospel is presented as the teaching peculiar to Christ and as the message that proclaims Christ, the Law cannot be included. For Christ Himself said: "The Law was given through Moses; grace and truth came through Jesus Christ" (John 1:17). Christ did not first give us the Law, but since the true knowledge of the Law is necessary before a person can accept the Gospel, He purified the Law of the false interpretations given by the Pharisees. See Luke 4:18-19. Here the Lord said not one word about the Law but mentioned only the teaching that is there for the poor, the sick, the crushed hearts, those in the prison of sin and of the devil. (See also Acts 17:18; 1 Corinthians 15:1-4; Romans 16:25-26; Galatians 1:6-7.)

3. When the message is directed to poor sinners, it is certainly Gospel in the narrower sense (Matthew 11:5; Luke 4:18).

4. When the effects of the Gospel are forgiveness, righteousness, and salvation by grace, it is Gospel in the narrower sense (Romans 1:16; Ephesians 1:13).

5. When faith is the correlative of Gospel, it is Gospel in the narrower sense (Mark 1:15; Mark 16:15-16). Even the latter passage uses Gospel in the narrower sense, for although the Lord adds: "He who does not believe will be condemned," that is not a part of the Gospel, but Law. He means to say that those who reject the Gospel must know that thereby they are hurling themselves into hell.

Twenty-eighth Evening Lecture

(May 15, 1885)

Preparing and delivering a sermon should always be done with fear and trembling, in the holy anxiety of not saying something false. The preacher must carefully scrutinize everything he has written to see whether it conforms to the Word of God and Christian experience. Let him not be enchanted by the beauties of style or rhetoric, but be especially concerned that his language is not false or subject to misunderstanding. Let the preacher be severe with himself and delete questionable passages, even though he worked hard to produce them. He may have to discard his whole sermon and start over. If he preaches what is false, he must correct it and publicly revoke it. Then, far from forfeiting respect, he will be cherished by the people as one who is most conscientious.

The apostle Paul says to all preachers: "A little leaven leavens the whole lump" (1 Corinthians 5:6). False teaching is a leaven, indeed a poison which, even in very small amounts, permeates the whole system and kills. Daily experience also teaches this. A very small dose of poison may have terrible consequences, while swallowing a whole piece of arsenic may do no damage. The amount of damage done by a single false statement in a sermon is beyond expression.

When, for example, a preacher wrongly reproves, and this is heard by pious, conscientious Christians who work out their salvation with fear and trembling, it may easily happen that such dear souls now become uncertain about their state of grace and doubt whether they will be saved. Then the preacher must not think that he will straighten out everything in a later sermon. No, the more the hearers look upon their pastor as orthodox and a genuine, experienced Christian, the less will they be able to surmount the trouble when he has shot the arrow of a false rebuke into their hearts.

Or he may offer false comfort where he should have rebuked, and false Christians enjoy it and compliment themselves on being good Christians. How terrible when a carnal-minded and secure person regards himself as a good Christian, even though the opposite is the case! He will go on in his blindness and finally be eternally damned.

A conscientious preacher may also have this experience: God permits him to make mistakes so that he will realize he cannot do without God's illumination and guidance. Therefore you must let every sermon be the product of fervent prayer. Do not try to write your sermon if you feel cold and lifeless and distraught. If only you will plead with God to snatch you out of this spiritual lethargy and grant you the Holy Spirit, then you will not merely write consoling words of which you feel nothing in your own heart. It is not enough to think that you have said everything that is in the Bible. You must be concerned in your preparation as to how you will cast your Gospel net in order to make a good catch.

Here preachers are greatly found wanting. Many waste much time in unnecessary matters during the week and then give less than their best in the pulpit. You can notice it: They say something only because they must say something; they don't care if it's helpful. That's terrible! The three quarters of an hour spent in the pulpit is extremely precious, a time that may be the deciding factor in the welfare and salvation of many people. Woe to the preacher who does not properly use his time to offer the best he can! If he does not have the conviction that he is preaching the truth, how can he expect to accomplish anything? . . . When a preacher has worked out his sermon, he should know: "That is a real fishhook for catching souls for Christ and bringing them to Him." But one who speaks without a plan and without a specific aim should not be surprised if he reaches no goal. Woe to the preacher and student who works frivolously and spouts the first thing that enters his mind! This happens especially in so-called extemporaneous speaking, by which I mean not only copying someone else's material, but also failing to reflect on the material. Extended meditation on the sermon subject will help give the preacher fluency. Yes, it will even be good for the preacher to emancipate himself in time from dependence on his manuscript and so give the Holy Spirit a chance to lay hold of him and suggest words and thoughts that had not come to him before.

So St. Paul writes to Timothy: "Do your best to present yourself to God as one approved, a workman who has no need to be ashamed, rightly handling the Word of truth" (2 Timothy 2:15). Thus the chief thing in preaching is properly to distinguish between Law and Gospel.

Thesis XVI

In the 12th place, God's Word is not rightly divided when it is suggested that shedding certain vices and performing certain works and virtues is a true conversion.

This is a very important thesis, for that is the crassest mingling of Law and Gospel there can be. If the sermon leads the hearer to think that if he stops robbing and stealing he is a good Christian, woe to the preacher who produces such ideas! The Gospel is turned into Law because conversion is made a work, whereas only the Gospel can produce it, namely by leading people to a living faith.

Rationalists are most guilty of this gross mingling. In fact, that is their religion, to say: "You must first get rid of your vices and exercise yourself in virtues, and then you will become a different person." But God's Word says: "You must first become a different person, and then you will turn from sin and do good works." To say that man must become holy through his works is paganism, neo-Judaism, and Islam. . . . Rationalists have the adage: "Genuine repentance is to quit practicing your vices." This can be understood correctly, as also our old teachers did. They said that those who boast of having the true faith and yet lead an evil life should know that forsaking their vices is the real repentance. But rationalists mean to say: "Don't worry, God just wants you to shed your vices; then you will be a true Christian."

That is disgraceful ethical teaching. Christianity puts it in one word: "Repent," change your attitude. With this word the Lord proceeds against sin and says: "You must completely change your attitude. Forsaking vices and doing good works is not what I demand, but you must have a different attitude, a different heart, a different spirit." That is what Christianity demands. It puts the ax to the root of the tree, while rationalism and the papacy only prune the branches of the poisonous tree, allowing ever new branches to sprout; but they are all poisonous. New branches must be grafted onto such a tree, and then there will be different fruits. As proof, let us hear some Scripture passages.

John 3:5-6: To the pharisaic righteousness of Nicodemus the Lord responded: "Truly, truly, I say to you, unless one is born of water and the Spirit, he cannot enter the kingdom of God. That which is born of the flesh is flesh, and that which is born of the Spirit is spirit." He meant: "You must become a different person."

Matthew 12:33: "The tree is known by its fruit." Before there can be good fruit, the tree must be good. So man must first become a new creature with a new attitude before he can produce good fruit. (See also Matthew 15:13; Jeremiah 4:3.)

1 Corinthians 13:3 is especially pertinent to our thesis. What matters primarily is not the outward works, but the love that motivates them. Even if I were so poor, utterly destitute, that I could do absolutely nothing, I could still be rich in good works before God, namely if my love urges me to the wish: "Ah, if I could only do good to all people! But according to God's will I must let others show love to me." In such a case God looks upon the willingness as a good work. . . .

On John 3:3 Luther writes: "Therefore we teach that all the works of man are nothing and in vain apart from the new birth. And for this reason we call this the most important element in the instruction of the people, namely, that first of all they must be reborn. . . . First they must be born anew and become new persons" *(Sermons on the Gospel of St. John, Luther's Works,* American Edition, Vol. 22, p. 279). [*Editorial note:* See the following pages in Luther regarding what is involved in the new birth, material which Walther quotes.]

Some falsely orthodox preachers think: "Ah, that is nothing but Pietism." No, that is Christianity!

[Later Walther comments:] In the new birth everything is God's work. If I enjoy my food, if I eat and sleep, that too is God's work—not only that which is hard for me to do. If I torment myself as a slave of the Law, that is nothing but martyrdom for hell. A Christian has the right attitude, and so everything he does is God-pleasing, for only good, sweet water comes from a good spring.

Another pertinent passage of Luther is from his *The Freedom of a Christian* (1520). . . . He writes:

> Good works do not make a good man, but a good man does good work; evil works do not make a wicked man, but a wicked man does evil works . . . as Christ also says, "A good tree cannot bear evil fruit, nor can a bad tree bear good fruit" [Matt. 7:18]. . . . So it is with the works of man. As the man is, whether believer or unbeliever, so also is his work—good if it was done in faith, wicked if it was done in unbelief. But the converse is not true, that the work makes the man either a believer or an unbeliever. As works do not make a man a believer, so also they do not make him righteous. But as faith makes a man a believer and righteous, so faith does good works *(Luther's Works,* American Edition, Vol. 31, p. 361).

These are matters we can easily understand, but Luther had to pass through very difficult struggles before he could sing this song. It is surprising that he was able thus to picture the relationship between faith and works as early as 1520.

Twenty-ninth Evening Lecture
(May 29, 1885)

Christ's word to the church in Laodicea (Revelation 3:15-16) is both noteworthy and frightening. In God's infallible judgment it is worse to be a lukewarm preacher than a cold one, worse to be lax and indifferent and to carry on his ministry for the living it provides than to be ungodly. If a preacher, though respectable, is a sleepyhead and without any real concern for the kingdom of God and the salvation of souls, this can only infect the poor hearers and eventually put the whole congregation to sleep. On the other hand, if a preacher evidently lives and teaches in an ungodly way, the good people will not follow him but turn from him in disgust. But although a preacher's lukewarmness does the church greater harm than open ungodliness, both will one day receive the same verdict: "I never knew you; depart from me, you evildoers" [Matthew 7:23].

But a truly faithful servant of Jesus Christ will one day hear the inexpressibly joyous message: "Well done, good and faithful servant; you have been faithful over a little, I will set you over much; enter into the joy of your master" [Matthew 25:21]. He dare not be lukewarm or cold. His heart must burn with love to Jesus, his Savior, and to His congregation which is entrusted to him, so that he can say with Paul: "If we are beside ourselves, it is for God" (2 Corinthians 5:13). . . . Every true preacher and servant of Christ will be filled with earnest zeal, even though his only return may be unpopularity and even bitter hatred. A true preacher will prefer that to being on good terms with everybody as a result of concealing or blunting the truth.

Thus, my friends, it cannot be denied: A preacher, especially a zealous one, must take his preaching very seriously, or else he commits a grave sin. But he can also sin by going beyond the Word of God in what he says about Christianity and its demands. That leads us to the 17th thesis.

Thesis XVII

In the 13th place, God's Word is not rightly divided when believers are pictured in a way that does not fit all believers at all times with regard both to strength of faith and to the feelings and the fruitfulness connected with it.

This mistake is made particularly by young preachers who have little experience. They want to make an impression and arouse the people out of their natural security. Therefore they think they cannot demand too much of those who are Christians, so that no hypocrite will consider himself a Christian. But here a preacher dare not go beyond God's Word, or else he can do dreadful harm. Christians are often quite different from the way they are (though sincerely) pictured in the sermon. The attempt is made to rouse the people and warn them against self-delusion. However, that must not be the final goal, which is to make the hearers certain that they have forgiveness of their sins before God and the hope of eternal life, so that they can confidently face death. Whoever does not have that as his final goal is not an evangelical preacher. Therefore, let him for God's sake be careful and not say that a person who does so and so cannot be a Christian, unless he is absolutely sure. A Christian often acts in a very unchristian way.

In Romans 7:18 and 14 Paul describes the Christian as consisting of two parts. He always wants to do what is right, but he often falls short. It is therefore contrary to the Bible to assert that a Christian does not have a good will if he does not accomplish all that is good. The chief thing for a person is to want to do the good. Frequently he may not get beyond that. Before he realizes it, he has gone astray, and he is ashamed of himself. But that is a long way from falling from grace.

A Christian feels himself enslaved under sin and therefore cries with the apostle, "Wretched man that I am! Who will deliver me from this body of death?" (Romans 7:24). Remember this for your own consolation and also apply it to your congregation for their consolation. It is a malady of our time that Christians are not sure of their state, because they are not given definite instruction. But when a Christian is shown what a miserable sinner he is, he will cling to Christ and refuse to listen to the devil when he tells him he has fallen from grace.

Philippians 3:12 tells us that this life is a constant pursuit without ever reaching the goal. The Christian life has its ups and downs. Temptations and trials increase, and the mature Christian is more conscious of his weakness.

Galatians 5:17 shows the conflict within the Christian. He falls short and sins from weakness, but the preacher must be careful not to deny that he is a Christian. (See also James 3:2.)

According to Hebrews 12:1 the Christian is constantly in the process of laying aside his sin which, however, continues to cling to him. He cannot rid his soul of it, and it makes him listless in sanctification. . . . (See also Isaiah 64:6; Job 14:4.)

Psalm 32:6 refers to the prayer of the godly for forgiveness of sin.

But why look for more passages? The Savior commanded all Christians to pray daily: "Forgive us our sins." Hence every new day lays new guilt on our hearts and consciences. One who pictures the Christian as being perfect—not like the Methodists, but in individual cases—presents a caricature of the Christian and does immeasurable harm. The most delicate conscience will think: "Alas, I am no Christian! I often suspected it, and today the preacher told me so." And perhaps nobody can erase that thought from this person's mind. He will labor until death, trying never again to fall into certain sins, but he does again and again. Therefore the preacher must give Christians the right means to rise quickly after a fall—unless it be willful transgression, which expels the Holy Spirit from the heart. But a Christian in danger will notice it right away and will flee to his heavenly Father and ask for forgiveness for Christ's sake, and he will soon become confident that God has forgiven him. He will say:

> Oh, my faith shall e'er enfold Him,
> Till I come where I behold Him,
> Till my Bridegroom calls for me.

Sometimes Christians are described as being perfectly happy all the time, while non-Christians are pictured as being most unhappy. I have often noticed this in your sermons, but neither of these descriptions is true. Many thousands of Christians are filled with fear and inner turmoil and feel acutely unhappy, while many non-Christians appear to have no worries at all.

156

You may treat topics like "The Blessedness of a Christian," but remember well: *This blessedness does not consist in having nothing but happy emotions.* Even in the midst of bitter feelings he can trust God to accept him and take him to heaven when he dies, and that is blessedness indeed. You must be concerned never to say anything that runs counter to Christian experience. You must put yourself in your hearers' place and ask what would alarm you and make you doubtful. . . . It is, of course, quite all right to present a vivid picture of an occasional foretaste of eternal salvation which a Christian may experience, but those are only brief moments in a Christian's life. If such blessed moments are correctly presented, they will not beget anxiety and doubt but an intense longing for such an experience. And such experiences come especially to those who have contended faithfully. They lay prostrate and thought all was lost when God overwhelmed them with such heavenly joy that they felt transported into heaven.

You must also remember that a Christian keeps his temperament also after his conversion, such as a quick temper. Hence you cannot say that a Christian is changed from a bear to a lamb in the sense that he lets everybody taunt and malign him and at once forgives them. No, a Christian often has his hands full with his temper. He may even get so angry that he cannot be calmed. Why? Because his temperament got the upper hand. Then you dare not think that such a person will go to hell if he should die that night. While a judgmental Christian is thinking thus, the culprit may be on his knees pleading for forgiveness and promising amendment. How awful, then, to pass a loveless judgment! Perhaps he will come the very next day and apologize.

Often the Christian is pictured as patient as Job. One may say: "Deprive a Christian of everything he has and he will say cheerfully, 'The Lord gave, and the Lord has taken away; blessed be the name of the Lord' [Job 1:21]." The preacher may think that is entirely Biblical. True, Job said it, but not all Christians can say it. If you say so in your sermon, you have told a shameful lie. . . .

Many preach about a true Christian as if he had no fear of death. That is terrible. Most Christians are afraid of death. It is a special grace for one to have no fear of death whatever and to think: "Let death come today or tomorrow; I am ready." . . .

Whatever you do, be careful not to draw a picture of the Christian in which you cannot recognize yourself. Even pride, which is one of the greatest vices, a sin against the First Commandment, may severely afflict a Christian. But we are all proud by nature. Yet one is more prone to it than another.

A person of choleric temperament, with a strong will and great energy, as a rule has much self-confidence and expects others to respect him for it. That is abominable arrogance. And yet it is found among true Christians. Just look at the Lord's disciples! They quarrel about which one is the greatest. It would be unbelievable if it were not in the Bible that the apostles quarreled like little children: "I am the greatest!" "No, I am the greatest!" Indeed, the mother of the sons of Zebedee naively asked the Lord to place one son at His right hand and the other at His left. But when the Lord rebuked them, they could have sunk through the floor for shame.

Furthermore, it is wrong to speak as if a Christian is always fervent in prayer as his favorite occupation. Far from it. It takes much inner conflict to pray with the conviction of being heard. Often the person's thoughts are elsewhere while he says the words. For that reason the Lord's Prayer has been called the greatest martyr. And true Christians are guilty too. To be sure, one who as a rule mindlessly rattles off the Lord's Prayer is not a Christian. A Christian will repent of his lack of devotion and start over. Yet we keep our flesh and blood. At times these may indeed be so well held in subjection that we fancy ourselves in heaven and feel as if our heart would melt in ecstasy as we talk with God.

Even the desire to become rich is often present in true Christians, and if they would not be warned and admonished, they would be lost. Businessmen especially are in danger of becoming misers.

What matters is whether one loves God's Word and his Savior and does not lead a dissolute life. Some want to create a saintly impression by outward gestures, always turning up their eyes to heaven and opening their mouth only to cite the Bible, and reading Scripture in their leisure time. Everyone will think: "That certainly is a good Christian!" That was Melanchthon's experience with the "heavenly prophets." One must not think that only those who put on a pious appearance are Christians. I do not deny that some of them are Christians, but many of them are wretched hypocrites. The Lord's disciples did not always speak or act piously. Yet the Lord did not regard them as unconverted but treated them as people who still had the Old Adam.

You may mention what *strong* and especially *faithful* Christians do. That may serve as a powerful incentive for those who have not advanced to that stage. Remember this when you receive new members. Do not regard them as ungodly if they do not at once engage in religious conversation. Many cling to their Savior even though they are unable to talk about it. Some may have had very little experience in spiritual matters and therefore have little to say.

In conclusion let us listen to a quotation from Luther's *Church Postil,*

(St. Louis Edition, XII, 911 f.). [*Editorial note:* We omit this for reasons of space.]

Thirtieth Evening Lecture
(June 5, 1885)

Many young men, highly gifted for the ministry and even inclined toward it, still do not want to become preachers because they think they will forfeit their happiness and their freedom. But that is a great delusion. Whoever desires to be saved must be ready to sacrifice his happiness and do without his freedom, if that is Christ's will. Not only the preacher, but every Christian must choose the narrow way that leads to heaven, forsake the world, combat and crucify the flesh, and work out his salvation with fear and trembling. Therefore by his unwillingness to become a preacher a young man gains little or nothing for his covetous flesh. A Christian must be a spiritual priest—even if he is not a preacher—if he does not want to reject God's grace.

It is, of course, true that one who wants to become a preacher must first have become a true Christian; this is indispensable. Paul closes the list of what is required of bishops, or preachers, with these words: "They must hold the mystery of the faith with a clear conscience" (1 Timothy 3:9). A preacher must have a clear conscience, cleansed by the blood of Christ through forgiveness and also by the sanctification of the Spirit. A preacher must have come to the great resolve to live not for himself but for Him who died and rose again. At his ordination, by which he is set apart for service in the sanctuary, he must bid an irrevocable farewell to the world. A preacher must be ready to renounce the world and give himself with full devotion to the Lord's service. . . .

It is a great calamity for a congregation to get a pastor who is orthodox but unconverted, who may present the pure doctrine but does not from experience believe what he preaches. From the pulpit he may lead his flock to good pasture, but he will be a poor pastor and watchman over souls, and an even worse example. He will not have the image of a Christian who denies and renounces both himself and the world. He may remain loyal to the pure doctrine, if that is to his advantage, perhaps even defend it. But let him experience ingratitude, ignominy, and persecution for the sake of the pure teaching, and he will soon fall away. It will become manifest that his Christianity sprang from a rotten root and that the congregation was deceived.

In times of emergency, when wolves and foxes attack, it is of prime importance for the shepherd to stand firm and be ready to sacrifice his life for the truth and for his flock. An unconverted person would find this ridiculous, to abandon his pleasant life in a pleasant job with pleasant income just because of some subtle point of doctrine. So he may view it, since he has never understood the true connection between doctrine and salvation. And if it involves teaching of a purely practical nature, having to do with a true knowledge and experience of the heart, such an orthodox preacher will speak of it like a blind man about color. He will either have an exaggerated view of Christianity or give it less than its due. We have heard how Christianity can be exaggerated. Today let us hear how a preacher can put Christianity on a lower level than its real nature requires.

Thesis XVIII

In the 14th place, God's Word is not rightly divided when the universal corruption of mankind is described as if the true believers were living in dominating and willful sins.

No orthodox teacher will say that a Christian could be a fornicator and an adulterer. Yet it is easy to be tempted to stray from sound doctrine when one wants to depict the universal corruption of humankind in a most forceful way. This is a mistake often made by zealous preachers. Students are also inclined to do this . . . as though Christians lived in manifest mortal sins! This can do great harm. . . . We must always add that man is like that by nature, or as long as he is not reborn. . . . But when you address a Christian congregation you dare not, for God's sake, speak as though all true Christians practiced such shameful vices.

We cannot be too careful. As harmful and dangerous as it was for the Pietists to set up many classes of people, and no one knew where he belonged, we must never neglect in our sermons to specify the two great classes, namely to distinguish between believers and unbelievers, pious and godless, converted and unconverted, regenerate and unregenerate. Scripture continually makes that classification. (See Mark 16:16; Luke 5:32; Matthew 5:45; Matthew 13:49.) Always only two classes!

This must sound forth in every sermon, so that the hearer knows he is either dead or alive, converted or unconverted. . . . It is therefore an accursed heresy of modern theologians to teach that a person could still be converted in Hades. May God in His mercy preserve you from this dreadful teaching! . . . Christ clearly teaches that there are only two gates and two ways and two goals, either life or death [Matthew 7:13-14]. It is therefore simply frightening when Law and Gospel are so badly mingled that these two classes are mixed up. The Law produces damned sinners; the Gospel, free and blessed people. . . . Every Christian who is baptized can

160

therefore apply to himself the Word: "This is My beloved son, with whom I am well pleased."

Passages like Romans 6:14, 1 Corinthians 6:9-11, 2 Peter 2: 20-22, Romans 8:13-14, Galatians 5:19-21, and Ephesians 5:5-6 clearly show the difference between Christians and unbelievers. The Christians, though sinners, are not dominated by sin. . . . Since such passages occur in the sermon pericopes, they must be carefully explained to the congregation. . . . The preacher should know his text well in advance of preaching it. Whoever waits until Wednesday or Thursday to look up next Sunday's pericope thereby betrays a shameful hireling's mentality. A true preacher thinks about next week's sermon as early as Sunday evening, unless he has visits to make that evening. He will take great delight in capturing one fortress of the devil after another. To be sure, he will not succeed in leveling them all, but you must have the earnest desire to do so. Otherwise many will remain in their spiritual misery, in their misery of sin, and you will be responsible. But if you do what you can by the grace of God, your Savior will not humiliate you because of your weakness, but by grace give you the crown of glory.

Most pertinent is what Luther says in the Smalcald Articles (Part III, Art III, par. 42-45; Tappert, pp. 309 f.). [*Editorial note:* We omit this quotation, where it is clearly stated that Christian faith and a life of manifest sin are incompatible. Walther continues:]

This should be obvious, but Calvinists teach what our thesis condemns. The Decrees of the Synod of Dort (V, 6) state: "According to His immutable purpose of election, God, who is rich in mercy, does not wholly remove the Holy Spirit from His own even when they sin grievously, nor does He permit them to fall entirely out of the grace of adoption as children of God and out of the state of justification." In other words, people living in mortal sin are still justified people who have kept the Holy Spirit. This is false, but we do agree that the elect cannot remain in such a state until their death, for otherwise they would not be among the elect.

Thirty-first Evening Lecture

(June 12, 1885)

The existence and origin of sin is one of the most difficult problems for the human mind. Even serious-minded pagan philosophers have wrestled with this matter. But since they had no inkling of God's original perfect creation and man's subsequent fall through Satan's temptation, they were able to discover neither the dreadfulness of sin nor its origin. At best they

161

recognized sin as an innate weakness and frailty of man. Others, attempting to go further, like Zoroaster, Manes, and many Gnostics, posited an original dual principle, good and bad, thus accounting for man's good and evil. But even so they were unable to recognize the fearful abomination of sin.

Unfortunately, there are many within Christendom, baptized and unbaptized, who do not know what sin is. Some, like the rationalists, maintain that man is by nature good and becomes evil only because of his environment. Others, like the pantheists, atheists, and materialists, assert that sin is something perfectly natural, like satisfying hunger and thirst. In fact, many of them say that sin was necessary for man's development toward self-consciousness. The infamous philosopher Hegel openly stated that without the fall into sin paradise would have been nothing more than a park for animals. He regarded sin as the transition from barbarism to self-conscious thought.

This blindness regarding sin is the chief cause for the nearly general rejection of the Gospel in our day. One who does not know sin in its dreadfulness will not be interested in the sacrificial death of the Son of God for the reconciliation and redemption of a sinful world, but will consider it unnecessary and a wretched fairy tale. Therefore it is one of the most important requirements of an evangelical preacher to know how to show his hearers the true nature of sin clearly and unmistakably as a dreadful calamity. Without such knowledge there can be no understanding of the Gospel. And certainly, one who has no true knowledge of sin is even less able to distinguish properly between Law and Gospel. This brings us to our next thesis.

Thesis XIX

In the 15th place, God's Word is not rightly divided when the preacher gives the impression that certain sins are not in themselves damnable but only venial.

Without clarity in this matter you will not be equipped for a proper discharge of the ministerial office.

As noted earlier, we must make a distinction between mortal and venial sins, or else we do not distinguish Law and Gospel properly. But this must be done with great care. We must show clearly that we make this distinction only insofar as there are certain sins that drive out the Holy Spirit. Then faith is also driven out, for there can be no faith without the Holy Spirit. Such sins we call mortal sins, since they result in spiritual death. Anyone can easily experience this. When he sins wilfully he notices that the Holy Spirit has departed, he cannot pray like a child of God, and can no longer bravely resist temptation. He will feel enslaved by sin. It is good to have at least this insight; then he can come back to God. But as long as he is in this condition, he is not in fellowship with God.

Venial sins we call those that a Christian commits without losing the Holy Spirit. They are sins of weakness and rashness, or they are often referred to as the everyday sins of Christians.

But we must for God's sake never give the impression that people need not be concerned about venial sins or ask that they be forgiven. That would be preaching the people into hell. It would make them carnally secure and drive the fear of God from their hearts. That is not proper evangelical preaching. It is altogether false to think that one who proclaims very little Law is a real evangelical preacher. Both must be preached, the Law severely and the Gospel sweetly. One who does not preach both dare not claim to be an evangelical preacher. He must know that he is a deceiver and is sowing the Gospel like seed into the sea, where it cannot sprout. The heavenly seed of the Gospel will sprout only in a broken heart. But it often happens that preachers create the impression that, since we are all sinners, we need not worry about venial sins. That is godless talk.

Study the implications of passages like Matthew 5:18-19, Matthew 12:36, James 2:10, Galatians 3:10, 1 John 1:7, and Matthew 5:21-22. They show clearly that no commandment of God can be slighted or ignored and that the transgression of every commandment puts the sinner under God's judgment and condemnation. Sin is "lawlessness," rebellion against the holy and almighty God, our most exalted heavenly Lawgiver. Anyone who sins wilfully despises the King's law and treads it underfoot, a capital crime. And though we do not despise God's law in this fashion, we do transgress it daily. This we must heartily deplore. . . .

[*Editorial note:* We omit a quotation from the Roman catechism and one from Socinus, together with Walther's comments.]

Here are a few testimonies from Luther. At the Leipzig debate his second thesis was: "To deny that man sins even when doing good; that venial sin is pardonable, not according to its nature, but by the mercy of God; or that sin remains in the child after baptism; that is equivalent to crushing Paul and Christ under foot *(Luther's Works,* American Edition, Vol. 31 p. 317). . . . In his *Explanations of the Ninety-five Theses* (1518) Luther wrote on Thesis 76: "I should have said more about venial sin because it is valued so lightly today that it is hardly considered a sin at all. And I am afraid that many will come to great destruction who snore so securely in their sins and do not see that they have committed really big ones. . . . One who does not constantly fear and act as if he were filled with mortal sins, will hardly be saved at all, for the Scripture says, 'Enter not into judgment with Thy servant, O Lord' [Ps. 143:2]. Not only venial sins, as they generally call them today, but even good works cannot endure the judgment of God, for both of them need the forgiving compassion of God . . . " *(Luther's Works,* American Edition, Vol. 31, p. 242).

Evangelical preaching magnifies sin. The preacher must judge sin most severely, for he must announce God's verdict. Never make light even of venial sins, but remember that we daily sin much and deserve nothing but condemnation. Yet God does not want to condemn you who believe in Christ. . . . It is terrible for one to say that his conscience doesn't bother him, when God's Word condemns him!

Dannhauer says: "Sin is as great as He is who thereby is offended" *(Hodosophia,* p. 195). That is an important axiom. . . .

Finally, our Christian experience teaches that no sin is in itself venial. A true Christian has an active conscience, which reproves him when he has done wrong and will not give him peace until he repents. . . . Hence also venial sin is an evil, a fire that can flare up and lead to damantion. *Little sins become big sins when we think little of them.*

Thirty-second Evening Lecture
(June 19, 1885)

When, my dear friends, rationalism in the last quarter of the previous century flooded the so-called Protestant church and the theological chairs at universities and pulpits everywhere, it was inevitable that people began to feel that it no longer made a difference whether a person was Lutheran or Reformed or Catholic. The few remaining sincere Christians, who believed and confessed the orthodox Christian faith, then joined hands like those rescued from a shipwreck, while most others went down. In that situation it was inevitable for the thought to arise that the time had come to put an end to doctrinal controversies among the churches, to break down the barriers between denominations, put aside distinctive confessions, and establish a general union, or at least a union of Protestant churches.

But what happened? Already in 1817 Claus Harms, who still had a few drops of Lutheran blood in his veins, published *95 Theses* as companions to Luther's, against rationalism and the Prussian Union. He said: "You want to enrich the Lutheran Church as a poor maid by means of a marriage. Do not perform the ceremony over Luther's bones! They will stir, and then, woe to you." This word came true. When the Union was consummated in Prussia, great numbers of Lutherans suddenly arose from their sleep . . . and declared they would never leave the church of their fathers. . . .

Those were glorious days in the darkness of the middle of this century! But the old, pure, true Lutheran Church did not emerge from those glorious struggles. Why? Because those men who wanted to preserve what they had did not have a clear understanding themselves. Consequently they moved from one extreme to the other, from rationalism and religious and ecclesiastical indifferentism to particularism and anti-Lutheran hierarchism. Those who were determined opponents of the Union and wanted to be true Lutherans claimed that the visible Lutheran Church was the one holy Christian church of the Creed, the church outside of which there was no salvation. . . . That was a sad and serious error, directly contrary to the Word of God and subverting the cardinal teaching of Christianity, the doctrine of justification by grace alone for Christ's sake through faith. In this error Law and Gospel were obviously mingled and are still being mingled. . . .

Thesis XX

In the 16th place, God's Word is not rightly divided when salvation is linked to membership in the visible orthodox church and salvation is denied to anyone who errs in any article of faith.

It is very hard to explain how, after so long a time of dominance by rationalism and the greatest religious indifferentism, people could get the idea that the visible Lutheran Church is the church as such, outside of which there could be no salvation. Yet there is an explanation. This error was the consequence of another error, namely the teaching that the church is a visible organization established by Christ on earth. It was taught that the church is nothing but a kind of religious state, ruled over not by kings and emperors, generals and mayors, but by superintendents, bishops, church administrations, pastors, deacons, synods, and the like. That error was the fruitful mother of other dreadful errors. . . .

The members of the church are built upon the foundation of the apostles and prophets (Ephesians 2:19-22). They are the ones who cling in firm faith to the Word of the apostles and prophets. One who does not have a living faith is no member of the church.

The Savior calls Himself a bridegroom. Whoever is not united with Him in his innermost heart is not a Christian and a member of the church, for the church is the bride of Christ.

Christ is also called the Head of the church. Hence only he can be a member of the church who receives light, life, power, and grace from Christ the Head. Whoever is not thus spiritually united with Christ does not have Him as his Head. Whoever runs his own life and is not governed by Christ as his Head is not a member of the church.

The apostle calls the church Christ's body. Therefore many faithful Lutherans said that a body must be something visible. But that is very bad exegesis. The point of comparison is not the visibility, but that the church ... is an organism of many diverse parts that are permeated by one faith and one life of faith. That itself proves beyond contradiction that the church is not something visible, but invisible. Only he is a member of the church who continually draws sustenance from Christ the Head.

Christ calls the church His flock. Hence no one is a member of the church who is not a sheep of Christ and does not follow His leading nor hear His voice.

It is said that Christ compared the church to a field where wheat and weeds grow. Yet the Lord did not say: "The field is My kingdom," but "The field is the world" [Matthew 13:38]. Therefore the church is not a fellowship of good and evil people. The Apology of the Augsburg Confession also calls attention to this situation (Art. VII and VIII, par. 12-19; Tappert, pp. 170 f.). ... *It is possible to see who is associated with the church, but it is not possible to see who the true members are.* Only God knows. To human eyes the church is invisible.

People who promote this error want to be good Lutherans in opposition to the papacy, but they are only exchanging weapons. At one time the papists defended this false teaching. Now Lutherans dare to counter with the claim: No, we, we, we are the church outside of which there is no salvation." Thus they can become objects of ridicule to the papists, for they are usurping a role formerly played by the pope and his crowd. It follows that either the papal church is the true church or that the church had disappeared when Luther came. But Scripture says that the true church cannot be destroyed; it will continue until judgment day. But there was no church called "Lutheran" until the 16th century. In fact, no church since the days of the apostles has had the pure doctrine the way our fathers had it. Hence, either Scripture is lying, or the papistic church was the true church and Luther's Reformation must have been a rebellion. That is the dilemma for those who want to maintain this false teaching about the church.

However, the chief thing is that those who link salvation to membership in the visible orthodox church thereby subvert the doctrine of justification through faith; of this there can be no doubt. Those who come to the Lutheran Church already have the true faith. To say that Luther did not have the true faith before he became a "Lutheran" is a dangerous error. As much as we esteem our church, may we be preserved from so disgraceful a fanaticism as to claim that the Lutheran Church is the only saving church. The true church is spread over the whole world and exists in all denominations. The church is not an external organism into which one must be inserted to be a member of the church. Whoever believes in Jesus Christ and is a member of His spiritual body is a member of the church. Nor can the church be disrupted. It remains one, even though separated by space and time.

But doesn't Scripture refer to external churches? True, there is the church at Rome, Corinth, Galatia, Philippi, Thessalonica, and the churches in Asia Minor to which St. John directed letters. All these were visible. Therefore many say that the church is visible. But this does not follow. Wherever Scripture speaks of the church as such it always speaks of an invisible fellowship. But then it applies the term "church" also to local groups where the invisible church is hidden. It is for the sake of the members of the invisible church that a visible organization is called "church." False Christians and hypocrites are not members of the church. In love we assume that all are Christians who profess to be, but we cannot look into their heart. That we leave to God. We will not judge a person unless he is *manifestly* ungodly. Then we will regard him "as a Gentile and a tax collector" [Matthew 18:17] and exclude him.

But now also the Lutheran Church is only a visible church, by synecdoche. It is, therefore, dreadful to say that one can be saved only in this church. . . . There are Christians in the Reformed churches and the Roman Catholic Church. God has promised that His Word will bear fruit where it is proclaimed (Isaiah 55:11). The church of Rome still confesses: "Christ is the Son of God who died on the cross to redeem the world." That truth is enough so that a person can come to saving knowledge. Whoever denies this must also deny that there are Christians in some Lutheran churches, for these also have errors. But God's Word is there and it is fruitful. It will always convert some souls to God.

Whoever holds this false teaching about the church grievously mingles Law and Gospel. The Gospel says, "Believe in the Lord Jesus Christ." The Law makes all kinds of demands. As soon as a demand is introduced alongside faith as necessary to salvation, Law and Gospel are mingled. I belong to the Lutheran Church because I want to hold to the truth. If I discover that the church to which I belong teaches errors, I must leave it, so as not to be contaminated and be a "partaker of other men's sins" [1 Timothy 5:22 KJV]. . . .

From the fact that people may be saved and be God's children in all the denominations it does not follow that one may remain in sectarian churches. Many think the admission that one could be saved in any of the denominations is a unionistic principle. However, since I must be saved through faith, it is possible to be saved in those denominations. But if I recognize the error and do not withdraw from that heterodox fellowship, I will be lost, because I will not forsake the error, even though I recognize it.

I remember when I came to faith. I also came to the United Church. Some wanted to bring me to the Lutheran Church, but I said, "I have faith, and I do not want to belong to any church that claims it alone can save." Then I received some good books to read and discovered that this is not the case. The Lutheran Church claims *it alone has the pure doctrine* of the Word of God, but it does not claim to be the only saving church. As soon as I saw that, I left the United Church and joined the Lutherans. I had long realized that the Lutheran Church had the truth, but I did not want to commit myself to such papistic principles. Now I learned that it was not the teaching of the Lutheran Church to condemn all who err in some article of faith as long as they do not know any better.

This is the teaching of our church, as is clear from the Preface to the *Book of Concord.*

> With reference to the condemnations . . . it is not our purpose and intention to mean thereby those persons who err ingenuously and who do not blaspheme the truth of the divine Word, and far less do we mean entire churches inside or outside the Holy Empire of the German Nation. On the contrary, we mean specifically to condemn only false and seductive doctrines and their stiff-necked proponents and blasphemers . . . . But we have no doubt at all that one can find many pious, innocent people even in those churches which have up to now admittedly not come to agreement with us. These people go their way in the simplicity of their hearts, do not understand the issues, and take no pleasure in blasphemies against the Holy Supper . . . " (Tappert, pp. 11 f.).

Remember this beautiful passage. If someone raises the objection to you that the Lutheran Church claims to be the only one that can save a person, and that it condemns all others, then refer that person to this passage in our Confessions. Note that the Formula of Concord condemned the teaching of the Reformed, but not the persons who err in simplicity. . . . The Lutheran Church repudiates any physical pressure or persecution with regard to those who differ in doctrine. It finds such a course abhorrent.

In a preface which Luther wrote in 1538 for the *95 Theses* of 1517, he reminisced about how extremely difficult it was for him to get to the point of opposing the church of Rome, because of its constant claims that it alone was the true church. [*Editorial note:* Walther quotes a long section from this preface (St. Louis Edition, XIV, 452 f.).]

God grant that you will not permit yourselves to be drawn into the false teaching that the Lutheran Church is the true visible church of Jesus Christ *in the sense that one can be saved only within it.* To be sure, the

168

Lutheran Church is the true visible church, but only in the sense that it alone has the pure truth. As soon as the idea is added that there is salvation nowhere else, the doctrine of justification by grace through faith in Jesus Christ is deleted and Law and Gospel are mingled. May God preserve you from this error for your own sake and also for the sake of those who will be entrusted to you!

Thirty-third Evening Lecture
(Sept. 4, 1885)

The first requisite for a theologian is obviously that he have a complete, exact, and clear knowledge of all teachings of the divine revelation. To call a man a theologian who does not have this knowledge is a contradiction. Theologians are supposed to be the spiritual physicians of mankind. A physician must know the medicines which nature provides for the cure of physical ills. So a theologian, as a spiritual physician, must know the spiritual medicines offered by the Word of God for spiritual illness; but these spiritual medicines are none other than the saving doctrines revealed by God.

But this is not all that is required of a theologian. He needs two other things just as much: 1. He must understand the mutual relationships of the teachings in order to be able to apply them correctly, and 2. he must have courage and love for his theological calling. A doctor who knows potent medicines but ignorantly mixes them together in such a way that one cancels the other will, instead of healing the patients, hasten their death. So a theologian who does not know which teachings he must combine and which he must keep separate may easily do souls more harm than good. And finally, just as a doctor will measure up to his heavy duties only if he truly loves his work and is not in it for the money, so a theologian will be faithful to his calling only if he is dedicated to it and sees his reward in that God helps him to save souls, diminish the rule of Satan, advance the kingdom of God, and populate heaven.

Therefore I have always considered it my sacred duty not only to present the pure doctrine in my courses in Dogmatics, but also to assemble the entire student body once a week to demonstrate the importance, significance, and practical application of those doctrines, and then above all also to give you a cheerful heart for your difficult calling. We call these Friday evening lectures "Luther Hours," chiefly because I want to give the floor especially to our beloved father Luther, the divinely destined Reformer of the church and the common teacher of our church. By the grace of God my students have hitherto been glad to attend these weekend lectures and were blessed by them, as many have solemnly assured me, not only in receiving clearer insights into Christian doctrine but also in being strengthened in their faith in the forgiveness of sins, in being God's children, and in their salvation. I hope that the new students will also have this experience! May God help me to speak a good word and let it bear fruit. But remember, you must join me in this prayer. You are not here to acquire secular learning but to become familiar with a teaching that will save you and through you save others.

This is a most serious matter. You must put off the shoes of an earthly and carnal mind and take your place with Mary at Jesus' feet and hear from Him the one thing needful [Luke 10:38-42]. May God grant it! And may God help me to be a help to you for all time!

In the course of the past year we considered twenty theses on the distinction of Law and Gospel. We still have five theses left, and these are by no means unimportant. We must finish with them before we take up another topic. . . . I hope that all of you are sincere Christians, or at least that the Word of God has drawn you and will make a deep and abiding impression on you when it confronts you with its divine power. Then, when you leave this school, you will not only be equipped with fine theological insights but will also have a heart aglow to proclaim what great things the Lord has done for mankind.

I hope the students from last year will not consider it tedious if I once more read all the theses which have already been discussed, so that the dear newly entered students will know what we are discussing and of what importance the remaining theses are.

(The first 20 theses were hereupon read, and a few short remarks and explanations were made about each thesis.)

Faith does not grow out of itself. True faith is so firm that even if heaven would cave in and hell open up below us, we could say: "Let heaven cave in and hell open us, I believe in Jesus Christ, true God, who has redeemed me, a lost and condemned person, with His precious divine blood. No devil and no hell can rob me of that!" A hypocrite's faith, on the contrary, will melt like March snow in the warm sun.

Many think they are strict Bible-Lutherans if they insist: "One who is not a Lutheran cannot be saved; at least in his dying hour he must accept Lutheranism or else he will go to hell." But one who says that is not a true Lutheran but an apostate from Lutheranism, for that is not our teaching. We teach that man becomes righteous and is saved by grace, and Lutheran teaching surely makes that clear to him. But one who in another denomination loves the truth can be a better Christian than many a Lutheran. Christ rules everywhere, also in the midst of His enemies.

Thesis XXI

In the 17th place, God's Word is not rightly divided when it is taught that the sacraments have a salutary effect even if they are merely performed (ex opere operato).

A most important thesis that condemns a great error. This is the teaching of the papists: "If you submit to Baptism, it will do you some good, even though you are not yet a believer, as long as you do not live in mortal sins. Baptism will give you grace and make God gracious to you." Also concerning the Mass they say: "As often as a person hears Mass, he receives some grace. At every Communion attendance he will receive grace just because he attends." That teaching runs directly counter to the Word of God, for the Gospel teaches that man is justified and saved by grace alone and only then is able to do good works.

If I become righteous and obtain grace by being baptized or receiving Communion, then I am saved by works rather than by faith alone (Romans 3:28). If Baptism and Communion are regarded as something we do, they appear as quite insignificant works, hardly worth mentioning. How terrible, then, to teach that I receive grace if only I use the sacraments. No, if you do not come in faith, your Baptism and Communion will condemn you. They are means of grace only because a promise is connected with these external signs. And this promise of grace can be received only by faith. To have water poured over me does not help me, nor to receive the consecrated bread and wine, not even because I receive Christ's body and blood. It will not help me but only harm me, if I come without faith, for then I will become guilty of the Lord's body and blood. All depends on my believing. . . .

False teachers say concerning the sacraments: "We admit that mere preaching and hearing will do you no good, unless you accept the Word in faith. But it is different with the sacraments. They have the great advantage that by their mere use God is graciously effective in me." That is ungodly teaching. Sacraments are nothing but the Word of God combined with outward signs. Augustine called the sacraments the "visible Word." As little as God's Word helps me if I do not believe, so little will Baptism help me without faith. To believe in your Baptism means to believe God, who has attached such a glorious promise to Baptism.

The objection of the enthusiasts to Lutheran teaching is therefore groundless. Lutherans do not teach that we must put our confidence in Baptism and the Lord's Supper. We teach that in Baptism and the Lord's Supper God makes a promise to you. Cling to that promise and do not doubt. But I can cling to God's promise only after I have become a poor sinner. To say that you must take comfort in your Baptism and you must be converted to Christ is one and the same. Only the Holy Spirit can bestow this true faith.

Thirty-fourth Evening Lecture
(Sept. 11, 1885)

Whoever speaks of pure doctrine as being extremely important is suspected of not having the true Christian spirit. To speak of "pure doctrine" is considered to be in bad taste. Even those theologians who rate as confessional refer to pure doctrine mostly in a derisive manner, as a catchword for a theology of the dead letter. One who seriously contends for pure doctrine and opposes false doctrine is regarded as a heartless and loveless fanatic. Why? Because, first of all, modern theologians know very well that they do not have what has always been labeled and in fact is pure doctrine. Second, because they even believe that pure doctrine does not exist except as an unattainable ideal in a Platonic republic.

We live in a time when people are "ever learning and never able to come to the knowledge of the truth," as the apostle says (2 Timothy 3:7 KJV). Our time manifests the mocking and skeptical spirit of Pilate, who asked, "What is truth?" but without waiting for an answer. . . . Such contempt of the truth, of pure doctrine, shows that we are living in an unspeakably tragic age.

The Word of God speaks very clearly about pure teaching. "Let him who has My Word speak My Word faithfully" (Jeremiah 23:28). . . . Our Lord Jesus Christ Himself said: "If you continue in My Word, you are truly My disciples, and you will know the truth, and the truth will make you free" (John 8:31-32). (See also Jude 3; 2 John 9-11; Titus 1:9-11; 1 Timothy 4:16; Galatians 5:7-9.)

Try to imagine what would have happened in the early church if men like Athanasius, Cyril, and Augustine had not earnestly opposed the heretics Arius, Nestorius, and Pelagius. Already in the fourth century the church would have lost the chief article of the Christian faith and come to ruin. To be sure, in the council of God this was impossible, but for that reason God had to raise up instruments such as those teachers of the truth. In their lifetime they were hated and persecuted as evil disturbers of Christendom, but for more than a millennium their names have shone brightly as witnesses to the saving truth, and in the glory of eternity they will shine "like the stars forever and ever" [Daniel 12:3]. Hence no one should be deterred from bearing witness to the truth, even though they are accused of having a false spirit.

Try also to imagine that Luther indeed knew the truth and bore witness to it in his own circles, but did not take up the battle against the abominations of the papacy that had intruded. What would have happened? Christendom would have remained under the spiritual tyranny of the Roman Antichrist, and all of us would now be his subjects.

There can be no question about it: We need both, defending the truth and combating error. To give you proficiency in both areas is one of the goals of these Friday evening lectures. God grant His blessing upon our deliberations!

Our thesis speaks of mingling Law and Gospel when it is taught that the sacraments are efficacious merely by being performed. The Gospel asks for nothing but faith in the promise, while the Law demands: "Do this, and you will live." But if the mere act of being baptized and receiving Communion conveys grace, the Gospel has been turned into Law, since I put confidence in what I do; and the Law has been turned into Gospel, since I promise poor sinners salvation for doing something.

It is hard to imagine, yet many teach that the sacraments are efficacious through the mere performance of the act. Even strict Lutherans make this mistake whenever they treat the sacraments. . . . But this is diametrically opposed to the doctrine of the Gospel. Here belong all those passages that say the Gospel requires nothing but faith and all depends on faith. But how can I say, then, that this or that work benefits me? If the preached Word does me no good unless I believe it, also Baptism and the Lord's Supper are of no avail without faith. Saying to a person that he is saved by faith alone is nothing else than saying that he is saved by grace.

However, most people put it this way: "To be saved, you need not do this or that work, but you must believe; God demands that of you!" But no, the apostle says explicitly: "It depends on faith, in order that the promise may rest on grace" (Romans 4:16). Remember this precious passage. Anything that conflicts with the teaching that we are saved alone by grace is an error that overturns the very foundation. God gives you forgiveness of sins, righteousness, life, and salvation as a gift. But what good is a gift to you if you do not accept it? But accepting it is not a work; it is simply taking what is offered.

Passages dealing specifically with the sacraments are, among others, Mark 16:16; Acts 8:36-37; Galatians 3:26-27; Romans 4:11. In all of them the accent is on the primary importance of faith. When Jesus says: "Do this in remembrance of Me," He calls for faith, for the true remembrance of Christ is to believe the promise: "Given and shed for you for the forgiveness of sins." Remember that as often as you go to Communion. If you think that by your attendance you have done your duty and performed a work acceptable to God, there was no blessing.

Our church is often accused of teaching that Baptism creates children of God merely by being performed, and that the Lord's Supper effects forgiveness merely by being performed. If that were the case, it would not be surprising if all true Christians would shy away from us. That would be dreadful. First we said that man is not saved by works, and now we would be saying that by performing these two small acts we receive the forgiveness of sins. Many people look at the calendar and think they must again do the Christian work of going to Communion. In this way they eat and drink judgment to themselves. It is the promise of grace connected with the elements that should entice us, and then we should approach in faith; then we will leave the Lord's Table with a blessing. . . .

Lutheran teaching on the sacraments is presented in Luther's Small Catechism. . . . In the Augsburg Confession, Art. XIII, it is stated: "They require faith, and they are rightly used when they are received in faith and for the purpose of strengthening faith" (Tappert, p. 36). See also the longer discussion in Apology XIII, where the necessity of faith in the promise is emphasized and the idea of a mechanical performance *(ex opere operato)* is rejected (Par. 18-23; Tappert, pp. 213 f.). . . . And we must reject the teaching of modern Lutherans like Kahnis and Delitzsch, who claim too much for the mere performance of Baptism and the Lord's Supper and disparage the need of faith. [*Editorial note:* We omit Walther's lengthy comments on the views of these two German professors.]

Thirty-fifth Evening Lecture

(Sept. 18, 1885)

Christ says: "I am the Way, and the Truth, and the Life; no one comes to the Father but by Me" [John 14:6]. Peter confirms this: "There is salvation in no one else, for there is no other name under heaven given among men by which we must be saved" [Acts 4:12]. To the Corinthians Paul writes: "I decided to know nothing among you except Jesus Christ and Him crucified" [1 Corinthians 2:2]. It is therefore a fearful sin if we do not entice the souls entrusted to us to Christ as their Lord and Savior. Words cannot describe the greatness of the sin of keeping someone away from faith in Christ. Wittingly or unwittingly, wilfully or ignorantly—a preacher guilty of this sin will rob people of eternal life and act like a ravenous wolf instead of a shepherd. There have been plenty of preachers who became aware of this fact on their deathbed, and many a one came to an end in bitter struggles and even in despair.

The worst offenders are the so-called rationalistic preachers who sacrilegiously mount their pulpits and instead of preaching Christ as the

Savior of all sinners present their wretched moralizing and spout bombastic phrases. . . .

The papists are just as bad. Instead of drawing people to Christ, the Savior and Friend of sinners, they present him as an even sterner lawgiver than Moses. When a poor sinner is distressed and asks for guidance, he is directed not to Christ but to Mary, the so-called Mother of Mercy. They have taught the people to be afraid of Christ and seek refuge with Mary or some patron saint. . . .

It is easy to avoid such crass teaching, but it is more difficult when it appears in more refined form. . . . This is the subject of our 22nd thesis.

Thesis XXII

In the 18th place, God's Word is not rightly divided when a false distinction is made between awakening and conversion, and not being able to believe is confused with not being permitted to believe.

In the first half of the 18th century the Pietists were especially guilty of this serious mingling of Law and Gospel. These included the Halle theologians and many others. . . . They kept people away from Christ by making a false distinction between awakening and conversion. They posited three classes of people: 1. unconverted; 2. awakened but not converted; 3. converted.

In spite of sincere intentions to remain faithful to pure teaching, the Pietists were wrong in this classification. It would be correct, if by the awakened they meant people who were occasionally stirred by the Word of God, but then erased this impression. There are indeed people who can no longer live in carnal security but who suppress this unrest, until the Lord smites them again with the hammer of the Law and makes them ready to receive the sugar of the Gospel. However, the awakened people of whom the Pietists were speaking are no longer among the unconverted. According to Scripture, there are only two classes, converted and unconverted.

If one did not follow Scripture, one could indeed call certain people awakened in distinction from true Christians. For instance, it is said of Herod Antipas that he heard John gladly, because he preached consolingly about the coming Messiah, and Herod at times also asked and followed John's advice. But he remained the old Herod. To please a miserable dancing girl Herod caused John the Baptist to lose his head. Another example is the procurator Felix, to whom Paul spoke earnestly "about justice and self-control and future judgment." Felix was struck in his conscience, but he quickly erased this impression. He told Paul, "Go away for the present; when I have an opportunity I will summon you" [Acts

24:24-25]; but he never did. Festus is another example. . . . And Agrippa, who even exclaimed, "In a short time you think to make me a Christian!" [Acts 26:28], so powerfully had Paul impressed him. Yet he remained unconverted. These people are not among the converted, and to call them awakened is a mistake. When Scripture speaks of awakening, it always has conversion in mind, as many passages make clear (e.g., Ephesians 5:14; Ephesians 2:4-6; Colossians 2:12).

Pietists, however, insist that unless one has experienced a thorough contrition, he is not yet converted but only awakened. Referring to David's soaking his bed with tears and going about all day bowed down, they say that one who has not gone through the same experience is not converted, but only awakened. . . . That is a false assumption. One may have become a true Christian without having experienced David's terrible agony. The Bible nowhere says that we must experience that to the same degree. According to Ephesians 1:13 we have been sealed with the promised Holy Spirit when we believe in Christ, no matter how weak our faith may be. Not everyone is given the same degree of elation and heroic courage.

To see that this is true, you need only read about the hearers at the first Pentecost. . . . They came to faith at once, and then these newly converted people "devoted themselves to the apostles' teaching and fellowship, to the breaking of bread and the prayers" [Acts 2:42]. The same is true of the Ethiopian eunuch . . . [Acts 8:34-39]. Note also the case of the jailer at Philippi . . . [Acts 16:23-34].

Now see if you can find a single example in Scripture where a prophet, an apostle, or some other saint pointed to a different way, saying: "Not so fast; first you must pass through various experiences!" No, they simply preached so that the people despaired of themselves and looked for help, and then they told them to believe in the Lord Jesus, and that was all.

Enthusiasts say: "That is not the proper order." Yes, it is not their order, but it is God's order. As soon as the Gospel sounded in the ears of those people, it entered their heart and turned them to faith. . . . A preacher who keeps the anxious sinner dangling, sometimes for months and even years, before allowing him to say that he believes is a spiritual quack and leads souls not to Jesus but to their own efforts. In a certain sense that is what the Pietists did. Especially preachers who are very zealous are in danger of committing this sin. They mean well, but they only torment poor souls. They should tell every grieving and despairing sinner: "It's simple. Just believe in Jesus your Savior, and all will be well."

According to Scripture it is not difficult to be converted, but it is difficult to remain converted. It is therefore wrong to apply to repentance Christ's word about entering by the narrow gate. Repentance is not a narrow gate we must squeeze through; it is something God gives. Our own contrived repentance is false and unacceptable to God. We must only use God's cutting Word, the Law, and then we shall have the first part of repentance. When the unconditional Gospel is then proclaimed, faith will soon result. You must accept the Gospel as soon as you hear it.

But then the conflict begins. False teachers make the mistake of putting the conflict before conversion. Then we are not yet able to fight. The struggle is difficult after we have come to faith. The narrow way is the Christian's cross, crucifying one's flesh, bearing the world's mockery and scorn, fighting against the devil, renouncing the world with its vanities, treasures, and pleasures. This is the difficult part, and this is why so many fall away. Many more than we think experience a conversion under the influence of the Word of God, but as soon as they leave the church they seek to suppress such feelings and try to convince themselves that it is nothing but fanaticism. Thus people harden themselves from Sunday to Sunday, and many lose their salvation. The Savior spoke of those who receive the Word with joy but fall away when tribulations and persecutions come [Matthew 13:20-21]. . . . Pietists say that those people were not yet converted. Yet the Lord said: "They believe for a while" [Luke 8:13].

Do not, therefore, believe that people can become secure when they are told how quickly one can come to conversion and repentance. On the contrary, consider the greatness of God's mercy. The lesson for converted Christians is: "You must fight daily and strive to make progress in the exercise of love, patience, and gentleness, and resist every sin." After conversion you may work with God. The enthusiasts place that cooperation before conversion. And that robs God of His honor.

[*Editorial note:* We omit two quotations from the Confessions: Formula of Concord, Solid Declaration, Art. II, par. 87 and 14; Tappert, pp. 538 and 523. Walther continues:]

Where there is but a spark of genuine longing for grace, there is faith, for faith is nothing but such longing. Then a person is not only "awakened" (in the wrong sense), but converted. Precisely because "God is at work" in us, "both to will and to work," the apostle exhorts us to "work out your own salvation with fear and trembling" [Philippians 2:12-13]. This is addressed to the converted, for the unconverted cannot work out their salvation.

Our opponents say that first God awakens a person and then gives him the power to convert himself and make his decision. That is nothing but a rehash of old errors. You are either dead or alive. Our current opponents claim that man must first receive a liberated will. But then he would have to become alive before he has been converted.

177

Luther shows us what the condition of those who come to faith must be. [*Editorial note:* We omit a long quotation from *The Bondage of the Will (Luther's Works,* American Edition, Vol. 33, pp. 61 f.). In it Luther says that a person must completely despair of being able to do the least thing toward his salvation. Walther concludes:]

A person must realize this, or else he receives the Gospel in vain. If he finds comfort within himself or thinks he can help himself, he is lost. Therefore the preacher must first bring the thunder of Law and then immediately proclaim the Gospel, lest many a precious soul despair and be lost.

Thirty-sixth Evening Lecture
(Sept. 25, 1885)

One would think that all people, since their fall into sin and indescribable misery, would with great joy receive the Scriptural teaching that man is justified and saved by grace alone through faith in Jesus Christ, and realize precisely from this teaching that the religion of the Bible must be the only true one, offering just what poor sinners need. Unfortunately, this is not the case, but the very opposite. Down to the present day the world has always taken offense at this teaching. Hence already Paul testified: "We preach Christ crucified, a stumbling block to Jews and folly to Gentiles" [1 Corinthians 1:23]. Though it was regarded by the world as a disgraceful message, Paul exclaimed: "I am not ashamed of the Gospel: it is the power of God for salvation to everyone who has faith" [Romans 1:16]. By nature every man harbors a blind and self-righteous Pharisee who thinks that the best and surest religion must be the one that demands the most of man, for salvation is so great that man must unquestionably do something very great to obtain it.

When the prophets of Baal displayed such great zeal in their devotion to Baal that they "cut themselves . . . with swords and lances, until the blood gushed out upon them" [1 Kings 18:28], the poor, blind people thought: "Those are the true prophets of God!"—until the prophet Elijah put an end to their hypocrisy. When the Pharisees and scribes taught that one must keep the whole law of Moses to the letter, yes, also the traditions of the elders, the people thought: "The religion of our Pharisees and scribes is better than that of Christ, who calls all sinners, even the worst, to Himself and offers them grace." And Paul had the same experience. . . .

It has always been thus. People are impressed by demands for works and by a display of sanctity. . . . They are prone to disparage the works of

God but hold the works of men in high esteem. That is a tragic consequence of the fall into sin. And it appears also in our own Evangelical Lutheran Church, if in more refined form. This is the point of the second part of Thesis 22 . . . namely that not being able to believe is confused with not being permitted to believe.

As a rule, the Pietists advised one who had come to an awareness of his sins not to believe too soon. They said: "Before you can believe, your contrition must be far more complete than it is now. You must be contrite not only from fear of punishment but also from love to God. Otherwise your contrition is null and void. You must first feel that God is beginning to have mercy on you; you must first hear His voice, 'Be of good cheer, your sins shall be forgiven!' Just keep on struggling until you have arrived. Then you can begin to take comfort." A terrible method! One must not first be converted and then believe; not first feel that he has grace, but first believe the Word of grace without feeling, and then feeling will come. God bestows these feelings by His grace. Some are without them for a long time. Hence this is not the right way to direct a person to salvation: to tell him that he dare not yet believe, even though he feels that he is a poor, lost sinner.

To be sure, no one can create faith himself, but God must do it. A person can be in a state where he cannot believe and where God will not grant him faith. One who regards himself as healthy and righteous cannot believe, for he is spiritually surfeited.

John 5:44: "How can you believe, who receive glory from one another?" the Lord asked the Pharisees. The desire for honor is a sin that makes faith impossible. . . . From this it does not follow, however, that a person is not *permitted* to believe. Everybody is always permitted to believe. Whoever tells the sinner he is not yet permitted to believe is either wicked or still blind in this regard.

To tell a person he is not *permitted* to believe is contrary, first of all, to Christ's complete redemption (1 John 2:1-2; 2 Corinthians 5:14). . . . But it is also contrary to the Gospel, for Christ commanded His disciples to go into all the world and preach the Gospel to every creature. To preach the Gospel is nothing but to tell every human being the good news that he is redeemed and righteous, and that everyone should just come and believe it and thus be saved. Is it not terrible, then, to tell someone that he is not permitted to believe? The Gospel belongs to everyone, and all are called upon to believe. Whoever does not believe makes liars out of God and all His prophets and apostles. . . . By raising Jesus Christ from the dead God absolved all mankind. How terrible to say that this indeed happened, but people may not believe it. That is a denial of Christ's resurrection.

It is also in conflict with the doctrine of absolution (Matthew 18:18; John 20:23). ... After Jesus Christ redeemed the whole world He also gave His disciples the authority to forgive everyone his sins. ... The Lord simply says: "If you forgive the sins of any, they are forgiven." ... This is the most consoling doctrine possible, a teaching based solidly on God's own blood that was shed on the cross. Sin has really been forgiven, and God does everything now to induce us to believe it. Our absolution has no other purpose than to cause the absolved to believe what is proclaimed from the pulpit. ...

The same is true of the sacraments. The water in Baptism saves us. By His body, given for us, and His blood, shed for us, the Lord promises us the forgiveness of our sins, but we must believe it, and then we may leap for joy as we leave the altar.

However, when not being able to believe is confused with not being permitted to believe, this also goes against the practice of the apostles, as the examples of the crowd at the first Pentecost and the jailer at Philippi demonstrate. ...

It is also a great folly for preachers to fall back on their good intention to get the sinner to experience a thorough conversion. They must keep in mind that God is wiser than they. He knew full well that when the comfort of the Gospel is spread in all hearts, many would think, "I can believe that too." Therefore we must not withhold this comfort. One must not starve the children because of concern for the dogs. We must cheerfully proclaim God's universal grace and then leave it up to Him, as to who will believe and who will abuse it. When the ground has been excavated, one must quietly lay the foundation of the building. Otherwise a rainstorm can close it up again. ... After the Law has made people aware of being sinners, we must quickly come with the Gospel and put it into people's hearts. That is the correct method, while the method of the Methodists is wrong.

[*Editorial note:* We omit three quotations from Luther: St. Louis Edition, XI, 1141, 1104, and 733f. Walther continues:]

Many people think, when they receive absolution: "That is very comforting, if I know that I am in the right frame of mind." That is not what God wants. Since redemption has been acquired for all, it must be given to all. It is as if God Himself stood before us, called us by name, and said: "Your sins are forgiven." How joyfully we would then go our way! We would exclaim: "Now no devil can make my salvation unsure."

But when a preacher absolves, it is really God who does it, although He does it mediately. The sects think that we believe our preachers receive a special secret power through ordination to look into people's hearts and thus pronounce absolution. That is not our teaching, but as often as I preach the Gospel, I absolve everybody. Of course, many will sit there and refuse to believe it, and thus depart as unforgiven and condemned sinners. The children of God, on the other hand, will think: "What a lovely sermon that was! I may calmly return home, for the heavy burden of my sins has been removed."

Thirty-seventh Evening Lecture
(Oct. 2, 1885)

One of the most necessary and important requisites of a preacher is, my friends, that he is filled with a sincere and burning zeal to discharge his office properly and accomplish something good, namely to pluck out of hell every soul entrusted to him, to lead those souls to God, make them truly pious, and bring them to heaven. A proper pastor must have permanently renounced any striving for wealth and honor and prestige in this world. He must find his greatest joy in seeing that his labor is not in vain in the Lord, and that must be the sweetest compensation for all his great anxieties and worries. He must daily and hourly make the sigh of faithful old Pastor Lollmann his own:

> O God, whose bread is feeding me,
> Would I were of some use to Thee!

Paul is the outstanding example of genuine zeal for his ministry, even to the extent of being willing to be cut off from Christ for the sake of his brethren (Romans 9:3). . . .

There is, however, also a false, ungodly, carnal zeal, that does not come from God and is not created by the Holy Spirit but has its basis in enmity against those who teach otherwise. That is why some are so zealous—or for selfish reasons, because they know such zeal will bring them acclaim, especially in certain congregations; or they are simply fanatics. How zealous were the priests and elders, scribes and Pharisees against Christ! They spared no effort to conduct their office in opposition to Him. That is why Paul said of the Jews: "They have a zeal for God, but it is not enlightened" (Romans 10:2). Think also of the zeal with which the false teachers tried to lead the Christians in Galatia astray. But Paul said they would bear their judgment (Galatians 5:10).

How zealous were the Anabaptists in Luther's time! For the sake of their religion they forsook house and home, wife and child, and many of them suffered drowning rather than recant their teaching. But all church history shows, and our experience, especially in this country, confirms the fact that the false spirits have a greater zeal to inculcate their teachings than orthodox teachers to bring the pure truth to men's hearts.

Why is this? The reason is easy to see. The preachers of false doctrine are not restrained, bur rather incited, by their reason and their flesh and blood, while preachers of the pure doctrine of God's Word are constantly held back by their reason and their flesh and blood. That makes their task a thousand times more difficult. It is easy enough to speak out of one's heart, but it is difficult to proclaim the truth on the basis of God's Word, after earnest searching in the same, after fervent prayer and earnest wrestling for the Holy Spirit's illumination. This is so difficult above all because it is so difficult rightly to divide the Word of truth, properly to distinguish between Law and Gospel and not mingle them in any way—something required of an approved workman in the Lord's vineyard. About such mingling we are warned in the 23rd thesis.

Thesis XXIII

In the 19th place, God's Word is not rightly divided when the attempt is made to induce the unregenerate by means of the demands, threats, and promises of the Law to renounce sin and do good works, and thus to make them pious, and to impel the regenerate toward the good by means of legalistic demands rather than by evangelical exhortation.

A study of Scripture will clearly show that this is a gross mingling of Law and Gospel entirely contrary to the purpose of the Law after the Fall.

Jeremiah 31:31-34: A glorious, precious passage! A veritable sun suddenly rising in the twilight of the Old Testament! . . . Insofar as God had made a covenant with Israel, it was a covenant of Law, although the prophets always preached the Gospel and pointed to the Messiah. Israel broke the covenant, failing to live up to the Law's demands. Now God promised a new covenant, to be established through the Messiah, a covenant of grace, in which God would forgive their iniquity and not remember their sin. . . .

Romans 3:20; 7:7-13: St. Paul shows that the function of the Law is to lay bare and make manifest man's sin, his innate sinful condition. That is all that the Law can do.

2 Corinthians 3:6: "The written code kills." The written code, or the letter, does not refer to the literal sense of Scripture, as many like to interpret, but to the Law, as the context shows.

Psalm 119:32: It is a matter of the Christian's own experience that only the Gospel ("When You comfort my heart," Luther's translation) provides the motivation and willingness to run the way of God's commandments. . . . How foolish, then, for the preacher to decide to hurl the thunderbolts of the Law and preach hellfire in order to improve conditions! Preaching the Law is necessary to terrify the secure sinner, but the Law will not renew the heart nor kindle love to God and the neighbor. At best it will produce only a forced obedience.

Galatians 3:2: False teachers regarded Paul's preaching of grace and faith as quite inadequate and incomplete and insisted on supplementing it with the Law. The Galatians were taken in. When Paul heard of it, he wrote to them and asked: "Did you receive the Spirit by works of the Law, or by hearing with faith?" . . . The answer was obvious. All their former peace and spiritual joy and confidence, as well as their sacrificial love, were products exclusively of the Gospel, not of the Law. . . .

Remember the apostle's words! If you want to put life into your congregation and fill the members with the Spirit of peace, joy, faith, confidence, sonship, and rest for the soul, do not, for God's sake, turn to the Law. Of course you must also make use of the Law, but never by itself. Do not offer the Law one day and save the Gospel for a later date. The Gospel must take over as soon as the Law has done its work.

The rationalists are the worst offenders in this awful mingling of Law and Gospel. There are, in fact, rationalistic preachers who think the Gospel is a dangerous teaching that only makes people secure and indifferent to sanctification, because all they hear is that man is saved through faith alone. So they earnestly preach morality to make people good. But the only result is, at best, that some are brought to a degree of respectability, so that they will abstain from gross vices and crimes. But that one must get a new heart, that one should truly love God and the neighbor—there is no inkling of that. . . .

But such a mingling of Law and Gospel is found also in many an orthodox church. In the first place, there are those who obtained certainty only after long and anguished struggle and refused to be comforted, because they had not come to know the true doctrine. Now, when such a man preaches, legalistic terms often intrude, so that the hearers feel that while he is a pious man, he makes demands upon them that they cannot satisfy.

In the second place, such mingling also takes place when the preacher notes that all his preaching seems to achieve nothing. There is no improvement in the life of the members. The preacher may then think that he has preached too much Gospel and decides to preach nothing but the Law for a while. But that is a mistake! Things will not get better. The people will become resentful. . . . At most, they will respond under coercion. But God does not want the obedience of slaves.

Even the most disreputable congregation can be reformed only by the sweetest Gospel. If a congregation has sunk to so low an ebb, it is always because the preachers did not preach the Gospel enough. No wonder nothing good is accomplished; for the Law kills, but the Spirit, the Gospel, makes alives.

Commenting on Romans 12:1, Luther says: "He does not say, I command you; for he is preaching to such as are already Christian and godly through faith in the new man. Such people must not be coerced with commands but exhorted to do willingly what must be done with the old, sinful man. One who does not act voluntarily in response to kindly admonition is no Christian" (St. Louis Edition, XII, 318).

Is it not terrible when a preacher does everything to produce dead works and turn his members into hypocrites before God? Only those are good works that flow from a free heart. . . . Only that gift is satisfying that comes from love. So God is repelled by works done by coercion. Luther continues: "One who compels unwilling people by means of the Law is not a Christian preacher but a worldly slave driver." . . .

Let no one think: "If someone preaches the Gospel to them, they will not do God's will. I must preach the Law and God's threats." If that is all you do, you have led the people straight to hell. Better not act the policeman in your congregation, but change the people's hearts, so that they will freely and gladly do what pleases God. . . .

See also Luther's fine commentary on Psalm 110:3: "Your people will offer themselves freely" *(Luther's Works,* American Edition, Vol. 13, p. 288).

Thirty-eighth Evening Lecture

(Oct. 23, 1885)

Many preachers, even good ones, think they have done the job when they have stirred up their hearers out of their natural security and led them to despair of their salvation. Now, to be saved, everyone needs to be jolted out of his false peace and comfort and hopes, and be led to despair of his salvation and his present condition. But all that is only preliminary. The chief thing is something quite different. The sinner must be brought to become very sure of his state of grace and salvation, so that the pardoned one can rejoice with pious Woltersdorf:

> I know, yes I know, and my heart e'er retains,
> That as sure as God in His kingdom still reigns,
> As sure as His sun continues to shine,
> So sure am I that forgiveness is mine.

There can be no doubt that this is an evangelical preacher's chief goal. It is his task to preach the Gospel to those entrusted to him, to bring them to faith in Christ, to baptize, absolve, and distribute Communion. Now, preaching the Gospel is nothing but telling people that they are reconciled to God through Christ and are fully redeemed. And a living faith of the heart is nothing but the divine certainty that sins are forgiven and heaven's gates stand open. Baptism is nothing but snatching a person out of the sinful world with the solemn assurance: "God is gracious to you, and you are His beloved child." Absolution is nothing but to say in the name and by the authority of Christ: "Your sins are forgiven." Giving the Lord's Supper is nothing but assuring the individual: "You, too, share in the great redemption."

Scripture shows that all true preachers aimed at having their hearers make the confident assertion: "I am a child of God and an heir of eternal life." Christ said to His disciples: "Rejoice that your names are written in heaven" [Luke 10:20]. Paul tells the Corinthians: "You were washed, you were sanctified, you were justified in the name of the Lord Jesus Christ and in the Spirit of our God" [1 Corinthians 6:11]. Peter wrote: "You were straying like sheep, but have now returned to the Shepherd and Guardian of your souls" [1 Peter 2:25]. And John said: "Beloved, we are God's children now; it does not yet appear what we shall be, but we know that when He appears we shall be like Him, for we shall see Him as He is" [1 John 3:2]. In all their dealings with the members of their congregations the apostles presupposed them to be dear children of God in spite of all frailties and failings.

It is much different today. Even the best preachers are quite content if their people are at the point of sensing their own lost estate. But it is truly terrible if the stricken sinner cannot say: "I know that my Redeemer lives! I know whom I have believed!"

The cause of this malady is that preachers mingle Law and Gospel and do not follow the apostle's admonition to be workmen who rightly divide the Word of truth [2 Timothy 2:15 KJV]. If the Gospel is preached with an admixture of Law, it cannot lead anyone to faith in the forgiveness of sins. And vice versa, if the Law is preached with an admixture of Gospel, it will not lead people to a knowledge of their sins and the need of forgiveness.

Thesis XXIV

In the 20th place, God's Word is not rightly divided when the unforgivable sin against the Holy Spirit is described as unforgivable because of its magnitude.

The Law alone condemns sin, but the Gospel absolves from all sins, excluding none of them. The prophet writes: "Though your sins are like scarlet, they shall be as white as snow" (Isaiah 1:18). The apostle Paul writes: "Where sin increased, grace abounded all the more"(Romans 5:20). Hence Luther sings the lovely words:

Though great our sins and sore our woes,
His grace much more aboundeth;
His helping hand no limit knows,
Our utmost need it soundeth.

(The Lutheran Hymnal, 329:5)

The sin against the Holy Spirit is mentioned in Matthew 12:30-32 (and parallels in Mark 3:28-30 and Luke 12:10) and in Hebrews 6:4-8 and 1 John 5:16. This sin is unforgivable not because the person of the Holy Spirit is more glorious than that of the Father and the Son, but because it is blasphemy against the *office* of the Holy Spirit, which is to call people to Christ and keep them with Him. Christians who in their weakness at times harbor blasphemous thoughts in their hearts must not think they have committed the unforgivable sin, for Christ says: "Whoever *speaks* against the Holy Spirit will not be forgiven." As the best preachers have experienced with regard to their members, the devil often torments even the best Christians by giving them evil thoughts against their heavenly Father and against the Holy Spirit. . . . But that is not the sin against the Holy Spirit.

I myself gave spiritual help to a girl who even uttered such thoughts, but at the same time threw herself on the floor and sighed and cried that God would deliver her from this. She did not come to rest until she saw that she was not doing this herself. Satan had not only shot fiery darts into her but had also taken possession of her lips.

According to Mark 3, to declare the work of the Holy Spirit to be the devil's work, even though one knows it is God's work, is to commit blasphemy against the Holy Spirit. This is certainly a most serious matter. Resisting the working of the Holy Spirit leads to the next step, which is hatred of God's way of salvation. Therefore take heed! Whenever the Holy Spirit knocks at the heart's door, open at once, no matter what the world may think of it. This is no joking matter. Unless the Holy Spirit brings us to faith, we will not receive it. One who rejects Him is beyond help, even God's help. For God desires to preserve His order of salvation. . . .

A most important passage is Hebrews 6:4-8. It shows that one who has committed the sin against the Holy Spirit can never come to repentance again. It is not God who puts man into this condition, but man gets there by his own fault. When this condition has reached a certain stage, God no longer works on the person. Then he is accursed and beyond the possibility of salvation, because he cannot come to repentance.

St. John (1 John 5:16) tells his Christians that they should no longer pray for one who has committed this sin. But since we cannot look into anyone's heart, we cannot say of anyone with absolute certainty that he has committed the unforgivable sin. . . .

As terrible as all this sounds, it also contains an inexpressibly great comfort. Someone may confess himself to be a wretched person who has committed the sin against the Holy Spirit. But he finds no pleasure in his condition; only terror. This shows that God has at least begun repentance in him and he needs only to cling to the promise of the Gospel. . . . As long as people are sorry for their blasphemous thoughts and works, God has surely begun the work of repentance in them. This is an irrefutable proof that they have not committed this sin. Such a person should be told that he is a dear child of God but is undergoing terrible trials. In general, when this matter is being treated, the accent should be on convincing people that they have not committed this sin, rather than on warning them against becoming guilty of it. . . .

Luther, commenting on 1 John 5:16, defines this sin as follows: "It resists the grace of God, the means of salvation, and the remission of sins. Where there is no acknowledgment, there is no remission. For the remission of sins is preached to those who feel sin and seek the grace of God. The others, however, are not troubled by scruples of conscience. Nor do they acknowledge and feel sin" *(Luther's Works,* American Edition, Vol. 30, pp. 324—25).

[*Editorial note:* Walther quotes extensively, in Latin, from Baier's *Compendium theologiae positivae.* We refer the reader to Francis Pieper, *Christian Dogmatics,* Vol. I, pp. 571—77.]

Whoever has committed this sin is condemned not so much for the sake of this sin but because of unbelief. . . .

Thirty-ninth Evening Lecture
(Nov. 6, 1885)

No calling is so despised and hated as that of the teacher of theology or religion. In the eyes of the world such people are primarily responsible for retarding the arrival of the golden age. The French encyclopedist Diderot, who died 100 years ago, wrote: "There will be no improvement in the world until the last king has been hanged with the guts of the last priest.". . . This word has remained the slogan of revolutionaries to the present day. And one may well expect that this word will be put into action. All signs point that way. You may live to see it happen.

If only theologians and teachers of religion had not demeaned themselves and become the objects of hatred by their own fault!

Unfortunately, that is the case. Both church history and our own experience confirm this view. All too many teachers of religion disgracefully misuse their sacred calling to gratify their worldly attitude, their quest for money and honor and power. As a result, either from fear or selfish ambition, they not only withhold and deny the truth, but proclaim the very opposite, and spread lies and error instead of the pure Gospel. In fact, there is no vice so repulsive, no crime so dreadful, but that teachers of religion have disgraced their office with it and caused unspeakable offense in the eyes of the world. But, my friends, do not let this fact deter you from further theological study!

Remember, first of all: The omniscient God foreknew this would happen. And yet, in His infinite wisdom, He arranged it so that this sacred office was not to be staffed by the holy angels but by fallen, sinful men. May God preserve us from being offended by this arrangement! Rather let us be filled with adoring wonder that God, even with such poor and often wretched servants, will not permit His church to be overcome by the powers of hell.

Second, remember that God has, nevertheless, given the highest honor to the teachers of religion. First of all, during His earthly ministry, when He filled this office Himself, the Son of God said to the first teachers for all time: "He who hears you hears Me, and he who rejects you rejects Me, and he who rejects Me rejects Him who sent Me" [Luke 10:16]. What marvelous credentials for the servants of the Word!

Furthermore, God has revealed that not only marriages were made in heaven, but also the relationship of ministers to congregations. Like Jeremiah [Jeremiah 1:5] and Paul [Galatians 1:15], all true preachers were designated by God from eternity to be His assistants in saving the souls entrusted to them.

Finally, no one has received more glorious promises than a teacher of the Gospel, a servant of the Word of God. Through Daniel God said: "Those who are wise shall shine like the brightness of the firmament; and those who turn many to righteousness, like the stars forever and ever" [Daniel 12:3]. One day the world will have to hear and see the elect and the angels saying to God: "This man was a faithful preacher and teacher. He proclaimed the saving Word of God to a lost world. On earth he was despised and maligned, but now he will shine like a star forever and ever."

O my friends, this should surely make us glad to remain faithful to our God who has called us into this office! To be sure, that applies only to the right kind of preachers. Let us, therefore, consider the last of our theses on the difference between Law and Gospel and the mingling of both. Here we speak of the first requisite of a true teacher of the Christian religion.

Thesis XXV

In the 21st place, God's Word is not rightly divided when the preacher does not in general let the Gospel predominate.

This is most important. Law and Gospel are mingled and spoiled for the hearer not only when the Law predominates but also when in general Law and Gospel are given equal space and the Gospel is not allowed to predominate. I confess to anxiety lest I spoil this precious subject for you. The more I have meditated on it, the less I have been able to find the right words—it is so precious. Let us now see from Scripture that in general the Gospel must predominate.

The first preacher of Christ after His birth was the angel who told the terrified shepherds: "Be not afraid; for behold, I bring you good news of a great joy which will come to all the people" (Luke 2:10). Not a syllable of Law, not a trace of prescriptions and God's demands upon man, but the very opposite, God's grace toward all people. The heavenly hosts sing joyfully: "Glory to God in the highest, and on earth peace, good will toward men" [v. 14 KJV]. . . . God asks nothing but that people will accept His gift with joy and be comforted by this Child. There a heavenly preacher gave us an example of how we should preach. We must let the Gospel predominate. We must indeed preach the Law, but only as preparation for the Gospel. Else we are not true servants of the Gospel.

Mark 16:15-16: Before our Lord ascended into heaven, He clearly stated the basis of His religion and instructed His disciples on their task. "Go into all the world and preach the Gospel to the whole creation," He said. The word "Gospel" itself means good news. The Lord explains its content: "He who believes and is baptized will be saved." Even the addition: "But he who does not believe will be condemned," is precious. For Jesus does not say: "He who has sinned too much and too long will be condemned," but only "He who does not believe." . . .

2 Timothy 4:5: Paul tells Timothy to "do the work of an evangelist." Such men are called evangelists because they are to preach nothing but the evangel, the Gospel, that is, the teaching by means of which they must seek to save people. Of course, they must also proclaim the Law, but only as a preliminary to preaching the Gospel. The Law is in the service of the Gospel, but it is not the real doctrine of Christ. "The Law was given through Moses; grace and truth came through Jesus Christ" (John 1:17).

2 Corinthians 3:5-6: "Not that we are competent of ourselves to claim anything as coming from us; our competence is from God, who has made us competent to be ministers of a new covenant, not in a written code but in the Spirit; for the written code kills, but the Spirit gives life." Paul is speaking of himself as an apostle. Christian preachers must bear in mind

that they are not Old Testament preachers. "The written code" is the Law. A New Testament preacher should as such preach only the Gospel, nothing more. When he preaches the Law, he is really performing a work foreign to his office. It is horrible blindness to say, as the papists do, that in Scripture two doctrines must be distinguished, namely the old law and the evangelical law. To speak of an "evangelical law" is a contradiction in terms. How can the Law be a joyful message? . . .

1 Corinthians 2:2: The sole topic of his preaching, said Paul, was "Jesus Christ and Him crucified." Day and night he thought about how he could bring Christ to the people and lead them to faith in Him. Jesus Christ was the Core and Center of all his message. This was written also for our sake. Therefore, when you bid farewell to a parish, you can do so with a clear conscience only if you, too, can say: "I decided to know nothing among you except Jesus Christ and Him crucified." Woe to him who has preached the Law to make people good, believing that the Gospel could not save people! He was an unfaithful servant.

1 Corinthians 15:3: For Paul "of first importance" was preaching "that Christ died for our sins." All else was secondary. Do not only listen to this, but resolve that when you have a congregation you will do the same thing: You will not stand in your pulpit as one announcing a funeral, but as one inviting to a wedding. If you do not mingle Law and Gospel, you will always mount your pulpit with joy. People will soon notice your attitude, and miracles will begin to happen. So many preachers never have this experience, and their hearers remain asleep and miserly, because not enough Gospel was preached to them. People who come to church in a free country like ours come because they want to hear the Word of God. Let the preacher follow God's will and determine to preach the sweet Gospel so attractively that it will be irresistible and people will resolve to remain with Jesus.

It is not enough for you to feel that you are orthodox and able to present the pure teaching. It will be of no help if you mingle Law and Gospel. And the most subtle form of such mingling is when we *also* preach the Gospel but do not let it predominate. As soon as you fail to do so, your hearers will go hungry and many will starve to death spiritually. You give them too little to eat, for the true bread of life is not the Law but the Gospel.

2 Corinthians 1:24: According to this passage you as a preacher will assist Christian people in their joy. What a precious text for an installation sermon! For God's sake, don't become one who torments people, makes them uncertain, so that they leave the church with a heavy heart. Prepare your sermon in such a way that you are not to blame if those who hear it remain hardened and unconverted. Never mind the criticism of enthusiasts

who may say that you are not preaching enough hell and damnation. Be of good cheer! You are doing the right thing, for you must help Christians in their joy and not subject them to the torture of the Law. The longer you preach that way, the more will people praise God that they have such a man as their pastor. In all of church history you will discover that few churches have had the success which our synod can show, in spite of its weaknesses and frailties. That was not due to our wisdom, our hard work, our self-denial, but *solely because we have truly preached the Gospel.*

As soon as a hearer's heart longs for grace and the joyful confidence: "Yes, then I, too, can still get to heaven," he is a believer. Many remain in their sins because they feel they cannot live up to the demands of holiness to get to heaven. As for you, just joyfully and freely preach the Gospel of God's grace in Christ Jesus, and the people will banish such thoughts.

This is the teaching of our Lutheran Confessions. Article IV of the Augsburg Confession teaches concerning justification "that we cannot obtain forgiveness of sin and righteousness before God by our own merits, works, or satisfactions, but that we receive forgiveness of sin and become righteous before God by grace, for Christ's sake, through faith . . ." (Tappert, p. 30). In the Smalcald Articles we read: "Nothing in this article can be given up or compromised, even if heaven and earth and things temporal should be destroyed. . ." (Part II, Art. I, par. 5-6; Tappert, p. 292).

In the preface to his *Lectures on Galatians* (1535) Luther writes: "In my heart there rules this one doctrine, namely, faith in Christ. From it, through it, and to it all my theological thought flows and returns, day and night" *(Luther's Works,* American Edition, Vol. 27, p. 145). You should memorize this quotation and diligently apply it. No one can preach the Gospel more sweetly and gloriously than Luther. His preaching not only consoles but is so positive that it must overcome all doubts in the hearer. He must believe he is a child of God and will be saved, though he should die that night. Pray God on your knees that He would help you so that when you enter the ministry you will be able to say the same about your preaching. Would to God this could be said of all preachers, including all the preachers in our own church!

Here, too, there are differences. Some have a legalistic strain and thereby do themselves and their hearers great harm. They do not perform their ministry with the proper joy and do not make joyful Christians of their people. But that is necessary; that works miracles. If you will richly preach the Gospel, you need not worry that the people will forsake your church if some spiritual charlatan should come and put on a boisterous performance in the pulpit. The people will say: "Our pastor has brought us what we do not find elsewhere. He is a true Lutheran preacher, who showers great treasures upon us every Sunday."

In a sermon on John 17:10 Luther observes that while many boast of the Gospel and talk much about it and confess that Christ is the Son of God and Savior, they do not really explain how Christ is received, "used," and kept. They very rarely treat this central truth, and if they do, they are most cold and inept about it. On the contrary, a true preacher will treat this article most of all, in fact, constantly, since on it depends everything we need to know about God and our salvation (St. Louis Edition, VIII, 798).

In checking their sermons on the amount of space devoted to the Law and the Gospel, many will discover that they have given the Gospel only a little space. But when a preacher leaves the pulpit without having preached enough Gospel so that a poor sinner, who may be in church for the first and only time in his life, could learn how to be saved—woe to that preacher; he will have that man's soul on his conscience!

Commenting on Psalm 68:18, Luther emphasizes the security of the child of God, since Christ has taken Satan captive (St. Louis Edition, XIII, 2014). How foolish it is for preachers who see no results to decide to preach nothing but the Law for a while to rouse the people out of their spiritual sleep. But that will do no good. Luther said he could well put up with the criticism that his preaching was too sweet and consoling. And if people said they were being kept from doing good works, Luther replied that he was preaching that by which alone people's hearts are changed so that they will do good works. . . .

Luther means to say that you should just preach the consoling Gospel and don't think that will send people to hell. One or the other may take it as a comfort for the flesh, but don't think such people will have a joyful death. They do not really have the Gospel in their hearts. But do not let such incidents confuse you. Just keep on preaching the Gospel, as Christ told His disciples: "Go into all the world and preach the Gospel to the whole creation." . . . God grant that one day people will say of you: "He preaches well, but his message is too sweet." Just don't spend too much time on the Law. Come quickly with the Gospel. When the Law has made the iron red-hot, then come quickly with the Gospel to forge it while it is hot. Once it has cooled off, it is too late.

In conclusion, Luther writes in his *House Postil* that as trees are judged by their fruit, so preaching must be judged by its fruit. . . . [*Editorial note:* We omit this quotation from the St. Louis Edition of Luther's Works, XIII, 800 ff., where Luther says that the fruit of true preaching is that the people learn to know Christ "as the only Mediator between God and us."]

192

www.ingramcontent.com/pod-product-compliance
Lightning Source LLC
Chambersburg PA
CBHW030528100426
42813CB00001B/183